DISCOVERIES IN THE JUDAEAN DESERT · XIV

QUMRAN CAVE 4

IX

DISCOVERIES IN THE JUDAEAN DESERT · XIV

QUMRAN CAVE 4

IX

DEUTERONOMY, JOSHUA, JUDGES, KINGS

BY

EUGENE ULRICH
UNIVERSITY OF NOTRE DAME

FRANK MOORE CROSS
HARVARD UNIVERSITY

SIDNIE WHITE CRAWFORD

JULIE ANN DUNCAN

PATRICK W. SKEHAN

EMANUEL TOV

JULIO TREBOLLE BARRERA

CLARENDON PRESS · OXFORD

1995

Oxford University Press, Walton Street, Oxford OX2 6DP
Oxford New York
Athens Auckland Bangkok Bombay
Calcutta Cape Town Dar es Salaam Delhi
Florence Hong Kong Istanbul Karachi
Kuala Lumpur Madras Madrid Melbourne
Mexico City Nairobi Paris Singapore
Taipei Tokyo Toronto
and associated companies in
Berlin Ibadan

Oxford is a trade mark of Oxford University Press

Published in the United States by
Oxford University Press Inc., New York

British Library Cataloguing in Publication Data
Data available

Library of Congress Cataloging in Publication Data
Data available

ISBN 0-19-826366-X

1 3 5 7 9 10 8 6 4 2

Printed in Great Britain
on acid-free paper by
St. Edmundsbury Press, Bury St. Edmunds

This volume is dedicated to individuals and organizations who have graciously supported its publication

Mr. and Mrs. Grant L. Cannon
Catholic Biblical Association of America
Mr. and Mrs. De Witt Fields
General Dynamics Corporation
Mr. and Mrs. Harvey Grace
Mr. and Mrs. Stanley F. Hart
Mr. and Mrs. Steve Lund
University of Notre Dame
James Rothschild Foundation, Jerusalem
Royal Academy of Letters, Sweden
Mr. Carl-Hakon Swenson

CONTENTS

TABLE OF PLATES

FOREWORD

FRANK MOORE CROSS and Patrick W. Skehan are primarily responsible, together with Jozef T. Milik and John Strugnell, for the identification and placement of virtually all the fragments of the gigantic puzzle that this volume represents, as well as those published in the other biblical volumes. Moreover, Cross supervised the dissertations which resulted in the editions of the Deuteronomy scrolls and charted the nuanced palaeographic analysis and typological system of dating of all the manuscripts.

Eugene Ulrich, responding to Cross's invitation in late 1985, began organizing and overseeing the completion of the editions and the volume as a whole. With Cross, he selected additional colleagues to edit the full corpus of biblical volumes expeditiously. He worked closely with each of the editors on the content, accuracy, and clarity of the editions, attempting to achieve a proper balance between the varying character of the individual manuscripts, the different views and approaches of each editor, and the consistency of the final volume. The process was a rewardingly collaborative experience.

Patrick W. Skehan had published an edition of 4QDeut^{q} as early as 1954, now updated by Ulrich. Sidnie White Crawford and Julie Ann Duncan produced the editions of the remaining Deuteronomy manuscripts. Ulrich edited 4QJosh^{a}, Emanuel Tov 4QJosh^{b}, and Julio Trebolle Barrera, who has published widely on the text of Kings, edited 4QJudg^{a}, 4QJudg^{b}, and 4QKgs.

Colleagues and friends too numerous to name have contributed to the multifaceted effort represented in this work. Emanuel Tov and Weston W. Fields deserve the gratitude of the public as well as of the editors for their work in securing funding to make the publication process possible. Émile Puech, with his expertise in palaeography and his customary generosity, helped several of the editors refine their difficult readings. Hartmut Stegemann and his student, Hans-Günther Waubke, enhanced the editions of 4QJosh^{a} and 4QKgs with their methodological expertise in positioning fragments through study of the patterns of deterioration. T. S. Muraoka and Jeffrey H. Tigay made a number of helpful suggestions for the Deuteronomy editions.

Our long-term graduate assistants, Peter W. Flint, Robert A. Kugler, Curt Niccum, and, especially for this volume, Catherine M. Murphy and Leslie W. Walck, have earned our lasting gratitude for their years of careful work and devoted enthusiasm. Special thanks also go to Beverly Fields, the initial formatter of the electronic editions. This volume was prepared for camera-ready publication by the authors and Fields in the early stages and in the final stages by Ulrich, Walck, and Murphy.

We are highly grateful to Her Majesty the Queen Doña Sofía of Spain for making possible the congress Manuscritos Mar Muerto Madrid, 18–21 March 1991, and to Professors Julio Trebolle Barrera, Luis Vegas Montaner, and Javier Fernández Vallina for their thoughtful work in organizing it. The congress, as rich in elegant hospitality as in academic productivity, succeeded in providing a significant impetus to the publication of the scrolls as well as a new level of valuable interaction and communication of knowledge among the individuals in the various countries publishing and interpreting the scrolls.

It is a pleasure to acknowledge with special appreciation for their long-term financial support the National Endowment for the Humanities, an independent federal agency in the United States; the Yarnton Fund for the Qumran Project of the Oxford Centre for Hebrew and Jewish Studies; and the University of Notre Dame's Department of Theology, Institute for Scholarship in the Liberal Arts, and Office of Advanced Studies. The authors are also grateful for support from Albright College, the Universidad Complutense de Madrid, Harvard University, the Hebrew University of Jerusalem, and Princeton Theological Seminary, as well as the American Council of Learned Societies, the Center for Jewish Studies at the University of Pennsylvania (formerly the Annenberg Research Institute), and the George Barton Fellowship Fund through the American Schools of Oriental Research.

Acknowledgement for technical help is offered to Philip Payne of Linguist's Software, whose generous gift of the Hebrew, Palaeo-Hebrew, Greek, Syriac, and diacritical fonts add to the handsome appearance of this volume; and to Tsila Sagiv of the Rockefeller Museum, and Bruce and Kenneth Zuckerman, Greg Bearman, Marilyn Lundberg, and Sheila Spiro of the Ancient Biblical Manuscript Center for their photographic skill and artistry and for their innovative work in producing digitized images of the scrolls. We are also grateful to General Amir Drori, Mrs. Ayala Sussmann, Joe Zias and the curators of the Rockefeller Museum, and to Claire Pfann who facilitated communications and the transfer of new photographs between Jerusalem and Notre Dame.

The editorial and technical staff at Oxford University Press—Hilary O'Shea, Jenny Wagstaffe, Rachel Woodforde, and Jane Williams—provided the expertise, friendly co-operation, and patience essential for producing a volume as complex as this.

All the authors wish to join in paying an affectionate tribute to Frank Moore Cross an outstanding teacher, mentor, and treasured friend. We also wish to offer a personal expression of our grateful appreciation to: Laura and Megan Ulrich, Ivan Hall, Sabrina Odessa, Evelyn and Jim Whitehead, Catherine Mowry LaCugna, Patricia Hackett, Dan Crawford, Robert L. and Betty Duncan, and Lika Tov. We also give warm thanks for the hospitality of our hosts and friends at the École Biblique et Archéologique Française and the Albright Institute of Archaeological Research in Jerusalem.

Notre Dame, Indiana, March 1995 EUGENE ULRICH

ABBREVIATIONS AND SIGLA

THE abbreviations and sigla used in this volume are similar in general to those used in *Biblia Hebraica Stuttgartensia* and in the Göttingen and Brooke-McLean editions of the Septuagint, with adaptations considered useful or necessary. Additional abbreviations of Qumran sigla are found in *The Dead Sea Scrolls on Microfiche: A Comprehensive Facsimile Edition of the Texts from the Judean Desert: Companion Volume* (ed. E. Tov with S. J. Pfann, S. A. Reed, and M. J. Lundberg; 2d ed.; Leiden: Brill and IDC, 1995) and in Joseph A. Fitzmyer, *The Dead Sea Scrolls: Major Publications and Tools for Study* (rev. ed.; Atlanta: Scholars Press, 1990) 1–8. Abbreviations of journals and other sources and reference works are in accord with the 'Instructions for Contributors' in the *Catholic Biblical Quarterly* 46 (1984) 393–408 and the *Journal of Biblical Literature* 107 (1988) 579–96.

א א̇ א̊	certain letter, probable letter, possible letter, respectively (for discussion see the INTRODUCTION)
°	a letter which has ink traces remaining but cannot be confidently identified
[ ]	space between fragments or where the surface of the manuscript is missing
vacat	interval, indicating that the writing space was intentionally left blank
ס	*setuma*, a closed section in 𝔐; used to denote a new section of text beginning on the same line as the end of the previous section
פ	*petuḥa*, an open section in 𝔐; used to denote a new section of text beginning on the line below the end of the previous section
קצה	designation of the space used to mark the end of a section of text in the Samaritan Pentateuch
(4) 20	indication in the margin of the transcription that verse 4 begins somewhere in line 20
20 f.6	indication in the margin of the transcription that frg. 6 begins in line 20
/////	erasure or damage on the manuscript
+	additional word(s)
>	word(s) lacking
\	division between lines in a manuscript
≈	is equivalent to
≠	is not, does not equal
*	original or reconstructed form
c	corrected reading
1°, 2°	first, second occurrence of a form
L. 2^{sup}	(word or letters written) supralinearly above line 2
II 4–5	the second extant column of the manuscript, lines 4–5
frg. 10 ii 4–5	fragment 10, column 2 (where frg. 10 preserves two columns), lines 4–5
$2{:}23^{init}$	at the beginning of v 23
$2{:}23^{fin}$	at the end of v 23
2:23[24]	the number in brackets is usually the Greek verse number
מצרים^{bis}	מצרים occurs twice

𝔐	the Massoretic Text (as in *Biblia Hebraica Stuttgartensia*)
𝔐^{A}	The Aleppo Codex
𝔐^{L}	Codex Leningradensis
𝔐^{ed}	the edition of the Massoretic Text (as in *BHS*)
𝔐$^{ms(s)}$	Massoretic manuscript(s)
𝔐^{q}	*qere* for the Massoretic Text, as opposed to 𝔐 (= *ketib*)
ɯ *or* ɯ^{vGall}	the Samaritan Pentateuch, ed. von Gall
ɯ^{Ken}	the Samaritan Pentateuch, ed. Kennicott
ɯ^{Sad}	the Samaritan Pentateuch, ed. Sadaqa
ɯ$^{ms(corr)}$	a correction in a Samaritan manuscript
ɯ^{ap}, 𝔊^{ap}, 𝔗^{ap}	reading of manuscript(s) attested in the critical apparatus of an edition
10:2b	second part of verse 2 in chapter 10
10:2^{b}	additional part of a verse, usually in the Samaritan text, as numbered by von Gall
ℭ	fragments from the Cairo Geniza (cited from *BHS*)
𝔊	the Old Greek (as in the text of the Göttingen editions, where possible, but the Brooke-McLean edition for Joshua-Kings)
𝔊*	the (reconstructed) original reading of the Old Greek
𝔊^{ed}	the reading in the Göttingen or Brooke-McLean edition in contrast to an alternate reading considered to be the original Old Greek reading
𝔊^{ap}	a reading in the critical apparatus
𝔊^{A}	Codex Alexandrinus
𝔊$^{B^{mg}}$	a marginal reading in Codex Vaticanus
𝔊$^{A+}$	Codex Alexandrinus and other manuscripts
𝔊$^{B\ 93}$	Codex Vaticanus and manuscript 93
𝔊$^{pc,\ mlt,\ pl}$	a few (*pauci*), many (*multi*), or very many (*plurimi*) manuscripts
𝔊^{O}	the hexaplaric recension of Origen
𝔊^{L}	the Lucianic text
𝔊^{C}	the catena group
𝔖	the Peshitta, ed. the Peshitta Institute, Leiden
𝔗	the Targum, ed. A. Sperber
𝔗^{O}	Targum Onqelos
𝔗^{N}	Targum Neofiti
𝔗^{J}	Targum Pseudo-Jonathan
𝔗^{P}	the Palestinian Targum
𝔗$^{F(P,V)}$	Fragmentary Targum (manuscripts Paris, Vatican Ebr. 440)
𝔙	the Vulgate, ed. Monachi Sancti Benedicti
α′ σ′ θ′ ο′	attestations to the versions of Aquila, Symmachus, Theodotion, the Seventy
ϵβρ′	the Hebrew text of Origen
Arab	the Arabic version
Arm	the Armenian version
Bo	the Bohairic Coptic version
Co	the Coptic version (= Bo + Sa)
Eth	the Ethiopic version
La	witness to the Old Latin version
Sa	the Sahidic Coptic version
Syh	the Syrohexapla

NOTE(S)	the note(s) to the transcriptions in the individual editions
VAR.	the variant(s) listed after each fragment or column in the editions
Orth.	the section on orthography in the introduction to individual editions
orth.?	a form that may show (only) an orthographic difference
var.?	a form that may be a variant

aliter	otherwise
delevit	deleted
gr	a manuscript in Greek
hab	the witness has the reading
litt	*littera(e)*, letter(s)
mend	*mendaciter*, falsely
om totum comma	the entire verse is omitted
point(s) jalon(s)	dot(s) made to guide the ruling of a manuscript
pr	*praemittit, -unt*, placed before
rell	*reliqui*, the rest of the manuscripts
tr	*transpone(ndum) -it, -unt*, the letters or words are (to be) transposed
v(v)	verse(s)
vid	*ut videtur*, as it appears from the evidence available
vs.	versus

Mus. Inv. 265	Museum Inventory number
PAM 43.291	Palestinian Archaeological Museum photograph number
IAA 225.837	Israel Antiquities Authority photograph number

Cross	Frank Moore Cross. 'The Development of the Jewish Scripts', *The Bible and the Ancient Near East*. Garden City, NY: Doubleday, 1961.
Cross, *ALQ*	Frank Moore Cross. *The Ancient Library of Qumrân and Modern Biblical Studies*, rev. ed. Garden City, NY: Anchor Books, 1961.
DSS Microfiche	*The Dead Sea Scrolls on Microfiche: A Comprehensive Facsimile Edition of the Texts from the Judean Desert: Companion Volume*, ed. E. Tov with S. J. Pfann, S. A. Reed, and M. J. Lundberg. 2d ed. Leiden: Brill and IDC, 1995.
Duncan	Julie Ann Duncan, 'A Critical Edition of Deuteronomy Manuscripts from Qumran, Cave IV: 4QDt^{b}, 4QDt^{e}, 4QDt^{h}, 4QDt^{j}, 4QDt^{k}, 4QDt^{l}'. Ph.D. dissertation, Harvard University [University Microfilms], 1989.
Madrid	*The Madrid Qumran Congress: Proceedings of the International Congress on the Dead Sea Scrolls, Madrid 18–21 March, 1991*, 2 vols.; ed. Julio Trebolle Barrera and Luis Vegas Montaner. Leiden: Brill/Madrid: Editorial Complutense, 1992.
QHBT	*Qumran and the History of the Biblical Text*, ed. F. M. Cross and S. Talmon. Cambridge, MA: Harvard University Press, 1975.
Qimron	Elisha Qimron. *The Hebrew of the Dead Sea Scrolls*. HSS 29. Atlanta: Scholars Press, 1986.
THGD	J. W. Wevers. *Text History of the Greek Deuteronomy*. Göttingen, 1978.
White	Sidnie Ann White, 'A Critical Edition of Seven Manuscripts of Deuteronomy: 4QDt^{a}, 4QDt^{c}, 4QDt^{d}, 4QDt^{f}, 4QDt^{g}, 4QDt^{i}, and 4QDt^{n}'. Ph.D. dissertation, Harvard University [University Microfilms], 1988.

INTRODUCTION

THIS volume continues the publication of the series of biblical manuscripts in the Jewish script from Qumran Cave 4. It presents the manuscripts of the Books of Deuteronomy, Joshua, Judges, and Kings. An earlier volume, *DJD* XII, contains those of Genesis to Numbers, while *DJD* IX contains the biblical manuscripts written in the Palaeo-Hebrew script and those in the Greek language.

Many of these manuscripts are older by a millennium than those which previously held claim to being the most ancient Hebrew manuscripts of particular biblical books. The importance of these scrolls, however, is due not only to their great antiquity, but principally to the new and richly illuminating advances they provide for our knowledge about the text of the Bible, the complex history of the biblical text, and the process by which the Scriptures were composed and transmitted to posterity. Thus, they will be permanently valuable, providing a more sound basis for the Hebrew text of the Bible and for the translation of the Bible into modern languages.

The System of Naming and Numbering the Qumran Scrolls

For a convenient description of the system for designating the scrolls, see *The Dead Sea Scrolls on Microfiche: A Comprehensive Facsimile Edition of the Texts from the Judean Desert: Companion Volume* (ed. E. Tov with S. J. Pfann, S. A. Reed, and M. J. Lundberg; 2d ed.; Leiden: Brill and IDC, 1995) and Joseph A. Fitzmyer, *The Dead Sea Scrolls: Major Publications and Tools for Study* (rev. ed.; Atlanta: Scholars Press, 1990) 1–8. It may be helpful to mention here several points with regard to the manuscripts contained in this volume.

The manuscripts are both sequentially numbered and descriptively named, with the numbers 4Q**1–127** assigned to the biblical manuscripts from Cave 4. For example, one manuscript of Deuteronomy has the number '4Q**29**' and the name '4QDeut^{b}'. The latter denotes a Hebrew manuscript from Cave 4 at Qumran, which contains Deuteronomy, and is the second (= a, b, c, . . .) exemplar of Deuteronomy from that cave. Manuscripts 4Q**45** and 4Q**46**, 4QpaleoDeut^{r,s}, missing from the numerical sequence in the Table of Contents are already published in *DJD* IX, while manuscripts 4Q**51–53**, 4QSam^{a,b,c}, will be published in *DJD* XVII.

Moreover, decisions had to be made about the classifications and titles of manuscripts although at times the evidence could not have been fully certain in the early years after the discoveries. For example, some manuscripts survive in only a single fragment or a few small fragments and are so small that they could conceivably derive, not from a biblical manuscript, but from a commentary or from another work which simply cited or excerpted a few verses. But, due to the paucity of evidence, they are here treated as biblical scrolls. Again, certain collections of fragments, after having received a manuscript designation, were discovered to include fragments that actually belonged to more than one manuscript (e.g. 4QDeut$^{k1, k2, k3}$). Yet others which include only biblical text were recognized as being, not manuscripts of biblical books, but manuscripts with excerpted texts for liturgical or other purposes (e.g. 4QDeut$^{j, k1, n}$).

Archaeological Provenance and Dating

The archaeological data concerning Cave 4 at Qumran has been presented by Roland de Vaux in *DJD* III. 3–36 and *DJD* VI. 3–29; see also his description of Cave 1 in *DJD* I. 2–40, and see *DJD* IX. 2. Though most of the fragments were purchased from the Bedouin, the manuscripts can nevertheless be definitively linked with Cave 4, because certain scrolls are constituted by fragments which derive from both sources. For example, a number of fragments of 4QDeut[c] were among those purchased from the Bedouin, while other fragments that are manifestly integral pieces of the same scroll were unearthed in the official excavation of the cave. Thus, the archaeological dating of the site establishes a *terminus ante quem* of 68 CE for all these manuscripts, and indicates a period from the middle of the second century BCE to that *terminus* for the manuscripts copied by the community at Qumran. No *terminus a quo* emerges for those which were copied elsewhere and brought into the community. In 1991 and again in 1995, the dating of the scrolls generally and of selected scrolls specifically was confirmed by radiocarbon tests.[1]

Introductions to the Individual Editions

Because of the diverse nature of the various manuscripts collected in this volume, most of the specific introductory information will be found, not in this general INTRODUCTION to the volume (which will be designated by small capital letters), but distributed in the introductions to the individual editions (which by contrast will be designated, for example, as 'the Judg[a] introduction'). These will provide information on the physical details and dimensions of the preserved fragments, as well as the contents, palaeography, orthography, scribal peculiarities, errors, and corrections.

Bibliography. Bibliographic data, where directly pertinent to an individual manuscript, are presented at the beginning of that edition. Although many of the manuscripts have previously been published, often there is no extensive bibliography directly related to them, and no attempt at an exhaustive list has been made, though the more relevant works are usually listed. For general bibliography, see the microfiche edition and the work of Fitzmyer mentioned above, as well as the burgeoning literature on Qumran. For bibliographic items briefly noted within the editions the full details may usually be found in the ABBREVIATIONS AND SIGLA or at the beginning of that particular edition.

Physical details. Since many questions—for example, regarding criteria for deciding which scrolls were copied at Qumran—remain unanswered, observations on the physical details of the manuscripts are recorded. Measurements are usually made from ruled lines where possible. Thus, the depth of a bottom margin, for example, is measured from the last ruled line of script (i.e. the tops of the letters, since Hebrew writing was suspended from the lines) to the deepest extant part along the bottom edge. For purposes of reconstruction, the number of letters per line and lines per

[1] See G. Bonani, M. Broshi, I. Carmi, S. Ivy, J. Strugnell, and W. Wölfli, 'Radiocarbon Dating of the Dead Sea Scrolls', *Atiqot* 20 (1991) 27–32; and A. J. Timothy Jull, Douglas J. Donahue, Magen Broshi, and Emanuel Tov, 'Radiocarbon Dating of Scrolls and Linen Fragments from the Judean Desert', *Atiqot* (in press).

column is estimated where possible. The calculation of the number of letters per line includes the spaces between words.

Biblical contents. The biblical contents of the manuscripts are listed both in the introduction to each manuscript and in the comprehensive Index of Biblical Passages and Index of the Contents of the Manuscripts.

Palaeography. The palaeographic descriptions of the manuscripts in the Jewish scripts and the dates assigned to them are based primarily on the programmatic study by F. M. Cross, 'The Development of the Jewish Scripts'.[2] Specific information will normally be referred to as, for example: (Cross, p. 137, Fig. 1, Line 3).

Orthography. The orthographic profile of each manuscript is provided in the introduction to that manuscript. So that the textual character of each scroll can be more clearly grasped, simple differences in orthography, where no change in meaning is involved, should be distinguished from textual variants, which do involve meaning. Thus, the orthographic differences are listed in the introduction, whereas the textual variants are catalogued within the edition, in the VARIANTS section following the transcription of each fragment or column. In accord with this line of reasoning, some data that are properly morphological, such as variation in the pronominal suffixes (e.g. כה– vs. ך–), are listed for convenience with the orthographic differences in the introduction, not in the VARIANTS section.

Scribal corrections. Noteworthy peculiarities of the scribe or the manuscript are described, including errors as well as corrections or insertions made by the original scribe or by a later hand.

Textual character. Some of the manuscripts are textually quite interesting, others less so. In assessing the textual character, the editors have differed somewhat in approach. In the editions the lists of VARIANTS are presented as objectively as possible. But to different extents we, as editors, have offered our assessment of the textual character resulting from our study and experience of the manuscripts, in the hope that this can aid the reader.

Identification. At the end of the introduction to each manuscript the museum inventory (Mus. Inv.) number and the photograph numbers are given, so that researchers may locate the original manuscript in the Rockefeller Museum and know the photograph numbers assigned originally by the Palestine Archaeological Museum (PAM) or more recently by the Israel Antiquities Authority (IAA), and can check, for example, in the microfiche edition. Often only the most useful photograph numbers are listed, usually reflecting those primarily used by the editor and represented in the Plates. For a subsequent, more comprehensive list, see the *DSS Microfiche.*

Transcriptions, Notes, and Variants

Transcriptions and Reconstructions. The transcriptions are made from a comparison of the original manuscripts with the published photographs and with older photographs where possible. The originals, of course, sometimes clarify features that are ambiguous on the photographs. On the other hand, the writing is often more clearly visible on the

[2] F. M. Cross, 'The Development of the Jewish Scripts', *The Bible and the Ancient Near East: Essays in Honor of William Foxwell Albright* (ed. G. Ernest Wright; Garden City, NY: Doubleday, 1961) 133–202.

infrared photographs than on the ancient skin. Yet again, the older photographs sometimes show parts of letters, especially around the edges of manuscripts, which have since broken off. Thus, occasionally readings are presented in the transcriptions with a higher degree of certainty than they appear to warrant on the strength of the published plates.

Letters are transcribed according to four degrees of certainty. Though there are many more shades of difference and though subjective judgement necessarily plays a role, an effort has been made to apply the following system and terminology consistently.

Letters that are 'certain' or virtually certain are simply transcribed. Letters are considered 'probable' if the ink traces very probably form one particular letter though they could also form a second or third letter with features identical to the preserved strokes; these are indicated by a dot above the letter (e.g. בׄ). Letters are considered 'possible' if some ink is preserved and it conforms to the suggested letter but could also form any of several other letters sharing that feature; these are marked with a circlet above the letter (e.g. ב֯). Claims made for letters so marked can be only as solid as the empirical basis supporting them. 'Unidentifiable' letters, that is, those for which ink remains on the manuscript but which cannot be indentified with confidence, are indicated by circlets in the middle of the line (e.g. ∘). As regards the unidentifiable letters, an attempt has been made to reflect the number of letters by the number of circlets, but this remains ambiguous, because at times it is difficult to determine whether, for example, two ink traces formed parts of one letter or of two.

Similarly, there are different types of reconstruction which require different types of interpretation. Letters and words placed within square brackets are not preserved but are restored according to the editor's judgement for the convenience of the reader. In biblical manuscripts some unproblematic words or parts of words are supplied for context, if there is no strong reason to doubt that they had originally been in the manuscript. For example, the remainder of a partly extant word is routinely supplied for context if 𝔐, 𝔪, and 𝔊 are in agreement. Similarly, if only a word or two is missing between fragments, the lost text is sometimes supplied in order to establish the relative arrangement of the fragments. The reconstruction of individual words in the text was guided by the following criteria: first, by comparison with other extant parts or features of the particular scroll; secondly, by comparison with 𝔐, 𝔪, or 𝔊, depending upon the scroll's characteristic affinity, whether in orthography or text.

For certain manuscripts the entire text is reconstructed. Such filling in of missing but unproblematic text should be regarded as an aid to the reader and not as a conclusion by the editor that the scroll agreed with the text of 𝔐, 𝔪, or 𝔊 in every detail.

Less frequently, there are reconstructions suggested at places where the text is problematic. For example, when the various textual traditions are compared and especially quantitative variants emerge as possible, sometimes the spatial evidence preserved on the fragments indicates that the scroll probably agreed with one tradition and disagreed with another. On occasions when the evidence is sufficiently clear, the indicated reading is reconstructed and the evidence is supplied in a NOTE. When 𝔐, 𝔪, or 𝔊 disagree in more serious matters and the reading of the scroll is difficult to

determine, the text has either been reconstructed and explained in the NOTES or left unreconstructed.

Left and right margins are signalled by the lack of brackets for text printed at the respective margins. Top and bottom margins are indicated as such if a sufficient amount of the margin is preserved. They are indicated in square brackets if the margin is certain despite the lack of immediate evidence (if, for example, a contiguous column has the corresponding margin); they are listed with a question-mark if there is cause, but not proof, to suggest their occurrence.

Space that was intentionally left blank by the scribe to mark a sense-division or paragraph-division is usually denoted by *vacat*. Often there is an accompanying NOTE which lists how the 𝔐 and 𝔪 traditions divided the text. In certain cases in the transcription, the distance between fragments has been reduced in order to fit the format of these pages.

Notes. Following the transcriptions, the NOTES provide various types of information. Sometimes, as dictated by the material, a general NOTE describes features of the fragment or column as a whole or in relation to the larger arrangement of the scroll. The NOTES on individual lines or readings serve a variety of functions. First, they clarify physical problems (for example, whether a dark line is ink as opposed to shadow, or whether a blank spot is a blemish on the skin prior to the scribe's writing or simply an area where the surface layer with the writing has been lost from the skin). Secondly, they contain textual speculation regarding reconstructed—that is, not extant—variants, including instances in which clues preserved on the manuscript indicate that the scroll probably differed from 𝔐, 𝔪, or 𝔊, even if the crucial evidence does not survive. Thirdly, they record data about space intentionally left blank to mark paragraph-divisions; often the comparative data describing divisions in 𝔐 and 𝔪, as relevant, are also provided. Where the traditional type of division is unknown, simply the general term 'interval' is used. In this connection it may be useful to consult in Kittel's Foreword to BH^3 (§I e; see also the *BHS* Foreword, §I.2) his note about the divisions in 𝔐 on the basis of manuscript Leningradensis (see *DJD* IX. 6).

Variants. The catalogue of VARIANTS lists only those readings where the manuscript is extant (certain or highly probable on the scroll) and differs from one of the major Hebrew texts—other Qumran scrolls, 𝔐, or 𝔪. Ideally, 𝔊 should also be included as one of the criteria, and some editors systematically have, while others have not, made variation from 𝔊 a criterion for inclusion in the catalogue of VARIANTS. In the latter case, however, the NOTES often mention some of the more significant divergences from 𝔊. Reconstructed variants are either mentioned only in the NOTES or are listed separately after the VARIANTS section. Again, purely orthographic differences are noted in the section on orthography in the introduction to individual editions and are not listed among the VARIANTS.

Readings from 𝔐 are based on *BHS*, and those from 𝔪 are based on von Gall's edition. Readings from 𝔊 are based on Wevers' Göttingen critical edition for Deuteronomy and on the Brooke-McLean editions for Joshua, Judges, and Kings. There is no attempt to present an exhaustive list of variants from all the Greek manuscripts but only those which may have relevance for the Qumran text. Testimony of the fragments from the Cairo Geniza (ℭ) is provided on the basis of the critical apparatus in *BHS*; for further

evaluation of that material, see M. C. Davis, *Hebrew Biblical Manuscripts in the Cambridge Geniza Collection* (Cambridge, 1978).

Photographs and Plates

The attempt was made to reproduce the photographic plates on a scale of 1:1, but where this has not been possible, scales are provided. The relative distance between separate fragments on a plate, however, has at times been reduced to fit the format of these pages. Occasionally, new or simply different photographs were used for the plates in contrast to those which served as the basis for the transcription and NOTES; most differences or improvements have been entered into the editions, but it was impractical to revise the entire volume in light of these slightly divergent photographs.

28. 4QDeut^a

(PLATE I)

Preliminary publication: Sidnie Ann White, 'A Critical Edition of Seven Manuscripts of Deuteronomy: 4QDt^a, 4QDt^c, 4QDt^d, 4QDt^f, 4QDt^g, 4QDt^i, and 4QDt^n' (Ph.D. dissertation, Harvard University, 1988 [University Microfilms]) 9–18. 'Three Deuteronomy Manuscripts from Cave 4, Qumran', *JBL* 112 (1993) 23–42, esp. 23–8. 'Special Features of Four Biblical Manuscripts from Cave IV, Qumran: 4QDt^a, 4QDt^c, 4QDt^d, and 4QDt^g', *RevQ* 57–58 (1991) 157–67, esp. 158–60.

ONLY a solitary fragment, containing portions of Deut 23:26–24:8, is preserved from this manuscript. Of average thickness, and yellowish-brown in colour with darker stains in spots, its height is 10 cm and its width 13.9 cm at the broadest points. The surface of the leather was originally well-prepared; now some wrinkling and shrinkage have occurred, leaving some cracks on the surface. The right side of the fragment has a sewn edge, and the width of the margin to that edge is 1.25 cm. The regularity of the lines of script indicates that the manuscript had been ruled, although the dry lines are no longer visible. The average distance between the lines is 0.9 cm, and the reconstructed width of the column can be estimated at 12.75 cm, with 51–61 letter-spaces per line.

Palaeography establishes this formal hand in the transitional period from the Archaic to the Hasmonaean, *c*.175–150 BCE (Cross, p. 166). The letter size is variable; for example, the *ʾalep* can be quite small, and the *taw* is still fairly large, while in later Hasmonaean scripts (e.g. in 4QDeut^c and 4QSam^a) letter-size becomes standardized. Thick and thin pen strokes (e.g. in *yod* and *mem*) are still in use in this hand. The script is slightly later than that of 4QSam^b and 4QJer^a, but earlier than that of 4QSam^a; for example, the bending to the left of the leg on medial *ṣade* in 4QDeut^a does not occur in either 4QSam^b or 4QJer^a.

The orthography of 4QDeut^a is usually archaic in character. *Yod* is used as a *mater lectionis* only for $*\bar{\imath}$ and $*ay > \bar{e}$. *Waw* is regularly used for $*\bar{u}$, $*aw > \bar{o}$, and the suffix of the third masculine singular, and it is occasionally used to mark $*\bar{a} > \bar{o}$ when accented (cf. להיות in line 6), but not for any short *u* vowel (cf. יעבר in line 8). This manuscript also displays the short pronominal forms ת–, ך–, and הוא. The following is a list of merely orthographical variants found in 4QDeut^a:

24:3 (4) כרתת] כריתת 𝔐𝔖
24:4 (7) תחטא] תחטיא 𝔐; תחטיאו 𝔖; תחטאו 𝔖^{mss} (orth. and var.)
24:5 (9) נקי 𝔐] נקיא 𝔖

The scribe left three short intervals to mark paragraph-divisions in lines 1 (before 24:1), 8 (24:4-5), and 10 (24:6-7), but none at line 9 (24:5-6) where 𝔖 also lacks an interval, but 𝔐 has ס (see NOTES). On the basis of the small amount of extant evidence, it is impossible to assign 4QDeut^a to a textual tradition.

Mus. Inv. 256. PAM 43.102; 41.143, 41.192, 43.070.

Deut 23:26–24:8

1 [תני[ך] על [קמת רעך *vacat*
2 [[24:1] תמצ[א חן בעיניו כי מצא בה ערות
3 [ו[שלחה מביתו [2]והלכה והיתה לאיש
4 [[3] ו[כתב לה ספר כרתת ונתן בידה ושלחה מביתו
5 [[אשר לקחה לו לאשה [4]לא יוכל בעלה הראשו[ן]
6 [ל[שוב לקחתה להיות לו לאשה אחרי אשר הטמאה כי
7]תועבה הי[א לפני יהוה ולא תחטא את הארץ אשר יהוה אלהיך נתן לך
8]נחלה [[5]כי יקח איש אשה חדשה לא יצא בצבא ולא יעבר עליו כ]ל[
9]דבר [נקי יהיה לביתו שנה אחת ושמח את אשתו אשר לק]ח[[6]ל]א תחב[ל
10]רחי[ם ורכב כי נפש הוא חבל [7]כי ימצא איש גנ[ב]
11 ישראל] והת[עמר בו ומכרו ומת הגנ[ב]
12 [8]השמר] בנגע ה[צרעת לשמר מאד ול[עשות]
13 [צוי[תם[ ]

Part of the right margin with stitched edge has been preserved. It is certain that the words at the left of the fragment are at the left margin, since both the last word of line 9 and the first word of line 10 are partly visible.

L. 1 (23:26) There is a short interval at the end of the line before chapter 24; ס 𝔐, קצה 𝔪.

L. 2 (24:1) Spacing does not allow the inclusion of the longer 𝔪 text ובא אליה (אשה).

L. 5 (24:4) הראשו[ן]. To the left of *šin* there is an ink trace which appears to be the head of *waw*, although it could conceivably be interpreted as a *nun* (הראשן).

L. 8 (24:4-5) There is a short interval before v 5; ס 𝔐, no interval 𝔪.

L. 9 (24:6) תחב]ל. The 2nd masc. sing. form of the verb (with 𝔊𝔖) is correct in this negative commandment (cf. יחבל 𝔐𝔪𝔗). There is no interval before v 6; ס 𝔐, no interval 𝔪.

L. 10 (24:6) There is a short interval before v 7; ס 𝔐, קצה 𝔪.

L. 13 (24:8) צוי[תם[. The head of final *mem* is extant on the leather. To its right traces of ink are discernible; reconstruction of the text according to the number of letter-spaces available suggests *taw*.

VARIANTS

24:1-2 (3) והלכה[2] ו[שלחה מביתו 𝔊 סס] ושלחה מב[יתו[2] ויצאה מב[יתו והלכה 4QDeut[k2]𝔐𝔪𝔊[O]𝔗;
ܘܫܒܩܗ ܘܬܦܘܩ[2] ܡܢ ܒܝܬܗ ܘܬܐܙܠ 𝔖 (*BHS* note 2[a-a] errs)

24:4 (7) יהוה 1° 𝔐𝔪𝔗𝔖] κυριου του θεου σου 𝔊

24:4 (7) תחטא 𝔐𝔗𝔖 (תחטיא 𝔐𝔗𝔖)] תחטיאו 𝔪𝔊 (orth. and var.)

24:5 (8) כ[ל] 𝔐[mss]𝔊𝔗[ms]𝔗[J]] לכל 𝔐𝔪𝔗𝔖

24:8 (12) ול[עשות 𝔐𝔪[mss]𝔗𝔖] לעשות 𝔐[mss]𝔪𝔊 (cf 15:5)

29. 4QDeut[b]

(PLATE II)

Preliminary publication: Julie Ann Duncan, 'A Critical Edition of Deuteronomy Manuscripts from Qumran, Cave IV: 4QDt[b], 4QDt[e], 4QDt[h], 4QDt[j], 4QDt[k], 4QDt[l]' (Ph.D. dissertation; Harvard University, 1989 [University Microfilms]) 9–31 and Pls. I–IA.

EIGHT fragments from three contiguous columns of this manuscript survive, preserving portions of Deut 29:24-27; 30:3-14; 31:9-17, 24-30; and 32:1-3. The leather is of average thickness, prepared on the recto but untreated for writing on the verso. Its colour varies from light beige to a deep reddish brown. On frg. 5 the leather is cracked and wrinkled, while the other fragments have also suffered, at various points, considerable damage to the surface with some effacing of script. Dry lines for ruling are no longer evident.

There are two margins preserved on these fragments. Frg. 2 preserves a margin between two columns which fluctuates from 0.4 to 0.8 cm, since the left margin of col. I is uneven. Frg. 5 displays a top margin virtually intact, measuring 1.3 cm.

Although only those two marginal clues survive from this manuscript, their arrangement is such that the approximate height, width, and quantity of text per column may be deduced. Reconstruction according to 𝔐𝔪𝔊 suggests that the width of the columns varies somewhat: col. I has 82–88 letters per line, col. II averages 73, and col. III averages 64. The width of col. III can be estimated at *c.*10.5 cm. A calculation of text as in 𝔐𝔪𝔊 between the corresponding lines of col. I and col. II indicates approximately 26 lines per column. The broad top margin of col. III pinpoints where col. II must have ended, suggesting that the words at the top of frg. 2 were from line 8 of the column. The average distance between lines of script is 0.7 cm, and thus the estimated height of the inscribed column is *c.*15.5 cm, and of the scroll *c.*18 cm.

4QDeut[b] displays an early Hasmonaean book hand, dating *c.*150–100 BCE. Letter-size is not yet uniform; compare especially *taw* and *kap*, which can be, on occasion, quite large. *ʾAlep* is still high and small, as is the *ʿayin*. The *waw* and *yod* are often distinguished by length in this MS, e.g. יהוה frg. 5 2, and היום 5 4. The forms of *mem*, medial and final, can still be quite long, primitively so in some instances. There is little, if any, thickening of the letters for ornamentation (see Cross, pp. 175–81).

The orthography of 4QDeut[b] generally conforms to the patterns of 𝔐 and 𝔪 (see Table 1). Unaccented $\bar{o} < *\bar{a}$ is usually not represented: מצותיו col. I 12, אלהיך I 15, הנשאים II 8, אנכי III 3, ושפטיכם III 5, but cf. the fem. pl. endings in אבותם I 1, and חקותיו I 14. Accented $\bar{o} < *\bar{a}$ is represented in האלות I 11, but cf. הזאת III 1. לא is always written without *waw*, with the exception of הלוא II 18. $\bar{o} < *u$ is not marked, either in accented or in unaccented syllables: כל e.g. II 12, לאמר I 17, and לכתב III 1. $\hat{o} < *aw$ is always marked (התורה III 1, מותי III 4) with the exception of במעד II 9, cf. 𝔐. $*\bar{u}$ is always marked (ההוא II 18 and 3rd masc. pl. verbs). *Matres lectionis* are always used to mark $\hat{e} < *ay$ (e.g. אלהיך I 15, דברי II 12, אחרי III 4) and $*\bar{\imath}$ (e.g. ברית III 2, אנכי III 3, מותי III 4, כי e.g. I 13, and masc. pl. endings) but cf. להכעסו III 8. The scribe employs the short forms of independent pronouns (הוא, etc.) as well as of pronominal suffixes (ך-, ת-, etc.).

TABLE 1: *Orthography*

Col., line	Deut	4QDeut^{b}	𝔐	𝔖^{ed}	𝔖^{mss}
I 1	29:24	]א֯בותם	אבתם	אבתם	אבותם
I 14	30:10	[ו]ח֯קותיו	וחקתיו	וחקתיו	וחקותיו
I 16	30:11	]ר֯חוקה	רחקה	רחקה	רחוקה
II 9	31:10	במעד	במעד	במועד	
II 18	31:17	הלוא	הלא	הלא	הלוא
III 4	31:27	הייתם	היתם	הייתם	
III 8	31:29	להכעסו	להכעיסו	להכעיסו	להכעסו

4QDeut^{b} is not extant at any point where 𝔐 𝔖 have displayed a paragraph-division. At frg. 5 9, however, a reconstructed paragraph-division corresponding to פ 𝔐 and קצה 𝔖 is a virtual certainty, and at frg. 2 ii 13 a probability (פ 𝔐, קצה 𝔖; see NOTE at 2 ii 14). Moreover, the position of the extant words in frgs. 5–8 10–13, containing the song of Moses, indicates that the scribe arranged the song stichometrically, with two hemistichs to a line (cf. 4QpaleoDeut^{r} in *DJD* IX. 131, 147).

There are deliberate marks in the margin in frg. 2 (see NOTES at I 15 and II 15), as well as possible corrections by the original scribe at 31:16 and 31:17 (see NOTES at II 16, 17).

The variant יבחר at 31:11 with 𝔐 against בחר 𝔖 indicates that this is a Judaean, not Samaritan, form of the Book of Deuteronomy.

Mus. Inv. 1089. PAM 43.064. IAA 204.599.

Col. I: Frgs. 1, 2 i, 3 Deut 29:24-27; 30:3-14

top margin?

1 (25)]]א֯בותם כ֯[רת [
2] ו[לא֯ חלק להם]26 [
3 (27)] אד[מתם] [

[lines 4–7 missing]

f.2 8] הע[מ֯ים אשר
9 (4)] ומש[ם יקחך 5והביאך
10 (6)]]את לבבך ואת֯ לבב
11 (7)] אלהי[ך את כל האלות האלה
12 (8)] א[ת֯ כל מצות֯יו אשר אנכי֯
13 (9)] ובפרי אדמתך ובפרי] בהמ֯ת֯ך לטובה כי י֯שוב
f.3 14 (10)]]א֯שר שש[ ]מ֯צ֯ותיו[ו]ח֯קותיו הכת֯ו֯בים

15 (11)] ת]שוב אל יהוה אלהיך בכל לבב[ך]מׄצוך היׄוׄם #
16] ולא]רׄחוקה היא ממך 12 לא בׄשמׄ[ים [
17] 13 ולא] מעבׄר לים היא לאמר מי יעבׄר[[
18 (14)] הדב]רׄ מׄאד [בפי]ךׄ וׄבׄלבׄבׄך ובידך לע[שותו 15 [

The left margin is preserved for this first extant column of the manuscript. Reconstruction suggests that frg. 1 began on line 1 or 2 of the column and that frg. 2 began on line 8. The column was wide, and frg. 3 would have been more distant both from the right margin and from frg. 2 than appears in the format of the transcription.

L. 12 (30:8) מצוׄתׄיׄו. There has been surface damage to the leather, resulting in the loss of parts of the *waw*, *taw*, and *yod*.

L. 12 (30:8) אנכיׄ. Most of the *yod* has been lost due to surface damage.

L. 13 (30:9) ובפרי אדמתך ובפרי] בהמׄתׄך. Although homoioteleuton is a possibility, spatial reconstruction indicates that this MS contained the complete phrase with 𝔪𝔊. For the sequence in 𝔐 see 28:11 where 𝔐𝔪𝔊 all read ובפרי בהמתך ובפרי אדמתך.

L. 13 (30:9) יׄשׄוב. The head of *yod* is visible above the hole. Surface wear has destroyed most of the *šin*, but the tops of the right and left strokes can still be seen.

L. 14 (30:9) [ ]אׄשר. In PAM 43.064 there appear traces to the right of *ʾalep*, but they are on a separate, tiny piece which does not belong to this fragment.

L. 14 (30:10) הכׄתׄוׄבׄים. Small pieces have been rejoined to the fragment incorrectly. The stroke above the bottom stroke of *kap* (which is placed too high) may either be the top of that letter, or of the *taw* following. The right side of *taw* has been lost with the surface. A trace of the tip of *waw* is discernible just above the leg of *taw;* the rest of the letter would have been on a small piece which is no longer joined to the fragment. Part of the top stroke of *bet* has been swallowed in the crack, making it appear more narrow; most of the bottom stroke has been lost with the surface, but the end of the stroke is just visible under the *yod.*

L. 15 (30:11) היׄוׄם #. Smearing of ink has occurred around the *he*. There are three strokes of ink at the end of this line which are not part of a letter but which appear to be deliberate, rather than accidental. These markings do not correspond in kind to any of the para-textual elements discussed by Malachi Martin in *The Scribal Character of the Dead Sea Scrolls* (Louvain: Publications Universitaires, 1958) 1. 144–203.

L. 16 (30:12) בׄשמׄ[ים. The baseline of *mem* is discernible just under the gap in the leather.

VARIANTS

29:24 (1) כׄ]רת] pr אשר 𝔐𝔪; cf 𝔊ℭ𝔖
30:4^{fin} (9) יקחך 𝔐𝔪𝔊^{AO}ℭ𝔖𝔙] + יהוה אלהיך* 𝔊^{BCdnt}
30:9 (13) בפרי אדמתך ובפרי] בהמׄתׄך 𝔪𝔊] ובפרי בהמתך ובפרי אדמתך 𝔐ℭ𝔖𝔙 (see NOTE)
30:9 (13) לטובה 𝔐𝔪𝔊^{Odt}ℭ𝔖] > 𝔊^{ABCn}
30:10 (14) ו]חׄקותיו 𝔐𝔪ℭ𝔖𝔙] + ומשפטיו* 𝔊
30:10 (14) הכׄתׄוׄבׄים cf ℭ^{OJ}𝔖] הכתובה 𝔐𝔪
30:11 (16) היא 𝔪ℭ] הוא 𝔐
30:11 (16) ממך 𝔊] > 𝔐𝔪ℭ𝔖
30:13 (17) היא 𝔪ℭ] הוא 𝔐
30:14 (18) ובידך 𝔊] > 𝔐𝔪ℭ𝔖𝔙

Col. II: Frgs. 2 ii, 4 Deut 31:9-17

8	(10)	[לו]י הנשאים֯] את ארון [	
9	(11)	במעד שנת ◦] [	
10	(12)	יבחר תקראו] [	
11		והטף וגרך] [	
12	(13)	א֯ת֯ כל דברי הת֯[ורה [	
13		] [	
14		14וי[אמר יהוה [	
15	(15)	◦] עמוד הע[נ]ן פתח ה֯א֯ה֯[ל [	f.4
16		16] א]ל֯ה֯י נ֯{א֯}כ֯ר֯ ה֯א֯[ר]ץ֯] [	
17	(17)	]]בו ביום הה֯וא◦◦◦] [	
18		] ואמר ביו]ם֯ ההוא הלוא על◦◦] [	

The right margin of this column is partly preserved, continuing from the previous column. The first extant part of frg. 2 ii is line 8, which aligns with the equivalent line in col. I (frg. 2 i). Frg. 4 could fall either on line 15 or line 16, depending on whether the intervening text corresponded to 𝔐𝔪 or to the slightly longer text of 𝔊. The material evidence seems to favour the former option: the similar contours of the top and left edges of frgs. 3 and 4 indicate that the line reading פתח ה֯א֯ה֯[ל (frg. 4 15) is in horizontal alignment with the one containing ת]שוב אל יהוה אלהיך בכל לבב[ך (frg. 3 15). There are several indistinct traces on this fragment; in particular the reading of line 16, where the surface has been much eroded, is now impossible to determine with any certainty. The letters which can be identified are distorted and, in some instances, are unevenly spaced (for instance, הה֯וא◦◦◦ in line 17, and הלוא in line 18). These factors suggest that the scribe may have been writing on a damaged surface.

L. 12 (31:12) הת֯[ורה. The surface has been lost where the short angular base of *taw* should be visible.

L. 14 (31:14) וי[אמר. Reconstruction indicates that the extant *waw* and *yod* belong to ויאמר, the first word of verse 14. The reconstructed text between the last extant part of line 12 and this point is somewhat short of filling two lines, suggesting the possibility of an interval in the MS; 𝔐 פ, 𝔪 קצה.

L. 15 (31:14) The two strokes seen at the margin here are ink; they appear to be deliberate rather than accidental. The horizontal stroke resembles a paragraphos, but it would apparently occur in the middle of v 14. The lower stroke may well be the initial letter in line 15, perhaps *waw* of ויתיצבו (compare the *waw* immediately above).

L. 15 (31:15) הע[נ]ן. For medial *nun* here, compare ב֯[עי]נ֯י, frg. 5 8 (see esp. IAA 204.599; cf. ע֯נ[ן also in 4QDeut[j] at col. III 1, 5:22). The faint lines to the right of medial *nun* in the photograph are not ink, the surface of the leather has been entirely destroyed here. (The dark trace in the photograph, above and to the right, is not ink.)

L. 15 (31:15) ה֯א֯ה֯[ל. The traces appear to be the remnants of *he, ʾalep, he*. The right leg of the first *he* is visible; the crossbar of the letter is caved in, and the left leg has been destroyed with the surface.

The lower left leg, and the diagonal of *ʾalep* are visible. Most of the second *he* is rubbed away, but the lower tips of the legs remain.

L. 16 (31:16) נ{א}כר. Much of the surface in this line has been lost, which may reflect an attempted erasure. The proposed decipherment would suit the spacing of the fragment but is problematic palaeographically, though the tail of the final *ṣade* in the following הארץ helps anchor it. The clearest ink strokes, 1 cm in from the right edge, are best seen as *kap,* and the following oblique stroke as *reš*. The letter preceding *kap* is smudged, with a diagonal stroke emerging from the bottom left, suggestive of *ʾalep*. The top half of a possible *nun* is preserved just before the smudge. Both the possibility of an erasure and the traces suggestive of *ʾalep* indicate that the scribe may have begun writing אחרים (אלהי), as in vv 18 and 20, for נכר (אלהי) of this verse.

L. 17 (31:17)]◦◦◦. The only thing which can be said with certainty is that 4QDeut^{b} is not reading עזבתים (cf. 𝔐ш𝔊). The strokes appear to have been overwritten, perhaps in an attempt at correction; note in particular the first letter (*waw* or *reš*?) following ההוא. The vertical stroke seen above this letter is ink. A possible reading is ו<ז>נח]תים, taking the stroke above the line as a supralinear *zayin* (cf. Zech. 10:6, which reads והיו כאשר לא זנחתים). This proposal is problematic from a palaeographical standpoint as the head of the *waw* is oversized (but compare frg. 5 6, ואע]ידה) and the right leg of *ḥet* somewhat long; considerable distortion of the letters, however, must be assumed in any case, since they suit no identification well.

VARIANTS

31:11 (10) יבחר 𝔐𝔊ℭ𝔖𝔙] בחר ш. This variant shows that this MS is not a Samaritan form of the text.

31:11 (10) תקראו 𝔊] תקרא 𝔐𝔊^{O}ℭ𝔙; 𝔖 [illegible]; יקרא ш

31:15 (15) פתח; cf Exod 33:9(ועמד פתח האהל)] pr על 𝔐ш𝔊(επι)ℭ𝔖

Col. III: Frgs. 5–8 Deut 31:24–32:3

1 [ ]משה לכתב את דברי התורה הזאת על ספר עד תמם 25ויצו משה א[ת

2 [ ]ברית יהוה לאמר 26לקח את ספר התורה הזאת ושמתם אתו מצד[ ]

3 [ ]אלה]יכם והיה שם בך לעד 27כי אנכי ידעתי את מריך ואת ערפך ה[קשה]

4 [ ]ע]מכם היום ממרים הייתם עם יהוה ואף כי אחרי מותי 28הק[הילו]

5 [ ] שבטיכם[וזקניכם] ושפטיכם ושטריכם ואדברה ב[אזניהם]

6 [ ]ה]אלה ואע[ידה בם את הש]מים ואת הארץ 29כי ידעתי א[חרי]

7 [ ]תשחתו[ן] וסרתם מן]ה[ד]רך אשר צויתי את[כ]ם וק[ראת]

(30) 8 f.6 [ ]הי]מ[י]ם[ ]כי תעש]ו את ה]רע ב[עי]ני יהוה להכעסו [ ]

9 [ ]קה]ל ישרא[ל את]דברי השירה הזאת[עד תמם *vacat* [

10 f.7 [32:1האזינו [ ]◦]◦[ ]◦ ואדבר◦[ ] ותשמע הארץ אמ[רי פי *vacat* [

11 f.8 [2יערף כמטר ל]קח[י תזל כט]ל אמרתי[*vacat* [

12 [כשעירם עלי דשא וכרביבים]עלי ע[שב *vacat* [

13 [3כי שם יהוה אקרא הבו]גדול[ה לאלהינו *vacat* [

On this piece the leather is blackened in some areas and its surface is corrugated and occasionally cracked and split. Photographs 42.064 and 204.599 [partial] should both be consulted; 204.599, which is more recent, shows a new join of two small pieces near the end, but at three points (see lines 6 and 8) small bits of leather are no longer extant. This column averages about 64 letter-spaces to a line. The extant material in lines 10–13 of the song of Moses indicates that the scribe was writing stichometrically, with two hemistichs to a line (cf. 4QpaleoDeut[r] in *DJD* IX. 131, 147).

L. 4 (31:27) עְ]מָכֶם. The surface near the edge of the leather has been almost entirely destroyed; the lower left portion of medial *mem* is visible, as well as the head and downstroke of *kap*. Only a trace of the top of final *mem* remains.

L. 5 (31:28) שִׁבְטֵיכם. The tips of the right and middle arms of *šin* are evident, as well as the base-stroke of *bet*.

L. 6 (31:28) ה]אֵלה. Most of the *ʾalep* has been destroyed with the surface, but a part of the left leg remains (for *he* see PAM 42.064).

L. 7 (31:29) תִּשחתִוֻן. The top of *nun* is just discernible.

L. 7 (31:29) הִ[ד]רך. Only the left leg of *he* is visible.

L. 8 (31:29) הי]מִ[י]םִ. The stroke below the *ḥet* of תִּשחתִוֻן (line 7) is tentatively identified as the top of final *mem*.

L. 8 (31:29) בְ[עי]נֹ. The faint lines following the gap in the photograph are the traces of *nun* and *yod*.

L. 9 (31:30) קה]לֹ. The stroke of *lamed* is barely visible on the edge of the leather.

L. 9 (31:30) דִּבְרִי. Only the head of *dalet* is visible. The downstroke of *bet* is split, and part of the lower stroke has been lost. *Yod* has been distorted due to numerous cracks running through the leather at this point.

L. 9–10 (31:30[fin]–32:1) The exant letters in line 10 indicate that the scribe left the end of line 9 blank and began a new line with the beginning of the poem in 32:1; פ 𝔐, קצה 𝔐𝔰.

L. 10 (32:1) °[ ]°[ ]° [. The first trace may be the *šin* of השמים. The third circlet represents two traces of ink, which are virtually one on top of the other.

L. 10 (32:1) ואדברה°. There are two dots of ink, one above the tear and one below, which are probably part of the *he* (cf. ואדברה 𝔐𝔰).

L. 10 (32:1) ותשמע הארץ. Most of the *ʿayin* has been swallowed in the crack. Of the *he* only the right side (note the evidence of the breakthrough) and the left corner remain on the leather.

L. 11 (32:2) כט]לֹ אמרתי[. The reading of *ʾalep* is doubtful, but the rest of the letters in this word are more certain. The preceding trace of ink high above the line and below the *taw* of ותשמע in line 10 is *lamed*.

L. 12 (32:2) עְ]שב. A small part of the right arm of *ʿayin* has been lost, but the reading is certain.

L. 13 (32:3)]גִּדֹוֹלֹ[ה. The left side of *gimel* is preserved (typically in this MS the left leg joins the downstroke near the top, see ונרך frg. 2 ii 11). The head of *dalet* is slightly distorted by a crack in the leather. The head of *waw* is just visible on the edge of the leather, as is the top of *lamed*.

VARIANTS

31:26 (2) לקח 𝔐] לקחו 𝔰 cf 𝔊ℭSD

31:26 (2) הזאת ℭℭ[J]] הזה 𝔐𝔰ℭ[ONS]

31:27 (4) יהוה 𝔐𝔰𝔊[848]ℭS] *האלהים 𝔊[ABOCdnt]

31:28 (5) [זקניכם] ושפטיכם 𝔊] > 𝔐𝔰ℭSD

32:3 (13)]גִּדֹוֹלֹ[ה] גדל 𝔐𝔰 (cf Ps 145:3, 6; 2 Sam 7:21, 23)

30. 4QDeut[c]

(PLATES III-IX)

Preliminary publication: Sidnie Ann White, 'A Critical Edition', 19–132; 'Special Features', 160–62.

THE LARGEST Deuteronomy manuscript from Cave 4 is 4QDeut[c]. It has the greatest amount of text from the most number of chapters, and consists of 55 identifiable fragments, and eleven which have not yet been identified. The original colour of the manuscript was a yellowish brown, now greyish brown on certain fragments, yellow with darker stains on others, and dark brown on others. The leather was of medium thickness and well-prepared, but now it is quite dry and cracked, so that the surface is extremely damaged at certain points. A certain amount of wrinkling and shrinkage has occurred. On some fragments (e.g. frg. 51) the leather has become so black that the letters are barely visible, while on others (e.g. frgs. 37–41) they are worn and faded. Vertical and horizontal dry lines are visible on the manuscript (e.g. frg. 5).

Portions of 23 columns are represented in this manuscript, having *c*.27 lines per column. There appear to be two column widths in the manuscript: a shorter width of approximately 36–46 letter-spaces, and a longer width of approximately 47–58 letter-spaces. Frg. 54 col. ii is a special case because it contains, in its one extant line, part of Deut 32. On the basis of the number of lines that column must have contained (estimated from the bottom line of frg. 54 col. i), chap. 32 seems to be written stichometrically, with one stichos of poetry (one-half verse in Hebrew) per line.

Five fragments have two partially extant columns: 3, 25?, 32, 45, and 54. Two fragments have an extant top margin: 4 and 46. Frgs. 16, 27, 45, 53, and 54 have preserved a bottom margin. A right margin is present on frgs. 5 (with remains of stitching), 27, 41, and 50, and a left margin on frgs. 5, 6, 20, 29, 36, 47, and 53 (with remains of stitching). The average distance between columns is 1.35 cm. The average distance from line to line is 0.9 cm.

The surviving fragments preserve portions of the following text of Deuteronomy:

3:25-26	11:3, 9-13, 18	26:19–27:2
4:13-17, 31-32	12:18-19, 26, 31	27:24–28:14, 20,
7:3-4	13:5, 7, 11-12, 16	22-25, 29-30,
8:1-5	15:1-4, 15-19	48-50, 61
9:11-12, 17-19	16:2-3, 6-11	29:17-19
9:29–10:2	16:21–17:5, 7	31:16-19
10:5-8	17:15–18:1	32:3

The hand of 4QDeut[c] is a typical Hasmonaean book hand, to be dated *c*.150–100 BCE (roughly the same date as 1QIsa[a]). This is a clear, precise script, with letters of uniform size and very little thickening of the letters for ornamentation. The letters which give the clearest indication of Hasmonaean date are: *ʾalep*, *gimel* (on which the left leg joins where the right leg curves inward), *ḥet*, *kap* (which can sometimes have a straight downstroke), *mem* (which can sometimes have a straight downstroke), *nun*, *ṣade* (where the bend of the tail has become a base stroke on the medial form), and *reš*, all of which have become standard sized.

4QDeut[c], in its extant portions, uses a fairly full orthography (see Table 1). It consistently uses *matres lectionis* to mark **aw* > *ô* (e.g. יוסיפו frg. 24 2, או 32 ii 7), **ay* > *ê* (e.g. בני 10 2, דב[ר]י 55 i 7), **ī* (e.g. כי 5 5) and **ū* (e.g. 3rd masc. pl. verbs, but cf. שבעות 32 i 7). The manuscript uses a *waw* to mark **ā* > *ō* when it is accented (e.g. שמוע 15 8), however, unaccented **ā* > *ō* (e.g. all forms of אלהים) is not marked. לא is never written with a *mater lectionis*. Short **u*, **a*, and **i* are never marked with *matres lectionis*. 4QDeut[c] uses the short forms of the pronominal suffixes, הוא, ך-, etc.

TABLE 1: *Orthography*

Frg., Line	Deut	4QDeut[c]	𝔐	ɯ[ed]	ɯ[mss]
2–3 i 2	4:14	[ו]אותי	ואתי	ואתי	
2–3 i 3	4:14	לעשותכם	לעשתכם	לעשותכם	
5 2	8:2	הוליכך	הליכך	הוליכך	הולכך
5 3	8:2	נסותך	לנסתך	לנסותך	
5 4	8:3	וירעיבך	וירעבך	וירעבך	
5 4	8:3	ויאכילך	ויאכלך	ויאכלך	ויאכילך
5 4	8:3	אבותיך	אבתיך	אבתיך	אבותיך
5 5	8:3	הודיעך	הודעך	הודיעך	הודיך
7–8 2	9:18	כראשונה]	כראשנה	כראישונה	
9 2	10:1	הראשו[נים	כראשנים	כראישונים	
12–15 4	11:10	ברגליך	ברגלך	ברגליך	
12–15 6	11:12	אותה	אתה	אתה	
12–15 8	11:13	שמוע	שמע	שמע	
16 2	11:18	לטוטפות	לטוטפת	לטטפות	לטטפת[Sad]
21 1	13:5	ואות[ו]	ואתו	ואתו	
24 2	13:12	יוסיפו	יוספו	יוספו	יוסיפו
32 i–33 6	16:9	שבעות	שבעת	שבעות	
32 i–33 8	16:10	נדבות	נדבת	נדבת	
35 1	17:7	בראש[נה	בראשנה	בראישונה	
36–41 10	17:20 (orth. or var.?) רום		רום	רם	ראם
43–45 i 5	28:1	שמוע	שמוע	שמע	
43–45 i 6	28:1	אנוכי	אנכי	אנכי	
43–45 i 7	28:2	והש[י]גוך	והשיגך	והשיגוך	
43–45 i 10	28:6	בבואך	בבאך	בבאך	
43–45 i 11	28:7	אויביך	איביך	איביך	

Intervals to mark paragraph-division in 4QDeut[c] appear at the following places:

Frg. 32 i 6 (16:8) interval] ס 𝔐, קצה ɯ

Frg. 35 2 (17:7) interval] ס 𝔐, קצה ɯ

Frg. 42 2 (26:19) interval] ס 𝔐, קצה ɯ

Frg. 54–55 i 4 (31:17) interval after וצרות] no interval 𝔐ɯ, קצה ɯ[mss]

It can be said with assurance that 4QDeut^c is not a manuscript of the Samaritan tradition, since, in the one instance in the chapters represented by this manuscript where 𝔪 purposely revises its text to agree with the parallel text of Numbers (chap. 10), 4QDeut^c does not agree with 𝔪, but follows the text of 𝔐 and 𝔊.

Mus. Inv. 237, 238, 243.

PAM 43.065, 43.067, 43.069; 40.610, 40.968, 41.189, 41.592, 41.939, 42.006, 42.630, 42.705, 42.716, 44.016.

Frg. 1 Deut 3:25-26

1] הארׄ[ץׄ הט]ובה [
2] והלב]נון 26ויתעבׄ[ר [
3]]יׄהׄו[ה [

Frgs. 2–3 col. i Deut 4:13-17

f.3 1 [לע]שות עשׂ[רת לח]ות אבנים
2 [14ו]אותׄי צׄו[ה]חׄקים ומשפטים
3 לׄעשותכם אׄ]ותם ה]ירדן שמה
4 (15)]]רׄאיתם כל תמונׄ[ה]
5] 16פן תשח]תון ועשיתם
6 (17)]]בהמה אשר

VARIANTS

4:14 (3) ה]ירדן] > 𝔐𝔪𝔊ℭ𝔖𝔙 (cf 4:26)

4:15 (4) כל תמונׄ[ה] 𝔐𝔪𝔊^{Odt}ℭ𝔙] ομοιωμα 𝔊^{ABC}𝔖

Frg. 3 col. ii Deut 4:31-32

2 (32) אשר נשבע[[
3 אשׂ]ר]בׄרׄאׄ[[

L. 2 נשבע[. The original scribe wrote *bet*, perhaps correcting from a *kap*.

Frg. 4 Deut 7:3-4

top margin

1] ל]בנך ^{4}כ[י [

2] אף יהוה]אלהי[כם [

VARIANT

7:4 (2) אלהי[כם] > 𝔐𝔪𝔊𝔗𝔖𝔙; ο θεος 𝔊^{V}

Frg. 5 Deut 8:1-5

1 (2)]]ה̊א̊[ר]ץ̊ אשר נשבע ∘∘∘] [

2 הוליכך יהוה אלהיך זה ארבעים שנה] [

3 נסותך ולדעת את אשר בלבבך התשמר מצות̊[יו אם לא ^{3}ויענך]

4 וירעיבך ויאכילך את המן אשר לא ידעת ולא ידעו אבותיך

5 למען הודיעך כי לא על הלחם לבדו יחיה האדם כי על כל מ̊ו̊[צא פי]

6 יהוה יחיה האדם ^{4}שלמתך{ך} לא בלתה מעלי̊ך̊] [

7 זה ארבעים שנה ^{5}וידע[ת ע]ם̊ ל̊[בבך [

Frg. 5 contains a right margin with the remains of stitching and a left margin at line 4.

L. 6 (8:4) Directly to the left of שלמתך is a faint, erased *kap*.

VARIANTS

8:1 (1)]ה̊א̊[ר]ץ̊ 𝔐𝔪𝔊^{Bdnt}𝔗𝔖𝔙] +αγαθην 𝔊^{AC}

8:2 (2) זה ארבעים שנה] 4QDeut^{e,f}𝔐𝔪𝔊^{Odt}𝔗𝔖𝔙] > 𝔊^{ABC}La

8:2 (3) נסותך] לנס(ו)תך 𝔐𝔪𝔗𝔙; και εκπειραση σε 𝔊; ܘܢܢܣܝܟ 𝔖

8:2 (3) ולדעת 𝔊𝔖𝔙] לדעת 𝔐𝔪𝔗

8:2 (3) את אשר 𝔐𝔗] אשר 𝔐^{ms}𝔪; ܟܠ ܕܐܝܬ 𝔖

8:3 (4) המן 4QDeut^{f}𝔐𝔪𝔊$^{AB^{*}O}$𝔗𝔖𝔙] +εν τη ερημω 𝔊$^{Bmg mss}$

8:3 (4) לא ידעת ולא ידעו 4QDeut^{f}𝔐𝔪𝔊^{O}𝔗𝔖𝔙 (ידעון 4QDeut^{f}𝔐)] ουκ ηδεισαν 𝔊

8:3 (5) מ̊ו̊[צא 𝔐𝔪𝔗] ρηματι τω εκπορευομενω 𝔊; ܕܢܦܩ 𝔖; *quod egreditur* 𝔙

8:4 (6) שלמתך] שמלתך 4QDeut^{e}𝔐𝔪𝔗

8:4 (6) לא בלתה 𝔐𝔪𝔊^{AOCdnt}𝔗] ουκ επαλαιωθη απο σου τα υποδηματα σου ου κατετριβη 𝔊^{B};
ܠܐ ܒܠܝܘ 𝔖

Frg. 6 Deut 9:11-12

[ ]אׄלי 1
[ ]יהו]ה אלי (12) 2
[ ]אשׁר 3

Frgs. 7–8 Deut 9:17-19

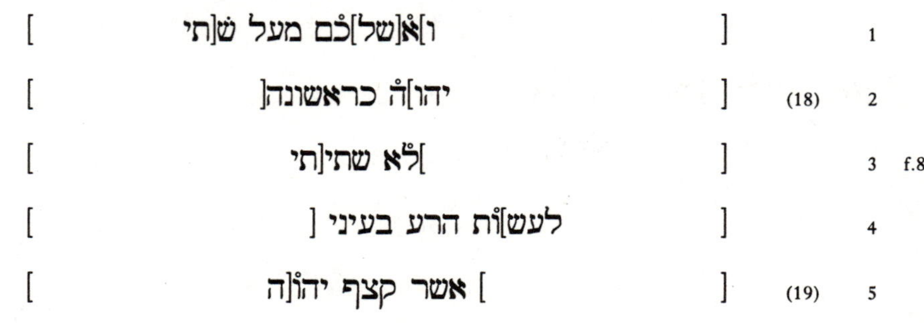
[ ]ו]אׄ[של]כׄם מעל שׄ[תי [1
[ ]יהו]הׄ כראשונה[[(18) 2
[ ]לׄ֯א שתי[תי [3 f.8
[ ]לעש]וׄת הרע בעיני [[4
[ ]אשר קצף יהו֯]ה [(19) 5

bottom margin?

VARIANTS

9:17 (1) [שׄ]תי 𝔐𝔪𝔊^Bdnt ℭ𝔖𝔙 **]** > 𝔊^AC

9:18 (2) יהו]ה֯ 𝔐𝔪ℭ𝔖𝔙 **]** + δευτερον 𝔊

Frg. 9 Deut 9:29–10:2

[ ]הנטוי]הׄ [10:1] בעת [[1
[ ]אב[נׄים הראשו[נים [2
א]שׁר
[ ]יהוה [[(2) 3

The identification of this fragment is dubious. Of all possible loci in 𝔐, the fragment fits Deut 10:1-2 the best, but it contains variants not found in any of the other witnesses.

L. 1 (9:29) הנטוי]הׄ. There is a trace of ink extant to the right of *bet* which may be *he*.

L. 3 (10:2) א]שׁר. This is a supralinear correction. The *reš* is clear on the leather. The left down-stroke and upper arm of *šin* are faintly visible. If *ʾalep* was visible, it has completely faded off the leather. This word would appear to be the אשר of 10:2 which occurs after הדברים. If this is the case, it would strengthen the argument that יהוה is a mistake for היו (see below), since if אשר was omitted by parablepsis, the natural place for its restoration would be over the following word. It is also possible that this correction signals a large haplography in the text after עץ at the end of v 1. The reconstruction of the text would place עץ at the end of line 2, a line of 45 letter-spaces (line 1 contains 44). This does not leave room at the beginning of line 3 for all of ואכתב על הלחת את הדברים אשר (assuming that יהוה is a mistake for היו). Therefore, most of this text must have been written, with אשר, above the line.

VARIANTS

10:1 (2) הראשו]נים] כראשנים 𝔐⅏𝔊ℭ𝔖𝔙.

10:2 (3) יהוה] > 𝔐⅏𝔊ℭ𝔖𝔙. This is a unique variant. According to the amount of space available in lines 2 and 3, יהוה should stand approximately where the other witnesses read הדברים in 10:2. It is possible that this is a variant text reading דברי יהוה. Slightly later in the verse היו appears. It is also possible that יהוה is a scribal error for היו. It should be noted that earlier in the verse, 𝔊^{B} has a 2nd person verb, γραψεις, instead of the 1st person verb ואכתב. If 4QDeut^{c} had a 2nd masc. sing. verb, the subject of which would be Moses, the phrase דברי יהוה would make better sense. However, the text of 𝔊^{B} is τα ρηματα, in agreement with 𝔐 et al. Finally, in v 4 we find the phrase הדברים אשר דבר יהוה, with the verb ויכתב. Therefore, יהוה here may be an anticipation of יהוה in v 4.

Frg. 10 Deut 10:5-8

1 [בארו]ןׄ [אשר ע]שיתי[ ]

2 [vacat]⁶ו]בני ישראל נסׄ[עו]

3 (7) [ו]יׄקבר שם ויׄ[כהן]

4 (8) [ו]מׄןׄ הגדגדה[ ]

5 [ש]בׄט[ ]

L. 2 (10:5) Although it is unusual to find an interval at the beginning of a line, there probably was one at the beginning of line 2 before ו]בני, the first word of v 6 (cf. similarly at 28:1), since there is a trace of final *nun* from בארו]ןׄ at the beginning of line 1, and v 5 ends at the end of line 1; interval 𝔐, קצה ⅏.

VARIANTS

10:6 (2–3) [מוסרה שם מת אהרן ו]יׄקבר שם ויׄ[כהן אלעזר בנו תחתיו] 𝔐𝔊ℭ𝔖𝔙] > ⅏

10:7 (4) ו]מׄןׄ הגדגדה[𝔐𝔊ℭ𝔖𝔙] משם ⅏

Frg. 11 Deut 11:3

1 [ ]3[°° אׄתׄ[יו]

2 [מ]לך מצרׄ[ים]

VARIANT

11:3 (2) מ]לך מצרׄ[ים 𝔐𝔊ℭ𝔖𝔙] > ⅏

Frgs. 12–15 Deut 11:9-13

1] נ]שבע יהוה[לא]ב[תיכם [
2]]זבת חלב ודבש 10כי ה]ארץ [
3] מצ]רים היא אשר[[
כנ]ן הירק
4]]ברגליך 11וה]ארץ [
5 (12)]]הרים[ובקע]ת למט]ר [f.13
6] יהו]ה אלהיך דרש אותה[[f.14,15
7] השנ]ה ועד אחרי]ת [
8 13] שמוע תשמ]עו [[
9]]◦ ◦[[

L. 2 (11:9)]זבת חלב. The left side of *ḥet* is visible on the plate. After the photograph was taken, a small piece with the preceding word זבת was joined to the fragment in the museum.

L. 4 (11:10)]ברגליך כנ]ן הירק. The *yod* is marked by correction dots, indicating that the correct reading is ברגלך, as in 𝔐. The original scribe inserted כנ]ן supralinearly, and presumably the final word הירק as well.

Variants

11:10 (3) היא 4QDeut^k1(היאה)𝔐] הוא 𝔐

11:10 (4)]ברגליך = ברגלך 𝔐ℭ] ברגליך 4QDeut^k1(ברגליכה)𝔐σ′(α′ Syh); τοις ποσιν (+αυτων 𝔊^B) 𝔊; ܒܪܓܠܝܟ S (orth. or var.?)

Frg. 16 Deut 11:18

1] דבר[י אלה על[[
2] והי[ו לטוטפות בין עיניכ[ם 19 [

bottom margin

Variant

11:18 (1) דבר[י אלה 𝔐𝔐ℭ𝔇] τα ρηματα ταυτα 𝔊; ܦܬܓܡܐ ܗܠܝܢ S

Frgs. 17–18 Deut 12:18-19

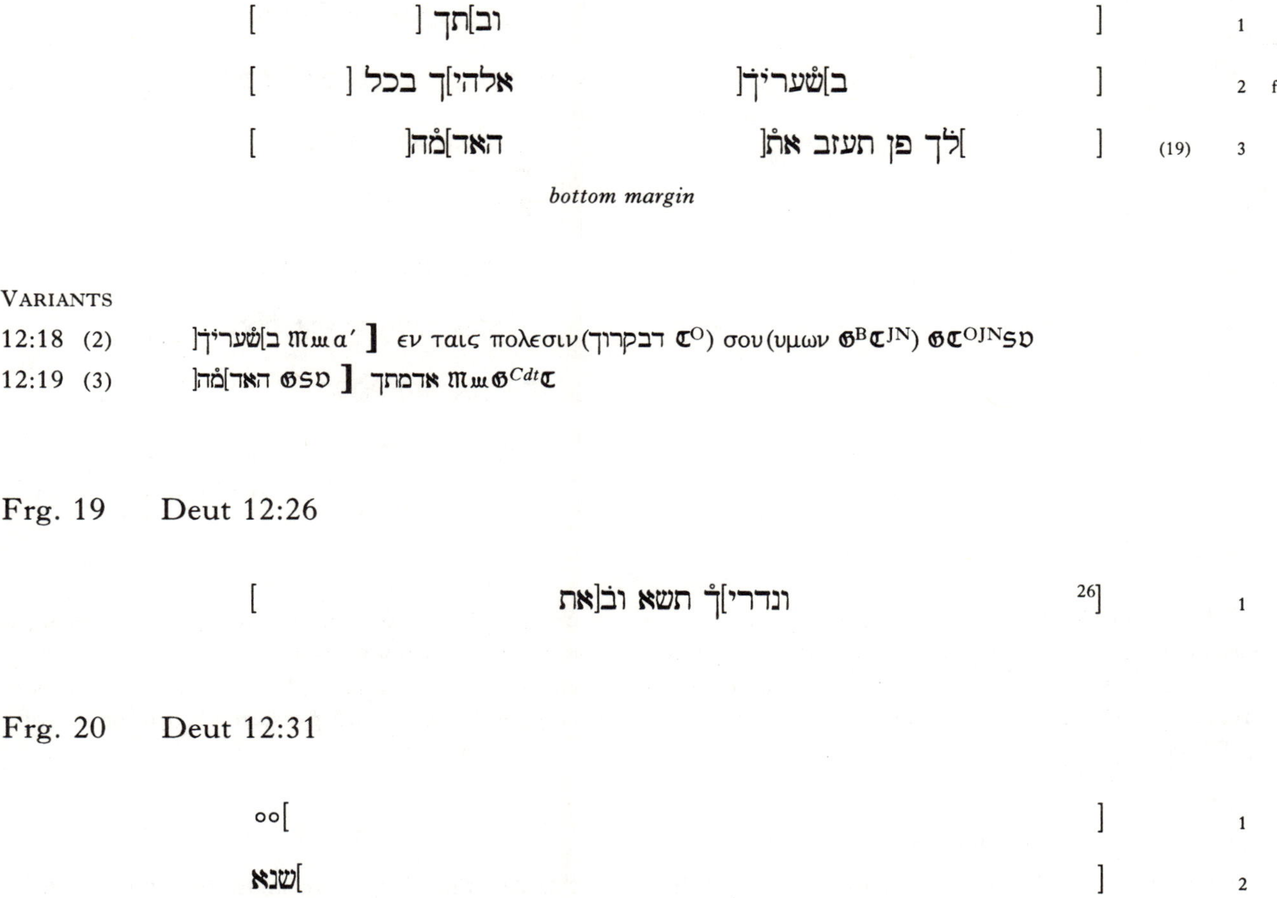

1] וב]תך [[

2] ב]שׂעריׄך[אלהי]ך בכל [[f.18

3 (19)]לׄך פן תעזב אתׄ[האד]מׄה[[

bottom margin

VARIANTS

12:18 (2) ב]שׂעריׄך[𝔐𝔪 α′] εν ταις πολεσιν (דבקרוך 𝔗O) σου (υμων 𝔊B𝔗JN) 𝔊𝔗OJN𝔖𝔙

12:19 (3) האד]מׄה[𝔊𝔖𝔙] אדמתך 𝔐𝔪𝔊Cdt𝔗

Frg. 19 Deut 12:26

1 26] ונדרי]ךׄ תשא ובׄ[את [

Frg. 20 Deut 12:31

1] [∘∘

2] [שנא

The identification of this fragment is made on the basis of palaeography and physical characteristics. There are only two places in Deuteronomy where שנא appears, at 12:31 and 16:22. This fragment cannot fit at 16:22, since the reconstruction of frgs. 32 and 34 col. ii, which preserve part of chap. 16, demands that שנא appear in the middle of a line. This fragment preserves a left margin after שנא; therefore it must be identified as 12:31.

Frg. 21 Deut 13:5

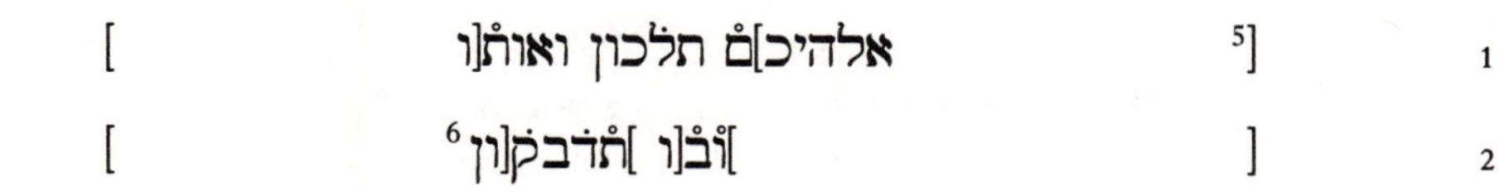

1 5] אלהיכ]םׄ תלכון ואותׄ[ו [

2]]ובׄ[ו]תׄדבקׄ[ון 6 [

VARIANT

13:5 (1) תלכו 𝔐] תלכון 𝔪

Frgs. 22–23 Deut 13:7

] בן]אביׄךׄ[או בן אמך] אׄוׄ בנך או אש]ת [1

]]אשר כנפׄ[שך בסתר לאמ]רׄ נׄלׄ[כה [2

VARIANTS

13:7 (1) בן אמך 𝔐ℭ𝔖𝔙] בן] אביׄךׄ[או בן אמך] 𝔪𝔊

13:7 (1) בנך או אש]ת] בנך או בתך או אשת 𝔐𝔪𝔊ℭ𝔖𝔙

Frg. 24 Deut 13:11-12

] (12) מ]צׄרים מבׄ[ית [1

]]יׄוסיפו לׄ[עשות [2

VARIANT

13:12 (2)]יׄוסיפו 𝔐ℭ𝔖] יוסיפו עוד 𝔪𝔊^{AOCdnt}; προσθησει ετι 𝔊^{B}

Frg. 25 col. i

]סׄתדׄ[ ]ת[1

]∘[2

It is not clear whether this fragment really contains two separate columns, or if the original join is correct. Since the first part of the fragment is unidentified, we have presented it as two separate columns for the convenience of the reader.

L. 1]סׄתדׄ[. The letter on the right is tentatively identified as *samek* because of the loop on its left. The letter identified as *dalet* may have a trace of a left downstroke as well as a right downstroke; if this is the case, then the letter might be identified as *he*.

Frg. 25 col. ii Deut 13:16

ואת בהמתה] [1

[ ]∘[ ]∘[ ] [2

VARIANT

13:16 (1) ואת בהמתה 𝔐𝔪𝔊^{Odt}ℭ𝔖𝔙] > 𝔊

Frgs. 26–27 Deut 15:1-4

1 [ ] *vacat* [ ] [
2 [ת]ע֯שה ש֯מ֯טה [2]ו֯זה ד[בר [
3 כ֯ל בעל משה֯ ידו אש֯[ר [
4 (3) [ל]א֯ יגש כי קרא שמ֯[טה [
5 (4) [ואשר]י֯היה לך את א֯[חיך [
6 [בך א]ביון כי ברך֯[[
7 אלהיך נתן ל֯[ך [

bottom margin

Variants

15:2 (3) בעל 𝔐𝔪𝔗S] > 𝔊
15:2 (4) [ל]א֯ יגש כי קרא 𝔊] לא יגש את רעהו ואת (את 𝔪) אחיו כי קרא 𝔐𝔪𝔗S𝔙; τον αδελφον σου ουκ απαιτησεις, οτι επικεκληται 𝔊
15:2 (4) שמ֯[טה 𝔐𝔪𝔊^{AOCdnt}𝔗S] η αφεσις 𝔊^{B}
15:3 (5) לך 𝔐𝔪𝔗S] + παρ αυτω 𝔊
15:4 (6) ברך֯ 𝔐] ברוך 𝔪

Frgs. 28–30 Deut 15:15-19

1] א]ת הדב֯[ר
2 (16)] כ]י֯ אה[בך
3 (17)]]באזנ֯ו f.29
4 (18)]]י֯קשה
5] מ]ש֯נ֯[ה]ש֯כר שכר
6] בכל אשר תעשה [
7 [19]]]ב֯בקרך [[f.30

Variants

15:18 (5) מ]ש֯נ֯[ה 𝔐𝔪𝔗S] εφετειον 𝔊
15:18 (5) שכר] שכיר 𝔐𝔪

Frg. 31 Deut 16:2-3

1 (3)]צאן ו]ב̊ק̊ר̊[[

2]תאכ[ל עליו ח̊]מץ [

VARIANT

16:3 (2) ל[תאכ] 𝔐𝔊𝔖𝔗^{O}𝔙] תאכלו ɯ𝔗^{N}

Frgs. 32 col. i, 33 Deut 16:6-11

1] אלה]י̊ך̊ לשכן שמו

2]]מ̊[ארץ]

3] 7]יהוה̊ אלהיך בו

4] [8]ש]ב̇עת̇ ימים מצות תאכלו

5] ליהו]ה̊ אל]ה[יך לא תעשה בו כל

6]מלאכה *va[cat* [9]שבעה שבעות תספר

7] ל]ספר שבעה שבעות [10]ועשית

8] מ]ת̊ת נדבות ידך אשר תתן

9]כ]אשר ◦]ברכך יהוה אלהיך [11]ושמח]ת לפני יהוה אלהיך f.33

והגר היתום ואלמנה

10]את]ה בנ̊ך̊[וה]לוי אשר בשערכ[ ]

11 ב̊קרבך ב̇]מקום]א̊להיך ל̇]שכן [

L. 1 (16:6) אלה]י̊ך̊. The head of a *kap* is discernible to the right of the *lamed* of לשכן. Although it is quite low on the line, it is too high to belong to line 2.

L. 2 (16:6)]מ̊[ארץ]. The bottom right corner of *mem* is extant. Based on the amount of space available, it is probable that 4QDeut[c] read]מ̊[ארץ \ מצרים] with 𝔊^{AOC}La, and not ממצרים with 𝔐ɯ𝔊^{Bdnt}𝔗𝔖𝔙, since, if we restored מצרים at the end of line 2, the beginning of line 3 would not be properly filled out. This reading in 4QDeut[c] may be a reminiscence from v 3.

L. 6 (16:8) The scribe left an interval before v 9; ס 𝔐, קצה ɯ. There is space available that would permit the longer readings of ɯ, 𝔊 or 𝔖, although with the interval it is unlikely.

L. 8 (16:10) מ]ת̊ת. The texts of 𝔐 and ɯ read מסת. The final *taw* is clear on the leather. However, the traces to its right cannot be interpreted as *samek*. *Samek* has a loop at the left, moving into the cross-bar; this trace is a slightly curved downstroke. It is, in fact, the same height and shape as the downstroke of the neighboring *taw*. Therefore, we have interpreted it as *taw*, and have restored מתת, which fits the context (see VAR.).

L. 9 (16:10) ◦]ברכך. It is difficult to determine whether this MS had יברכך with 𝔐𝔗 or ברכך with ɯ; 𝔊 is similarly ambiguous with ευλογησεν (fut. or aor.?), although 𝔊^{AFMVmss} have ηυλογησε(ν).

L. 10 (16:11) בשערכׄ[is crossed out, so the the MS now agrees with 𝔊^{B}ℭ^{N} (see VAR.).

L. 10 (16:11) והגר היתום ואלמנה is written supralinearly.

VARIANTS

16:6 (1) שמו 𝔐ℭ] את שמו 𝔪

16:8 (4) שׄ[בׄעׄת] ששת 𝔐𝔪𝔊ℭ𝔖

16:8 (4) מצות תאכלו] תאכל מצות 𝔐𝔪𝔊ℭ𝔖𝔙

16:8 (5) בו כל 𝔊] > 𝔐ℭ𝔙; כל 𝔪; ܒܗ 𝔖

16:9 (6) שבעות 𝔐(שבעת)𝔪𝔊^{B} Laℭ𝔖𝔙] + ολοκληρους 𝔊^{AOCdnt}

16:10 (8) מׄ[תׄת] מסת 𝔐𝔪ℭ𝔖; καθοτι 𝔊; *oblationem* 𝔙 (see NOTE)

16:10 (8) נדבות ידך] נדבת ידך 𝔐𝔊^{ACdnt}ℭ𝔙; נדבת ידיך 𝔪𝔖; η χειρ σου ισχυει 𝔊^{B} La

16:10 (8) תתן 𝔐𝔪𝔊^{ms}ℭ𝔖𝔙] δω σοι 𝔊; δωσει 𝔊^{ms}

16:11 (10) [את]ה בׄנׄךׄ[ ] אתה ובנך 𝔐𝔪𝔊^{AOCdnt}ℭ𝔖𝔙; > אתה 𝔊^{B}

16:11 (10-11) בׄקרבׄךׄ \ וה[לוי והגר היתום ואלמנה אשר 𝔊^{B}ℭ^{N}] וה[לוי אשר בשערכׄ[4QDeut^{c*};
והלוי אשר בשעריך (εν ταις πολεσιν 𝔊) והגר והיתום והאלמנה אשר בקרבך 𝔐𝔪𝔊ℭ𝔖𝔙

Frgs. 32 col. ii, 34 Deut 16:21–17:5

1 °°[ ]
2 21לא תטע לׄךׄ[ ]
3 תעשה לך 22ולׄ[א]
4 17:1לא תזבח ליהׄ[וה]
5 דבר רע כי תועׄ[בת]
6 2כי ימצא בקרבׄ[ך?]
7 איש או אשׄהׄ אׄשׄרׄ [ ]
8 בׄריתו 3וׄילׄ[ך]
9 לירח אׄ[ו]
10 ודרשת היׄ[טב]
11 בישראל 5והׄ[וצאת את]הׄאׄישׄ[ ] f.34
12 אשׄ[ר עשו את הדבר הר]עׄ הׄזׄה אלׄ[ ]
13 [ ]°[ ]

L. 3 (16:21) תעשה. *Taw* is written thickly, apparently correcting a *he* or a *reš*.

L. 11 (17:4-5) Reconstruction results in a very short line of only 39 letter-spaces. Since the beginning of line 12, אשׄ[ר, is on the leather, it cannot be moved to the end of line 11. There are no variant texts which would suggest a longer reading to fill out the line.

VARIANTS

16:22 (3) ולו]א 𝔐𝔪𝔗𝔖] ου 𝔊𝔙

17:2 (6) כי 𝔐𝔪𝔗𝔙] εαν δε 𝔊𝔖

17:2 (6) בקרב̇[ך? 𝔐𝔪𝔊𝔗^O𝔙] > 𝔊^B; ܒܝܢܬܗܘܢ 𝔖𝔗^N Arab

17:5 (12) אש]ר עשו את הדבר הר[ע̇ ה̇זה אל[𝔐𝔪𝔗] > 𝔊

Frg. 35 Deut 17:7

[ ]בראש]נה[ ] 1

[ ]מק[ר̇בך *t* [*vacat*] 2

L. 2 (17:7) The scribe left an interval before v 8; ס 𝔐, קצה 𝔪.

VARIANT

17:7 (2) מק[ר̇בך 𝔐𝔪𝔗𝔙] εξ υμων αυτων 𝔊 = ܒܝܢܬܗܘܢ 𝔖

Frgs. 36–41 Deut 17:15–18:1

[ ]∘ ∘[ ] 1

]מל̇ך לא תוכל לתת] 2

[ ]ל̇א אחיך[הוא [16]רק לא] ירבה לו [ ] 3 f.37

[ ] 4

[ ] הזה עוד[[17]] 5 f.38

[יר]בה לו מ̇[אד [18]] 6

[מש]נ̇ה̇ התורה[הזאת על]ספר מל̇[פני] (19) 7 f.39,40

[ ]בה[כ]ל̇ ימי חייו למען יל̇[מד] 8 f.41

[לש]מ̇ר את כל דברי̇[התורה]ה̇זאת ואת̇[9

[[20]לבלתי רום ל̇ב̇[בו מאחיו ולבלת]י̇[10

[יאריך ימים̇[11

[[18:1]לא יה̇[יה 12

[אשׁ̇[13

Line 2 preserves a left margin, while lines 10–13 preserve a right margin.

VARIANTS

17:15 (3)]אחיך 𝔐𝔪^{vGall}𝔊ℭ𝔖] אחי 𝔪^{Sad}; מן אחוכון ℭ^{J}

17:19 (8) בה 𝔪] בו 𝔐

17:20 (10) רום 𝔐] רם 𝔪; ראם 𝔪^{mss} (orth. or var.?)

Frg. 42 Deut 26:19–27:2

1] לשם ו]לׄתׄהלה ולׄתפ[ארת [

2]לך *vacat* [27:1]ויצו מׄ[שה] [

3] כל]הׄמצוה הזאת[[

4] [2] תע]ברו את הׄ[ירדן [

L. 2 (26:19) The scribe left an interval before 27:1; ס 𝔐, קצה 𝔪.

VARIANTS

26:19 (1) לשם ו]לׄתׄהלה ולׄתפ[ארת 𝔊] לתהלה ולשם ולתפארת 𝔐ℭ𝔖𝔙; לתהלה לשם ולתפארת 𝔪

26:19 (2) לך 𝔊^{mss}𝔖] > 𝔐𝔪𝔊ℭ𝔙

27:1 (3) כל]הׄמצוה הזאת[ ] כל המצוה 𝔐𝔪ℭ𝔖𝔙; πασας τας εντολας ταυτας 𝔊^{Bdnt} (> πασας 𝔊^{C}; > ταυτας 𝔊^{C}La)

Frgs. 43–45 col. i Deut 27:24–28:7

1] [24]א]רור [

2] [25]ארור לׄקׄחׄ שחד f.44

3] [26]א]רׄוׄר אשׄ[ר [

4] הז]אתׄ לׄ[ע]שׄ[ות אותם ו]אׄמרו כׄ[ל הע[ם אמן f.45

5] *vacat* [28:1]ו]היה אם שמוע תשמע בקׄול יהוה אלהיך לׄעׄשות את

6] אנוכי מצוך היום ונתנך יהוה אלהיך

7] האר]ץׄ [2]ובאו עליך כל הברכות האלה והשׄ[יג]וך

8] אל]הׄיך [3]ברוך אתה בעיר וברׄוך אתה

9] [4] פר]יׄ בטנך ופריׄ אדמתך ופרי בהׄמתך שגר אלפיך

10] [5]ב]רוך טנאך ומשארתׄך [6]בׄרוך אתה בׄבואך

] בצ[אׄתך 7 יתן יׄהוה את אויביך הקמׄ[ים]עליך 11

] י]צאו אליך ובשבעה דׄ[רכים [12

bottom margin

L. 7 (28:1) [עליון] 𝔐𝔪𝔊ℭ𝔙] > 𝔖. It is possible that 4QDeut^c did not contain עליון, since the space available between the final *ṣade* of הארץ and the reconstructed right margin of line 7 becomes crowded with the inclusion of עליון.

VARIANTS

27:26 (3) אשׁׄ[ר 𝔐𝔪ℭ𝔙] πας ανθρωπος οστις 𝔊𝔖

27:26 (4) ו]אׄמרו 𝔪𝔊] ואמר 𝔐ℭ𝔖𝔙

28:1 (5) ו]היה 𝔐𝔪𝔊^B Laℭ𝔖𝔙] + ως αν διαβητε τον Ιορδανην εις την γην η κυριος ο θεος υμων διδωσιν υμιν 𝔊

28:1 (5) לׄעׄשות] לשמר לעשות 𝔐ℭ; לשמר ולעשות 𝔪𝔊𝔖𝔙

28:4 (9) ופרי בהׄמתך 𝔐𝔪ℭ𝔖𝔙] > 𝔊

28:7 (11) יׄהוה 𝔐𝔪ℭ𝔖𝔙] κυριος ο θεος σου 𝔊

Frgs. 46–47 Deut 28:8-11

top margin

] א]תׄך את הברכׄ[ה [1

] ל[ׄו (9) 2 f.47

] א]להיך 3

] נק]רׄא עליך (10) 4

] ו]בׄפׄרי אׄ[דמתך] (11) 5

L. 1 (28:8) הברכׄ[ה. The leather is split and twisted so that the downstroke and base of *kap* are in front of its head.

VARIANT

28:11 (5) ו]בׄפׄרי אׄ[דמתך ובפרי בהמתך בפרי בטנך = επι τοις εκγονοις της κοιλιας σου και επι τοις γενημασιν της γης σου και επι τοις εκγονοις των κτηνων σου 𝔊^{B(d)nt} La] בפרי בטנך ובפרי בהמתך ובפרי אדמתך 𝔐𝔪𝔊^{AOC}ℭ𝔖𝔙

Frg. 48 Deut 28:12-14

1 (13)]]רׄבים ואתהׄ[[
2] ו]הׄי[ית רק[למעלה ולא תׄ[היה [
3 (14)] אנכ]יׄ[מצ]וׄךׄ היו[ם [

L. 2 (28:13) ו]הׄי[ית רק[למעלה. The *he* and the *yod* of והיית are clear on the right edge of the fragment. After that, the leather is split and shrunken; before the shrinkage occurred, there must have been a larger space for the missing letters.

Frg. 49 Deut 28:20

1 (19)]]°°[[
2 20ישלח יׄ[הוה [
3 בכל מׄ[שלח [

Frg. 45 col. ii Deut 28:22-25

1 בׄשׄחׄפׄת ובקׄ[דחת [
2 (23) ירדפוך עד[[
3 (24) אשר תחׄ[תיך [
4 (25) השמים ירׄ[ד [
5 ב[ד]רׄךׄ אׄחׄ[ד [
6 לׄ[כל [

VARIANT

28:22 (2) ירדפוך ш] ורדפוך 4QDeut^g𝔐𝔊; וירדפונך 𝔗; ܘܢܪܕܦܘܢܟ 𝔖; *et persequatur* 𝔙. The *yod* of 4QDeut^c is certain.

Frg. 50 Deut 28:29-30

1 [בֿצהרים כ[אשר

2 (30) [עשוק וגזול֯[

3 [[ישג]ל֯נ֯ה בי֯[ת

VARIANT

28:30 (3) [ישג]ל֯נ֯ה 𝔐𝔗𝔖] ישכבנה 𝔐^{q}; ישכב עמה 𝔪; εξει 𝔊^{ed}; λημψεται (cum var) 𝔊^{mss} (cf Isa 13:16)

Frg. 51 Deut 28:48-50

1 [[ישלחנו י]ה֯[ו]ה֯ בך ברע֯ב֯ ו֯ב֯[צמא

2 (49) [ ]צוארך עד השמיד֯[ו [

3 (50) [ ]הארץ כ֯א֯ש֯ר֯[[

4 (51) [ ]פ֯נ֯י֯ם֯[[

L. 1 (28:48) ברע֯ב֯. The 'breakthrough' of *ʿayin* is extant next to the base of *bet*. The tops of both letters have moved to the left of their bottom portions, owing to the split in the leather.

L. 1 (28:48) ו֯ב֯[צמא. The leather is split at this point, so that the tops of the letters are to the left of their bases. A portion of the head of *waw* and a portion of its downstroke are extant. The head of *bet* is clear, and a portion of its base is extant.

L. 2 (28:48) השמיד֯[ו. The sharp corner of the right shoulder of *dalet* is present on this letter, but there is also a bend to the left at the bottom of the downstroke. We have assumed that this is a ligature to the following *waw*.

VARIANTS

28:48 (1) בך 𝔐𝔪𝔊^{BOCdnt}𝔗𝔖𝔙] > 𝔊^{A}

28:48 (1) ו֯ב֯[צמא ובעירם 4QDeut^{c}𝔐𝔪𝔊^{AOCdnt}𝔗𝔖𝔙] > 𝔊^{B}

Frg. 52 Deut 28:61

1 [ו]כ֯ל֯ מכה[[

Frg. 53 Deut 29:17-19

1] לעב]ד̊
2] [18]והי]ה̇ בשמעו
3]]יהיה לי כי
4] [19]לא י]א̇בה יהוה
5]]◦ הוא ודבקה בו כל

bottom margin

The fragment contains a left margin with stitching.

L. 5 (29:19) The leather is brittle and has cracked in several places. Although on the photograph, the first letter appears separated and goes beneath the baseline, the leather is joined and aligned more exactly in the museum, so that ה̊הוא (𝔐𝔪ℭ) is quite possible.

VARIANTS

29:19 (4) יהוה 𝔐𝔪ℭ𝔖] ο θεος 𝔊

29:19 (5) ודבקה] ורבצה 𝔐; ורבצו 𝔪; και κολληθησονται 𝔊; וידבקון ℭ; [illegible] 𝔖

Frgs. 54–55 col. i Deut 31:16-19

1]]וקם העם הזה וזנה א̊ח̊רי̊[[
2]]שמה בקרבו ועזבוני והפרו את[ברי]ת̊י̊[[
3 (17)]]ביום ההוא ועזבתיך והסתרתי פני
4] ל]א̊כל ומ[צאוהו]ר̊עות רבות וצרות *vacat* ואמרו f.55
5]]יהוה ב̊[קרב]י̊ מצאוני הרעות האלה[[18]ו]א̊נ̊[וכי] (supralinear: א[להי])
6] פנ]י ממנ̊[ו ביום]ההוא על כל הרעה אשר ע̊[שה]
7] [19]וע]ת̇ כ̊תבו לכם א̇ת̇[דב]ר̊י השירה
8] ישרא]ל̊ שימוה בפיהם ל[מען]תהיה לי

bottom margin

L. 5 (31:17) There are only *c.*14 letter-spaces at the beginning of line 5 before יהוה, and this would not be enough space for all the words in 𝔐 et al.

L. 5 (31:17) א[להי]. The *ʾalep*, and presumably all of אלהי, was written supralinearly, apparently by the original scribe.

VARIANTS

31:16 (2)]שמה 𝔐𝔪𝔊^{AOdnt}ℭ𝔖𝔙] > 𝔊^{BC}La

31:16 (2) בקרבו 𝔐𝔪𝔊^{AOCdnt}] > 𝔊^{B}; ביניהון ℭ = ܒܓܘܗܘܢ 𝔖 = *in ea* 𝔙

31:16 (2) ועזבוני 𝔪𝔊ℭ(וישבקון)] ועזבני 𝔐𝔖𝔙. A definite pattern emerges in 4QDeut^{c} at this point to use the 3rd common pl. verb and 3rd masc. pl. suffixes, except at 31:18, where it appears to read, against all the other witnesses, ממנו.

31:16 (2) והפרו 𝔪𝔊ℭ] והפר 𝔐𝔖𝔙

31:17 (3) ועזבתיך] ועזבתים 𝔐𝔪𝔊ℭ𝔖𝔙

31:17 (4) ל]אֹכל 𝔐] לאכלה 𝔪

31:17 (4) ואמרו] ואמר 𝔐𝔪𝔊ℭ𝔖𝔙

31:17 (5) יהוה א[להי] 𝔊] אלהי 𝔐𝔪𝔖𝔙; שכינת אלהי ℭ

31:18 (6) פנ]י ממנ[ו] פני 𝔐𝔙; פני מהם 𝔪𝔊ℭ𝔖. *Mem*, *mem* and *nun* are extant; ממנו is the least difficult reading.

31:19 (7) וע]תׄ] ועתה 𝔐𝔪𝔊ℭ𝔙; > 𝔊^{B}; ܡܟܝܠ 𝔖

31:19 (7) לכם 𝔐𝔪𝔊^{O}ℭ𝔙] > 𝔊; ܠܗܘܢ 𝔖

31:19 (7) דב]רׄי השירה 𝔊] השירה 𝔐𝔪ℭ𝔖𝔙

31:19 (8) שימוה] שימה 𝔐𝔪^{Sad}ℭ; ושימה 𝔪^{vGall}𝔖; και διδαξατε αυτην 𝔊𝔙

Frg. 54 col. ii Deut 32:3

הב]ו גדל לאלהינו [1

bottom margin

On the basis of the number of lines that this column must have contained (estimated from the bottom of the previous column to this extant bottom line), chap. 32 seems to be written stichometrically, with one stichos of poetry (one-half verse in Hebrew) per line (see the 4QDeut^{c} introduction).

VARIANT

32:3 (1) הב[ו] 𝔐𝔊ℭ𝔖𝔙] והבו 𝔪

Unidentified Fragments

The unidentified fragments were placed by the original team of editors with 4QDeut^{c} on the basis of similarities in handwriting.

Frg. 56

1]אתׄ עמ[

2]ךׄ לתתׄ[

Frg. 57

1]◦ותׄיך ◦[

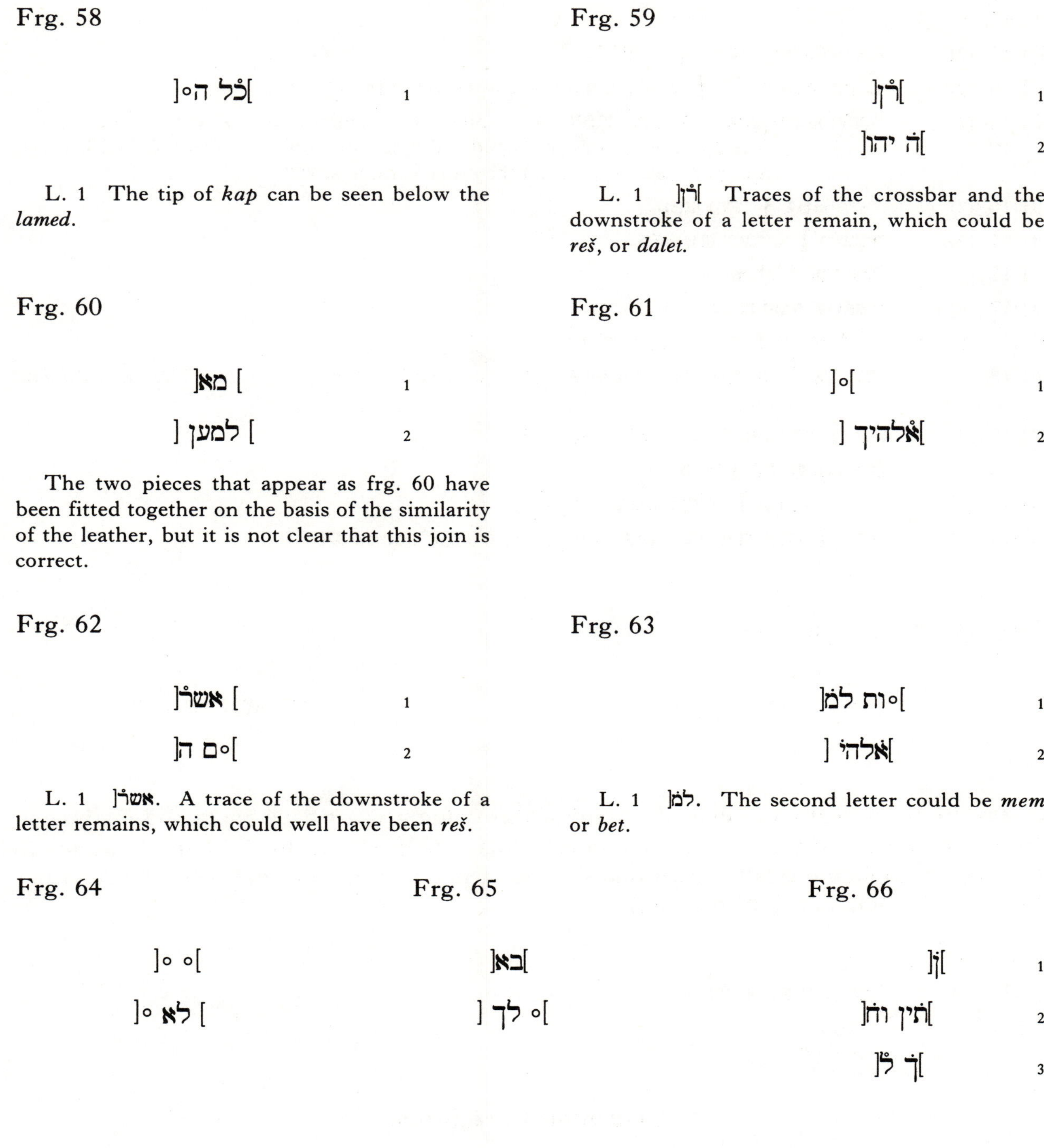

Frg. 58

]כ֯ל ה◦[

L. 1 The tip of *kap* can be seen below the *lamed*.

Frg. 59

]ר֯ן[

]ה֯ יהו[

L. 1]ר֯ן[Traces of the crossbar and the downstroke of a letter remain, which could be *reš*, or *dalet*.

Frg. 60

] מא[

] למען [

The two pieces that appear as frg. 60 have been fitted together on the basis of the similarity of the leather, but it is not clear that this join is correct.

Frg. 61

]◦[

]א֯להיך [

Frg. 62

] אשר֯[

]◦ם ה[

L. 1 אשר֯]. A trace of the downstroke of a letter remains, which could well have been *reš*.

Frg. 63

]◦ות למ֯[

]א֯להי [

L. 1 למ֯]. The second letter could be *mem* or *bet*.

Frg. 64

]◦ ◦[

] לא ◦[

Frg. 65

]בא[

]◦ לך [

Frg. 66

]ן֯[

]תין וח֯[

]ך ל֯[

31. 4QDeut^{d}

(PLATE X)

Preliminary publication: Sidnie Ann White, 'A Critical Edition', 133–54. 'Three Deuteronomy Manuscripts', *JBL* 112 (1993) 28–34. 'Special Features', *RevQ* 57–58 (1991) 163–4.

THE MANUSCRIPT is yellowish-brown, now stained grey in some places and blackened in others. The leather was of average thickness and well-prepared, but a certain amount of wrinkling and shrinkage has taken place, causing some damage to the surface.

Two partially damaged, contiguous columns containing portions of Deut 2:24-36 and 3:14–4:1 are preserved. There is a sewn edge at the left margin of col. II, and horizontal dry lines are visible. The height of the preserved part of the manuscript is *c.*16.9 cm. The average width of the inscribed column is 10.8 cm; col. I contains 59–68 letters per line, and col. II has 53–63. The width of the left margin of col. II from the inscribed text to the edge of the fragment is 1.0 cm, while the width of the margin between the columns is 1.2 cm. The distance between lines of script averages 0.8 cm, and reconstruction suggests *c.*27 lines per column.

Palaeographical study of this manuscript places it in the middle Hasmonaean period, *c.*125–75 BCE. The letters are of standard size and unornamented. The script is characterized by the use of ligatures for certain letters, particularly medial *nun*. Several features of the script are important for dating: the base-stroke of *bet* is penned from right to left; *dalet* has a very deep-cornered head, typical of the Hasmonaean form; *ṭet* is made in two strokes, with a slight spur formed by the juncture of the base and the right downstroke; and *yod* is short, with a triangular head. Medial *kap* appears in two forms, with the late Hasmonaean form of a straight, slightly slanted downstroke predominating. Finally, the flaring tick common on the head of *qop* in earlier scripts has practically disappeared.

The orthography of 4QDeut^{d} is consistently shorter than the traditions of either 𝔐 or ⅏ (see Table 1). The manuscript regularly uses *matres lectionis* to indicate **aw* > *ô* (e.g. עוד col. II line 17). However, this usage is not clear for the *Hipʿil* of verbs I-*yod* (e.g. תסף II 16). A *yod* is used to mark **ay* > *ê* (e.g. בני II 3, בעריכם II 7, עיניך II 10) and **ī* (e.g. כי I 11, and סיחן I 7). A *waw* is usually used to mark **ū* (e.g. עשו I 9, אסור I 8, גבול II 3). Accented **ā* > *ō* is sometimes indicated by a *mater lectionis* (e.g. חשבון I 7), but this usage is not consistent: accented **ā* > *ō* is consistently not marked with *waw* in verbs III-*he* (e.g. הראת II 10). Unaccented **ā* > *ō* is never marked with *waw* (e.g. לא, all forms of אלהים, and all examples of the participle). A *mater lectionis* is not used to indicate **u* > *o* (e.g. כל II 6). The manuscript consistently displays the short forms of the pronominal suffixes (ת–, ך–, etc.).

The only extant interval to mark paragraph-division in 4QDeut^{d} appears at 3:29 (II 20). No intervals occur corresponding to those in 𝔐⅏ at 2:30; 3:17; or 3:22 (see NOTES).

Mus. Inv. 323.

IAA 204.600; PAM 43.221; 41.195, 41.198, 42.165, 42.630, 42.706, 43.066, 43.160.

TABLE 1: *Orthography*

Col., line	Deut	4QDeut^{d}	𝔔	𝔐	𝔐 mss	𝔖 ed	𝔖 mss
I 7	2:26	קדמת		קדמות		קדמות	קדימות, קדומת
I 7	2:26	סיחן		סיחון		סיחון	
I 8	2:27	ושמאל		ושמאול		ושמאל	
II 5	3:18	חלצים		חלוצים		חלוצים	
II 6	3:19	ומקנכם		ומקנכם	ומקניכם	ומקניכם	ומקנכם
II 9	3:21	יהושע		יהושוע		יהושע	
II 10	3:21	הראת		הראת		הראות	
II 11	3:21	הממלכת		הממלכות		הממלכות	
II 11	3:22	תׄיׄראם (orth. or var.?)		תיראום	תיראם	תיראם	תיראום
II 13	3:24	החלת		החלות		החלת	
II 13	3:24	להראת	4Q^{e} להראות	להראות		להראות	
II 14	3:25	נא		נא		נה	
II 15	3:25	הטבה		הטובה		הטובה	
II 16	3:26	תסף		תוסף		תוסף	תוסיף
II 17	3:27	וצפנה		וצפנה		וצפונה	
II 19	3:28	ינׄחׄל (orth. or var.?)		ינחיל		ינחל	יניחל, ינחיל
II 19	3:28	אתם		אותם		אתם	

Col. I Deut 2:24-36

5 [וה]תׄגׄר בו מלחׄ[מה 25]

6 [ ] השׄמׄים אשר ישמעׄוׄן אׄ[ת שמעך]

7 (26) [ ]מדבר קדמת אל סיחן מלך חשבון [ ]

8 (27) [בד]רׄך בדרך אלך לא אסור ימין ושמאל 28 אׄ[כל בכס]ףׄ

9 [ו]שתיתי רק אעברהׄ בׄרגלי 29 כאשר עשו לי

10 [ ]הישבים בׄעׄרׄ[עד אשר אעבר א]ת הירדן

11 [אל הא]רׄץ אשׄ[ר יהוה אלהינו נתן לנו 30 ולא] אבה סיחׄ[ן מלך חשבון ה]עׄברנו בו כי

12 [הקשה יה]וׄהׄ[ ]לׄמׄעׄן תתו [ב]ידׄך כיום ה[זה 31 וי]אׄמׄרׄ

13 [ ]ארצו החל רש לרׄ[שת את א]רצו

14 32[33 ויתׄ]נׄהו יהוה אלהינוׄ[ ]נו

15 (34) [עריׄ]וׄ בעתׄ ההׄיׄ[א ונחרם את כ]ל

16 [35 רק] הבׄהמׄהׄ[בזזנו לנו ושלל הע]רׄים

17 (36) [והע]יר אשר בנחל ועד הגלעדׄ[ל]אׄ היתׄהׄ

The left margin is partly extant, continuing over to the next column. The line numbers correspond to those of col. II.

L. 6 (2:25) א]ת. 𝔪 reads את שמעך, while 𝔐 reads שמעך. The traces of the letter cannot be *šin*, with a stroke coming down from the left, but this can be the downstroke of *ʾalep*.

L. 12 (2:30) יה]ו֯ה֯[. There are two traces of ink extant on the bottom of the fragment. Spatial reconstruction suggests *waw* and *he*.

L. 12 (2:30) No interval follows v 30 in this manuscript; ס 𝔐, קצה 𝔪.

L. 14 (2:33) נו[ ]. Two ancient variants are attested: לפנינו in 𝔐𝔪𝔊^{ABOC}𝔗𝔖, and בידינו* = εις τας χειρας ημων in 𝔊^{dnt}La; they are conflated in some Hexaplaric MSS. It is impossible to tell which of the variants was present in this MS, but it did not contain the conflate text.

L. 15 (2:34) ה֯ה֯י֯א. The cross-bar of each *he* is extant. A trace of ink is discernible to the left of the second *he*. The confusion between הוא and היא, which is found in 𝔐, does not occur in this MS.

VARIANTS

2:25 (6) ישמע֯ו֯ן 𝔐] ישמעו 𝔪
2:25 (6) א]ת שמעך 𝔪] שמעך 𝔐𝔗 (see NOTE)
2:27 (8) בד]ר֯ך בדרך 𝔐𝔪𝔗] בדרך 𝔊𝔙; ܒܐܘܪܚܐ ܐܘܪܚܐ 𝔖
2:31 (13) רש לר]ש֯ת 𝔐𝔪𝔊^{O}𝔗] κληρονομησαι 𝔊 (cf 𝔖)
2:33 (14) ויתנ֯]הו 𝔐𝔪𝔊𝔗𝔖𝔙] και παρεδωκεν αυτους 𝔊^{C}
2:34 (15) ה֯ה֯י֯א 𝔐^{q}𝔪] ההוא 𝔐 (see NOTE)
2:36 (17) בנחל 𝔐𝔪𝔊𝔗𝔖] בתו֯ך ה֯נחל **4Q364**
2:36 (17) ועד הגלע֯]ד 𝔐𝔪𝔊^{ms}𝔗𝔖𝔙] και εως ορους του Γαλααδ 𝔊

Col. II Deut 3:14–4:1

1] ח]ו֯ת֯[יאיר ע]ד֯ הי֯[ום הזה]
2 15] 16 ולגד]י֯[נת]ת֯י מן הגלעד עד נח֯[ל]
3] הנח]ל֯ גבול בני עמון 17והערבה וה[ירדן וגבול]
4 [מ]כנרת ועד[ים הערבה ים]המלח תחת אשדת הפסגה מזר֯[חה 18]ואצו אתכם
5 [בע]ת֯[ההיא לאמר יהו]ה֯ אלהיכם נתן לכם את הארץ֯ הז֯את לרשתה חלצים
6] א]ח֯י֯כ֯ם בני ישראל כל בני חיל 19רק֯ נ֯ש֯[יכ]ם טפ֯[כם] ומקנכם ידע֯ת֯י֯
7 [כי מ]קנה רב לכם ישבו בעריכם אשר נתתי לכמ֯[20עד]א֯שר יני֯ח י֯הוה ל֯[אחיכם]
8 [ככם] וירשו גם הם את הארץ אשר יהוה א֯ל֯ה֯[י]כ֯מ֯ נתן להם בעב֯[ר הירדן]
9 ושבתם איש לירשתו אשר נתתי לכם 21ואת י֯הושע צויתי בעת[ההיא]
10 לאמר עיניך הראת את כל אשר עשה י֯[הוה א]ל֯היכם לשני המלכים֯ הא֯[לה]
11 כן יעשה יהוה לכל הממלכת אשר אתה[עבר שמה 22]ל֯א תי֯ראם כי יהוה
12 אלהי֯כ֯ם֯ ה֯ו֯א הנלחם לכם 23ואתחנן א[ל יהוה בעת הה]י֯א לאמר 24אדני
13 יהוה אתה החלת להראת את֯[עבדך את גדלך ואת]ידך החזקה אשר
14 מי אל בשמים ב֯א֯[ר]ץ֯[25א]ע֯ברה נא ואראה

את הארץ הטבה אשר בעבׄ[ר   הטוב]הׄזה והלבנון 26ויתעבד
יהוה בי למענכם ולא שמע[ר]בׄ לך אל תסף דבר
אלי עוד בׄדׄבׄ[ר הזה 27ע]לׄהׄ על ראש הפסגה[וש]א עיניׄךׄ ים וצפנה תימנה
ומזרחהׄ[וראה בעי]נׄיׄךׄ כי לׄאׄ תעבר את הירדן הזה 28וצׄ[ו א]תׄ יהושע וחזקהו
[ואמצהו כי]הוא יעבר לפנׄיׄ העם הזה והוא ינׄחׄל אתם את[האר]ץׄ[אשר]
[תראה 29ונשב] בׄגיא מול בית פעור *vacat* [   ]
[4:1ועתה ישראל שמע]אל הׄ[חקים ו]אל המשפטיםׄ[   ]

The right and stitched left margins are partially preserved.

L. 4 (3:17) No interval follows v 17 in this manuscript; interval 𝔐, קצה ⅏.

L. 12 (3:22) No interval follows v 22 in this manuscript; ס 𝔐, קצה ⅏.

L. 14 (3:24)]ץׄ[ר]בׄאׄ[ו. The original scribe wrote *waw* supralinearly.

L. 14 (3:25) וארא‍ה. There is a spot of ink on the leather above the *waw*.

L. 15 (3:26) ויתעבד. The final letter appears to be a clear *dalet*, and thus a mistake for *reš* (see VAR.).

L. 20 (3:29) A major interval follows v 29 in this manuscript; פ 𝔐, קצה ⅏.

VARIANTS

3:16 (2) עד 1° 𝔐^mss⅏^mss𝔊𝔙] ועד 𝔐⅏𝔗𝔖

3:18 (4)]ואצו 𝔐] ואצוה ⅏

3:19 (6) נׄשׄ[יכ]ם טפׄ[כם] 𝔐^ms] נשיכם וטפכם 4QDeut^m𝔐𝔊𝔗𝔖𝔙; טפכם ונשיכם ⅏

3:19 (6) ומקנכם 𝔐⅏^ms] ומקניכם 𝔐^mss 𝔗⅏ (orth. or var.?)

3:20 (7) יׄהוׄה 𝔐⅏𝔊^mss𝔗𝔖𝔙] + אלוהיכמה 4QDeut^m𝔊; + ο θεος ημων 𝔊^*dnt*

3:20 (8) וירשו 𝔐] ויירשו ⅏

3:21 (10) עיניך 𝔐⅏𝔗𝔖𝔙] οι οφθαλμοι υμων 𝔊

3:21 (10) א]לׄהיכם 𝔐𝔊 La𝔗𝔖𝔙] ο θεος ημων 𝔊^mss; > 𝔐^mss⅏

3:22 (11) תׄיראם 𝔐^mss𝔗⅏𝔙] תיראום 𝔐⅏^mss𝔊𝔗𝔖; φοβηθηση 𝔊^B* (orth. or var.?)

3:22 (12) אלהׄיׄכׄםׄ 𝔐⅏𝔊 La^100𝔗𝔖𝔙] ο θεος ημων 𝔊^AB

3:23 (12) הה]יׄא 𝔐^q⅏] ההוא 𝔐

3:24 (13) ואת]ידך החזקה 𝔐⅏𝔗𝔙] και την χειρα την κραταιαν και τον βραχιονα τον υψηλον 𝔊; ܘܐܝܕܟ ܥܫܝܢܬܐ ܘܕܪܥܟ ܪܡܐ 𝔖

3:25 (15) הטבה 𝔐⅏𝔗𝔖] + ταυτην 𝔊; *hanc optimam* 𝔙

3:25 (15) הטוב \ ]הׄזה 𝔐⅏𝔊^O𝔗𝔙] tr 𝔊(vid)𝔖; > τουτο 𝔊^B*

3:26 (15) ויתעבד] ויתעבר 𝔐⅏𝔊𝔗𝔖 (see NOTE)

3:26 (16–17) תסף דבר \ אלי עוד בׄדׄבׄ[ר הזה 𝔐⅏𝔗] προσθης ετι λαλησαι τον λογον τουτον 𝔊; ܬܘܣܦ ܬܘܒ ܠܡܡܠܠܘ ܥܡܝ ܦܬܓܡܐ ܗܢܐ 𝔖

3:27 (17) על ראש 𝔊] ראש 𝔐; אל ראש ⅏𝔗𝔖; *cacumen* 𝔙

3:27 (17–18) ים וצפנה תימנה \ ומזרחהׄ] ימה וצפ(ו)נה ותימנה ומזרחה 𝔐⅏𝔊𝔗𝔙; ܠܡܥܪܒܐ ܘܠܓܪܒܝܐ ܘܠܬܝܡܢܐ ܘܠܡܕܢܚܐ 𝔖

3:28 (19) ינׄחׄל אתם ⅏] ינחיל אותם 𝔐; ינחיל(יניחל ⅏^ms) אתם ⅏^mss; κατακληρονομησει αυτοις 𝔊 (orth. or var.?)

32. 4QDeut[e]

(PLATE XI)

Preliminary publication: Julie Ann Duncan, 'A Critical Edition', 34–50.

THE SURVIVING fragments of this manuscript preserve portions of Deut 3:24, 7:12-16, 7:21–8:4, and 8:5-7, 10-11, 15-16. In its pristine form the leather was light beige with a matte finish, but the back of the leather was untreated for writing. Most of the fragments have been stained to a deep brown with a glossy surface, and some have a corrugated surface. There are no dry lines visible, but the regularity of the inscribed lines indicate that the manuscript had been ruled.

4QDeut[e] consists of two large fragments and six small ones, three of which remain unidentified. Frgs. 2–5 preserve portions of three contiguous columns, with frg. 2 preserving the lower part of the first column, frgs. 3 and 4 the lower part of the second column, and frg. 5 the top of the third column. Frg. 1 preserves a top margin measuring 1.7 cm, while frg 5 preserves a top margin of 1.5 cm and a right margin extending 1.4 cm. Frgs. 2 and 3 are wide enough to preserve intercolumnar margins, which vary from 1.0 to 1.7 cm, since left margins in this manuscript are ragged. Frg. 2 preserves a bottom margin of 2.0 cm, and frg. 4 one of 1.8 cm. The average distance between the tops of lines is *c.*7 mm. Column-width ranges from 48 to 60 letter-spaces. The text between the last preserved line at the bottom of col. I and the beginning of the extant material in col. II is estimated to have required 7 lines. Adding that to the 15 preserved lines in col. II indicates 22 lines per column for this manuscript.

4QDeut[e] is written in a formal script, showing some degree of semiformal influence, which may be dated to the late Hasmonaean period (*c.*50–25 BCE). The most advanced features in the palaeography of this hand are to be seen in *bet*, the base-stroke of which is clearly drawn left to right in some forms; *ṭet*, which has achieved the broad base of the Herodian form and is drawn in two strokes; *qop*, the tail of which is drawn upward and loops into the head; and *šin* whose right arm is regularly bent back. The earliest palaeographical forms may be seen in *dalet*, which appears still to be made in a single motion; *samek*, which is still unclosed; and final *kap*, in which the head is ticked and generally remains narrow. More generally, the letters are suspended from a ceiling line rather than ruled by a baseline, and letter size, while becoming more uniform, still vacillates, as is particularly evident in the slightly oversize *taw* and *mem*.

The orthographic practice of 4QDeut[e] corresponds to that of 𝔐 (see Table 1), with one exception: החלת with ꟺ against החלות 𝔐 at 3:24 (frg. 1 1). *Matres lectionis* are used to mark **ū* (e.g. ברוך I 20, מ֯הו֯מ֯ה֯ II 11, הוא II 14, and 3rd masc. pl. verbs) as well as **ī* (ותירשך I 19, איש II 12 and masc. pl. endings) and *ê* < **ay*, (לאבתי֯ך֯ I 18 and שנאיך I 22, etc.). But *ō* < **ā* in unaccented syllables is not represented, e.g. לאבתי֯ך֯ I 18, שנאיך I 22, אלהיך II 14, מצותו II 19, and the negative particle לא is always spelled without *waw* (e.g. I 22, etc.). Nor is *ō* < **u* marked with *waw* in unaccented syllables (e.g. מכל and כל I 20, 21, and ג֯דלה II 11); no instances of *ō* < **u* are preserved in accented syllables. 4QDeut[e] uses the short forms of the independent pronouns (e.g. הוא) and of the pronominal suffixes as well (e.g. ך-, ת-, etc.).

TABLE 1: *Orthography*

Col., frg., line	Deut	4QDeut^e	4QDeut		𝔐	𝔐^mss	𝔐^ed
1 1	3:24	ה֯חלת	4QDeut^d	החלת	החלות		החלת
II 2 ii, 3 i, 4 10	7:22	כל]ת[ם֯	4QpaleoDeut^r	כל]ותם	כלתם		כלותם
II 2 ii, 3 i, 4 11	7:23	מה֯ומה֯	4QpaleoDeut^r	מהומה֯	מהומה		מהמה
II 2 ii, 3 i, 4 11	7:23	*השמ֯ד֯ם	4QDeut^f	השמדם	השמדם		השמידם
			4QpaleoDeut^r	השמ]ידם			
II 2 ii, 3 i, 4 19	8:2	†מצותו	4QDeut^f	מצותיו]	מצותו	מצותיו	מצותיו
II 2 ii, 3 i, 4 20	8:3	ידע]ו֯ן֯	4QDeut^c	ידעו	ידעון	ידעו	ידעו
			4QDeut^f	ידע֯ון			

* Orth. or var.?; cf. also 4QDeut^g, 28:24 (10 4). † See Qimron §322.141.

Frg. 3 9 displays an interval before 7:22, although 𝔐 𝔐 have none at that point (see NOTE). Spatial reconstruction at col. III 16 also suggests that this manuscript contained an interval before chapter 8; פ 𝔐, קצה 𝔐.

4QDeut^e preserves one correction at 7:23 (frg. 3 i 11), where final *mem* appears to be written over another letter (see NOTE).

Mus. Inv. 233. PAM 43.068.

Frg. 1 Deut 3:24

top margin

[ ]י֯ה֯ו֯ה֯ אׄתׄהׄ הׄחלת להראותׄ אׄ]ת [1

Frg. 1 preserves a top margin.

L. 1 (3:24) להראותׄ. The edge of the leather on which *taw* is written is partially destroyed.

Col. I: Frg. 2 i Deut 7:12-16

]]ו֯שמ[ר יהוה אלהיך ל]ך֯[א]תׄ ◦[[17

[נשב]עׄ לאבתיך֯ 13 ואהבך וברכך והרבך ובר]ך [18

] דג]נך ותירשך ויצהרך שגר[א]ל֯[פי]ך֯ ועשתר֯]ת צאנך על ה]אׄדׄמׄה֯[ ] 19

אׄ]שר נש]בע לאבתיך לתת לך 14 ברוך תהיה מכל העׄמ֯י֯]ם ל]אׄ י֯הׄי֯ה 20

בך עקר ועקרה ובבהמתך 15 והסיר֯[ ]י֯הוה ממך כל[חלי]וכל מ֯]דוי מ]צ֯רים 21

הרעים אשר ידעת לא [י]ש֯י֯]מם]בך ונתנם בכל שנאיך 16 ואכלת את 22

bottom margin

Frg. 2 i preserves a right margin, a left margin, and a bottom margin, while traces from the following column are preserved on lines 20, 21, and 22 (see col. II). The fragment is from the first of three partly preserved contiguous columns. The lines are numbered on the assumption of 22 lines per column (see the 4QDeut^{e} introduction).

L. 19 (7:13) דג[נ֯ך. The letter preceding *kap* is damaged but may be identified as *nun* (versus *yod*, cf. 𝔪^{mss}); a split in the leather has destroyed the middle part of the stem of *nun*, creating a distortion in the photograph.

L. 21 (7:15) מ֯]דוי. Part of the surface around the *mem* has been destroyed.

VARIANTS

7:13 (19) ותירשך 𝔐𝔊^{ABCOdnt}𝔗^{O}𝔖𝔙] תירשך 𝔪𝔊^{mss}𝔗^{NJ}
7:13 (20) לאבתיך 𝔐𝔪𝔊^{C}𝔗𝔖𝔙] pr יהוה* 𝔊^{ABOdnt}
7:15 (22) אשר 5QDeut*𝔐𝔪] +ראיתה ואשר 5QDeut^{corr} *s.m.* 𝔊(sub ÷ 𝔊^{G}Syh)

Col. II: Frgs. 2 ii, 3 i, 4   7:21–8:4

8] 21לא תערץ מפנ]י֯הם f.3
9] ונו]ר֯א] *vacat* 22ונש֯ל֯ יהוה
10] מע]ט֯ מעט לא תוכל כל[ת]ם֯[מ]ה֯ר פן תרבה
11 (23)]]ב֯ידך והמם מה֯ומ֯ה֯[ ]ג֯דלה עד השמ֯ד֯ם
12 (24)] מ]ת֯חת ה֯שמים לא֯ יתיצ֯ב איש
13 (25)] תשר]פ֯ון בא֯ש לא תחמד כ֯ס֯ף
14] תוע]ב֯ת יהוה אלהיך הוא 26ולא
15] שק]ץ֯ תשקצנו ותעב תתעבנו
16 (8:1)] מצו]ך היום תשמרון
17] את הא]ר֯ץ אשר נשבע י֯[הוה]
18 (2)] אלהי]ך זה ארבע֯ים שנה
19] הת]שמר מצותו אם לא
20 3ו֯י֯[ענך ידע]ו֯ן֯ א֯ב֯[תי]ך f.2
21 למ֯[ען [
22 י֯[הוה יחוה האדם 4ש]מ֯לתך לא בלתה מע֯[ליך [f.4

bottom margin

Frg. 3 preserves a left margin, as well as traces from the following column in lines 8–11, and 14–17. Traces from the beginning of lines 20–22 of this column have also been preserved on the left margin of frg. 2. The bottom margin of the column is preserved on frg. 4.

L. 9 (7:21) ונו]רׄא. The leather between the end of this word and ונׄשל יהוה is partially destroyed, but the extant portion shows an interval before v 22; no interval 𝔐ш.

L. 10 (7:22) כל]ת[םׄ[. The horizontal stroke after *lamed* is the baseline of final *mem*, the downstroke having been lost with the surface.

L. 11 (7:23) והמם. Final *mem* appears to be written over another letter here, which was perhaps a medial *mem*—note the peak underneath the cross stroke of the head, which may be the left oblique of medial *mem*.

L. 13 (7:25) כׄסׄף. The top of *kap* and the upper right of *samek* have been rubbed away along with the surface.

L. 16 ($7{:}26^{fin}$) A reconstruction of this line indicates that an interval occurred at the end of chap. 7 in this MS; פ 𝔐, קצה ш.

L. 20 (8:3) The available space suggests that this MS read]לא ידעת ולא ידע]וׄן אבׄ[תי]ך with 4QDeut[c,f] 𝔐ш𝔊[O]𝔗𝔖𝔙 (> *לא ידעת 𝔊[ABC]).

VARIANTS

7:22 (10) כל]ת[םׄ[5QDeut𝔐ш] לכלותמׄהׄ[4QDeut[m]

7:22 (10) פן תרבה \]עליך חית השדה 𝔐ш𝔗𝔖𝔙] ινα μη γενηται η γη ερημος και πληθυνθη επι σε τα θηρια τα αγρια 𝔊. 𝔊 may be the result of parallel influence; compare Exod 23:29: פן תהיה הארץ שממה ורבה עליך חית השדה.

7:23 (11) בׄידך[𝔊(εις τας χειρας σου)] לפניך 4QpaleoDeut[r]𝔐ш𝔗𝔖

7:23 (11) השמׄדׄם 4QDeut[f]𝔐] השמ]ידם 4QpaleoDeut[r]ш (orth. or var.? cf. $7{:}24^{fin}$; 4QDeut[g] at $28{:}24^{fin}$; Josh 11:14)

7:25 (13) תחמד 𝔐ш𝔊𝔗𝔖𝔙] תחמדוׄ 4QpaleoDeut[r]

8:2 (18) זה ארבעׄיׄם שנה 4QDeut[c,f]𝔐ш𝔊[Odt]𝔗𝔖𝔙] > 𝔊[ABC]La

8:4 (22) ש]מׄלתך 𝔐ш𝔗] שלמתך 4QDeut[c]

Col. III: Frgs. 3 ii, 5. Deut 8:5-7, 10-11, 15-16

top margin

5וידעתׄ] עם [1 f.5

מיסרךׄ] 6ושמרת [2

אתו 7כׄ]י יהוה [3

] [4

] [5

Line	Verse	Text	
6		] [	
7		] [	
8	(10)	]◦ [	f.3
9	(11)	יה֯]וה אלהיך [	
10		י֯]הוה אלהיך לבלתי [	
11		מצ֯]וך היום [12] [	
12		] [	
13		] [	
14		[15] ה֯]מוליכך [	
15	(16)	א֯ש֯]ר אין [	
16		מ֯ן֯] במדבר [	
17		לה֯]יטבך באחריתך [17] [	

Frg. 5 preserves the top and the right margins. Traces from the beginnings of lines 8–11, and 14–17 of this column are preserved on the left edge of frg. 3; their relationship to the material preserved on frg. 5 is indicated in the transcription.

L. 1 (8:5)]וידעת֯. The peculiar traces at the edge of the leather are explained by surface damage, which has destroyed part of each of the legs of *taw*, creating an impression of two thin legs with hooks.

L. 3 (8:7) כ֯]י. The surface on the edge of the leather has been stripped away, with the result that only a trace remains of the upper part of *kap*.

Unidentified Fragments

Frg. 6

הטו]ב֯ ואת֯ ה֯]

A comprehensive examination of the text of Deuteronomy indicates that this fragment must preserve one of two passages:

30:15 את החיים ואת הטו]ב֯ ואת֯ ה֯]מות ואת הרע

or 34:3 ואת הנג]ב֯ ואת֯ ה֯]ככר בקעת ירחו.

Frg. 7

] והלכתْ]

The downstroke of the letter at the edge of the leather appears shorter than it is owing to surface loss; it can be identified as part of the right corner of *taw*. The fragment preserves one of the following verses:

8:19 את יהוה אלהיך] והלכתْ] אחרי אלהים אחרים
14:25 וצרת הכסף בידך] והלכתْ] אל המקום
or 16:7 ופנית בבקר] והלכתْ] לאהליך (cf. also 26:2, 29:9).

Frg. 8

]∘∘ ∘[

]∘∘ ∘ ∘ ∘[

This fragment apparently preserves the space between two lines, but the letters are not identifiable.

33. 4QDeut[f]

(PLATES XII–XV)

Preliminary publication: Sidnie Ann White, 'A Critical Edition', 155–214.

4QDEUT[f] consists of thirty-five identifiable fragments and six which have not yet been identified. The original colour of the manuscript was between a yellowish and a reddish brown, now faded to buff or yellow in some places and blackened in others. The surface of the leather, which is of average thickness, was originally smooth and glossy; it has wrinkled in places, and some shrinkage has occurred. The surface is worn and faded in spots. One unusual feature of the leather is that it is sprinkled with small black dots which are not ink, but on the photographs these can be misleading. Horizontal dry lines are visible on certain fragments (e.g. 1, 6, 9, 13, 17), and a vertical dry line on frg. 39.

There are at least twelve partially extant columns. Top margins are preserved on frg. 2 measuring 1.5 cm and on frg. 9 measuring 1.1 cm, and possibly one bottom margin on frg. 6 although not enough leather remains to be sure. Right margins are extant on frg. 4 measuring 1.5 cm, frg. 9 measuring 2 cm, and frg. 39, and left margins are present on frgs. 13 and 22. Frg. 9 displays a stitched right edge, and frg. 38 preserves portions of two columns. The distance between tops of lines ranges from 0.6 cm to 0.8 cm. The columns preserved generally tend to have a width of either *c.*43–53 or *c.*53–63 letter-spaces per line. Two columns are exceptions, however, having greater widths: the column with frgs. 29–31 has *c.*66–69 letter-spaces, and the column with frgs. 32–35 has *c.*75–88.

The surviving fragments preserve portions of the following text of Deuteronomy:

4:24-26	18:6-10	23:21-26
7:22-25	18:18-22	24:2-7
8:2-14	19:17–20:6	25:3-9
9:6-7	21:4-12	26:18–27:10
17:17-18	22:12-19	

Palaeographical study places 4QDeut[f] in the late Hasmonaean period (*c.*75–50 BCE). The letters are generally uniform in size, although final *mem* can be quite large, and *ʿayin* slightly smaller than normal. Letters tend to be broad and squat, with a thick ductus. The latest letter-forms present in the manuscript are *bet* (in which the base is penned in a separate stroke from left to right), *gimel*, and medial *mem*, which is made in one stroke, with a tick being added to the left oblique. There is no difference between the medial and final forms of *ṣade* in this hand.

The orthographic practice (see Table 1) of this scribe is to use *matres lectionis* for **aw* > *ô* (e.g. המוציאך 6 16, but והרידו 17 1), **ay* > *ê* (e.g. מלכיהם 2 3, אליהם 10 1), **ū*, **ī*, and sometimes **ā* > *ō* when accented (e.g. [ע]ללות 20 2, but cf. לא). *Matres lectionis* are not used for unaccented **ā* > *ō* (e.g. נתן 9 4), **u* > *o* (e.g. כל), **a* and **i*, nor does the scribe use the long forms of verbs, pronouns, or suffixes.

TABLE 1: *Orthography*

Frg., line	Deut	4QDeut^{f}	4QDeut	𝔐	𝔐^{mss}	ɯ
1 4	4:26	העידתי		העידתי		העדתי
2–3 3	7:23	השמדם (orth. or var.?)	השמ̇ד̇ם 4QDeut^{e} השמ]ידם 4QpaleoDeut^{r}	השמדם		השמידם
4–6 2	8:2	מצותיו]		מצותו	מצותיו	מצותיו
4–6 10	8:9	במסכנות		במסכנת		במסכנת
4–6 12	8:10	הטובה̇]		הטבה		הטובה
9 3	18:8	ממכרי]ו		ממכריו		ממכרו
17–19 1	21:4	ו̇הרידו		והורדו		והורידו
17–19 4	21:6	הקר̇בים		הקרבים		הקרובים
17–19 7	21:9	ה[נ]ק̇י		הנקי		הנקיא
20–23 2	22:14	[ע]ל̇לו̇ת		עלילת		עלילת
26–28 2	24:3	]כריתות		כריתת		כריתת
32–35 5	27:3	]ת̇בו̇א̇[		תבא		תבוא

Intervals to mark paragraph-division appear at the following places:

Frg. 4–6 7 (8:6) interval] no interval 𝔐 ɯ

Frg. 13–16 5 (19:21) interval] ס 𝔐 קצה ɯ

Frg. 17–19 8 (21:9) interval] ס 𝔐 קצה ɯ

Frg. 24–25 3 (23:21) interval] ס 𝔐 קצה ɯ

Six supralinear scribal corrections have been preserved: מעלך to מע[ל'ך̇ (4–6 5), גפן to 'גפן̇ (4–6 9), נשת to נ^ח^שת (4–6 11), הנער to הנער^ה^ (20–23 4), ושח to וש^מ^ח (26–28 7), and מצוה to מצוה ^את[כם^ (32–35 7). 4QDeut^{f} cannot be placed within any textual tradition.

Mus. Inv. 317, 322. PAM 43.062, 43.058, IAA 204.600; PAM 42.636, 42.709, 43.065.

Frg. 1 Deut 4:24-26

1 [ ]○[ ]

2 [ ]הוא אל קנ̇[א *vacat*]

3 [25 ונושנת]ם̇ בא̇ר̇ץ והשחתם ו̇[ע]ש̇יתם פסל̇[ ]

4 [י]ה̇וה אלהיך להכעיסו [26] העידתי בכ̇ם̇[ ]

5 [ ]מ̇ה̇ר מעל הארץ אשר אתם עב̇[רים]

6 [ע]ל̇[יה כי ה]ש̇[מד ת]ש̇מ̇ד̇ו̇ן̇[[27]]

VARIANTS

4:25 (4) אלהיך 𝔐𝔗^{O}] אלהיכם ɯ𝔊𝔗^{N}𝔖𝔙; του θεου ημων 𝔊^{C}

4:26 (5) מ̇ה̇ר[𝔐ɯ𝔊^{O}𝔗𝔖𝔙] > 𝔊

Frgs. 2–3 Deut 7:22-25

top margin

1 [א]להיך את הגוים האלה מ[פניך]
2 [תרב]ה֯ עליך חית השדה 23ונתנם י[הוה]
3 [גד]ל֯[ה ע]ד֯ השמדם 24ונתן מלכיהם֯[ ]
4 [ ]ל֯[פניך]ע֯ד֯ ה֯[שמדך]
5 (25) f.3 [עליה]ם֯ ולקח֯[ת]
6 [ ]°°[ ]

The top margin of this column is preserved.

L. 5 (7:25) ולקח֯[ת]. There is an apparently unintentional dot of ink above the hook of the *lamed*.

VARIANTS

7:22 (1) האלה 𝔪] האל 𝔐

7:23 (3) השמדם 4QDeut^{e}𝔐] השמ]ידם 4QpaleoDeut^{r}𝔪(orth. or var.? cf. 7:24^{fin}; 4QDeut^{g} at 28:24^{fin}; Josh 11:14)

7:24 (4) ל֯[פניך 𝔐^{ms}𝔪] בפניך 𝔐𝔊𝔗𝔖

Frgs. 4–6 Deut 8:2-14

1 [אלהי]ך֯[זה אר]ב֯ע֯י֯ם ש[נה]
2 (3) [אשר בלבבך ה֯תשמר מצותיו[
3 [המן אשר לא ידעת ולא ידעון א֯[בתיך
4 (4) [ל֯[ב]ד֯ו יח֯[י]ה האדם כי על֯[כ]ל֯
5 (5) f.5 [מע]ל֯ך֯ ל֯ך֯ ורגל[ך לא בצק]ה זה א֯ר֯ב֯[עים]
6 (6) [י]הוה אלה֯[י]ך֯]
7 f.6 [ולי]ר֯אה אתו vac]at]
8 [אר]ץ֯ טובה ורחבה ארץ[7]
9 8א]ר֯ץ חטה ושערה גפן ות֯[אנה]
10 (9)]ל֯א במסכנות תאכל ב[ה]לחם ולא]
11 ברז]ל ומהריה תחצב נשת 10ואכלת]
12 [הא]ר֯ץ הטוב֯ה֯[ ]

13 [ ]אלהיך לבלתי שמרֹ[11]
14 [ ]פן תאכל ושבעת ובתֹ[ים 12[ ]
15 (13) [וכס]ף וזהב ירבהֹ[ ]
16 [אלה]יֹך המוציאך מֹ[ארץ 14]

The right margin of this column is preserved.

L. 5 (8:4) מע]לֹיֹךֹ לךֹ. The arm of *lamed* under the *he* of האדם, line 4, is clear. Following this the remains of *yod* are written supralinearly, followed by the remains of the head of final *kap*. Following this word, the arm of *lamed* and the head of final *kap* again appear. It seems that the scribe wrote *lamed*-final *kap* twice, then, realizing his mistake, went back and inserted a *yod* above the first *lamed*-final *kap*, which were probably part of מעליך. It is possible that the second *lamed*-final *kap* is crossed out below the extant portion of the leather.

L. 7 (8:6) interval 4QDeut^n **]** no interval 𝔐𝔴.

L. 9 (8:8) ג֯פ֯ןׄ. *Waw* is written supralinearly.

L. 11 (8:9) נ֯ח֯שת. *Ḥet* is written above the *šin*.

VARIANTS

8:2 (1) זה אר]בֹעֹים ש]נה 4QDeut^{c,e}𝔐𝔴𝔊^{Odt}ℭ𝔖𝔙 **]** > 𝔊^{ABC}La

8:3 (3) המן 4QDeut^{c}𝔐𝔴𝔊$^{AB^*O}$ℭ𝔖𝔙 **]** + εν τη ερημω 𝔊$^{B^{mg}mss}$

8:3 (3) לא ידעת ולא ידעֹון (𝔴 ידעו) 4QDeut^{c}𝔐^{ms}𝔴) לא ידעת ולא ידעון 4QDeut^{c}𝔐𝔴𝔊^{O}𝔖𝔙 **]** ουκ ηδεισαν 𝔊

8:4 (5) ורגל]ך (𝔴 ורגליך) לא בצק]ה 𝔐𝔴 **]** οι ποδες σου ουκ ετυλωθησαν 𝔊; ומסנך לא יחיפו ℭ^O;
ܘܪܓܠܝܟ ܠܐ ܐܫܦ 𝔖; *et pes tuus non est subtritus* 𝔙

8:6 (7) ולי]רֹאה 𝔐𝔴𝔊ℭ𝔖𝔙 **]** ולאהבה 4QDeut^n

8:7 (8) טובה ורחבה 4QDeut^{j,n}𝔴𝔊 **]** טובה 𝔐ℭ𝔖𝔙

8:7 (8) ארץ 2° 4QDeut^{n}𝔐𝔴ℭ𝔖𝔙 **]** οὗ 𝔊

8:8 (9) ג֯פ֯ןׄ 4QDeut^{n}𝔐Laℭ𝔖 **]** גפן 𝔴𝔊𝔙

8:8 (9) ותֹ]אנה] 𝔐𝔊^{Cdt}ℭ𝔖 **]** תאנה 4QDeut^{n}𝔴𝔊

8:9 (10) לחם[4QDeut^{n}𝔐𝔴Laℭ𝔖 **]** τον αρτον σου 𝔊𝔙

8:9 (10) ולא 4QDeut^{n}𝔊𝔖𝔙 **]** לא 4QDeut^{j}𝔐𝔴𝔊^O Laℭ

8:9 (11) ומהריה 4QDeut^{j,n} 5QDeut **]** ומהרריה 𝔐𝔴. הר comes from the geminate root הרר, and the second *reš* normally reappears before suffixes. However, in later Hebrew the form with one *reš* becomes more common (see Qimron, p. 26).

Frg. 7 Deut 9:6-7

1 (7)] הטוב]ה הזאת [
2] י]הוה א]להיך [
3] א]לֹ[[

VARIANT

9:7 (3) א]ל[**]** עד 𝔐𝔴𝔊ℭ𝔖𝔙

Frg. 8 Deut 17:17-18

1 [נשים]ו֯לא יס[ור [
2 [לו מ]א֯ד֯ [18]ו֯ה֯[יה [

L. 2 (17:17-18) מ]א֯ד֯ ו֯ה֯[יה. This line is difficult to restore. The head of *dalet* seems clear, and the last two traces of ink on the line may be interpreted as the head of *he*. Therefore we have restored according to the other witnesses, but the restoration is very tentative.

Frg. 9 Deut 18:6-10

top margin

1 (7) אשר הוא גר֯[[
2 (8) בשם יהוה אל[היו [
3 (9) יאכלון לבד ממכרי[ו [
4 (10) אלהיך נתן לך לא ת֯[למד [
5 בנו ו֯[בתו] באש ק֯[סם [

The top margin and stitched right margin of this column are preserved.

VARIANTS

18:8 (3) יאכלון (𝔐 יאכלו) 𝔐𝔪^{vGall}𝔊^{V}𝔗S] יאכל 𝔪^{Sad}𝔊𝔙

18:8 (3) לבד ממכרי[ו (𝔪 ממכרו) 𝔐𝔪𝔊^{Odt}S] πλην της πρασεως 𝔊; דיתה שבתא דכין אתקינא 𝔗^{O}; *praeter quod venale est circa civitatem* La; *excepto eo quod in urbe sua* 𝔙

18:10 (5) ק֯[סם 𝔐𝔪𝔊^{ABOC}𝔗𝔙] pr και 𝔊^{dnt}LaS

Frgs. 10–12 Deut 18:18-22

1 (19) [ב]פיו ודבר אליהם את[[
2]]ידבר בשמי אנ֯[כי אדר]ש֯ מעמו[[20] [f.11
3]]לא צויתיו לדבר֯[ואשר]ידבר֯[בשם אלהי]ם֯[[f.12
4 (21)] ב]ל֯[בבך הד[בר אשר לא ד֯[ברו [
5 [22]] יבו]א֯ הוא ה֯ד֯[בר [

VARIANTS

18:19 (2) ידבר[𝔐𝔪𝔗S𝔙] + הנבי' 4QTest 𝔊(+ εκεινος 𝔊^{B})

18:20 (3) צויתיו 𝔐𝔪𝔊^{AOdt}𝔗S𝔙] προσεταξα 𝔊^{BCn}La

Frgs. 13–16 Deut 19:17–20:6

(18)] והשפטי]ם אשר[[

] ו]הנה עד שקר ה]עד]שקר[ענה]בא[חיו 19 [f.14

] לא]חיו ובערת הרע מקרבך 20והנש[א]רים [

] לע]שות עוד כ[דבר ה]רע הזה בקר[ב]ך 21לא[[f.15

]]בעין שן בשן[יד ביד ורגל ברגל [*vacat*] [

20:1] למ[ל]ח]מה על א[יביך ו]רכב ועם רב[[

] מאר]ץ מצרים 2והיה

(3)] א]ל[יהם] שמעה

] א]ל

(4)]]◦ ◦[[f.16

(5)] להל]חם לכם עם איב[יכם [

] ל]אמ]ר מי האיש אשר[[

(6)] במל]חמה ואיש אחר[[

] ויש]ב לבי[תו [

The left margin of this column is preserved.

L. 5 (19:21) interval] ◦ 𝔐, קצה ⅏; add 𝔊 (see VAR.).

VARIANTS

19:19 (3) ובערת 𝔐⅏𝔊^{Bdnt}La𝔗𝔙] εξαρειτε 𝔊^{AOC}; ܘܬܒܥܘܢ S

19:19 (3) מקרבך 𝔐⅏𝔗S𝔙] εξ υμων αυτων 𝔊

19:20 (4) לע]שות עוד 𝔐𝔗] עוד לעשות ⅏𝔊S

19:20 (4) בקר[ב]ך 𝔐⅏𝔗] εν υμιν 𝔊; ܒܝܢܬܟܘܢ S. The reading of 𝔊 (מקרבכם*) is materially impossible in this MS.

19:21 (4) לא[⅏𝔊S𝔙] ולא 𝔐𝔗

19:21 (5) [ברגל] 𝔐⅏𝔊^{BOn}La𝔗S𝔙] +καθοτι αν τις δω μωμον τω πλησιον ουτως δωσετε αυτω 𝔊^{ACdt}

20:1 (6) ועם ⅏𝔊S𝔙] עם 𝔐𝔗

20:3 (8) שמעה] שמע 𝔐⅏ (see Qimron, p. 47)

Frgs. 17–19 Deut 21:4-12

] 4והרידו זקנ[י] הע[יר] ההי[א את]העגלה[אל] נחל[[

[ו]לא יזרע וערפו שם את[הע]גלה ב[נחל 5ונ]גשו ה[כהנים [

3 [ב]חר יהוה אל[היך]לשרתו ו[לבר]ך בשם [יהוה ע]ל[[f.18,19
4 [נ]גע 6וכל זק[ני העיר ההי]א הקרבים אל החלל[[
5 (7)] י]דינו לא שפכו את הד[ם [
6 8] פ]דית יהוה ואל תתן דמ[[
7] 9ואת]ה תבער דם ה[נ]קי מ[קרבך [
8] [vacat 10כי תצא למלח[מה [
9 (11)] ב]שביה אש[ת [
10 (12)] ו]גלח[ה [

L. 8 (21:9) interval] ס 𝔐, קצה 𝔪

VARIANTS

21:4 (1) ההי]א 𝔐q𝔪] ההוא 𝔐
21:4 (2) וערפו שם 𝔐𝔪ℭS] και νευροκοπησουσιν 𝔊
21:5 (3)]לשרתו ו[לבר]ך 𝔐𝔊ℭS𝔙] לשרת ולברך 𝔪; לשרת* La
21:5 (3) בשם [יהוה 𝔐𝔪ℭS] επι τω ονοματι αυτου 𝔊𝔙. This MS has the final *mem*, so it must have agreed with 𝔐𝔪.
21:7 (5) שפכו 𝔐q, mssℭ𝔪𝔊ℭ𝔙] שפכה 𝔐S
21:8 (6) יהוה 𝔐𝔪𝔊B Laℭ S] + εκ γης αιγυπτου 𝔊AOCdnt
21:9 (7) דם ה[נ]קי] הד[ם הנקי 1QDeutb𝔐𝔪(הנקיא)𝔊ℭS; אשדי דם זכי ℭO; משדי דם זכאיי ℭP
21:10 (8) כי 𝔐𝔪ℭ𝔙] εαν δε 𝔊S
21:11 (9) ב]שביה 𝔐𝔊ℭS𝔙] בשביו 𝔪

Frgs. 20–23 Deut 22:12-19

1] ת]כסה ב[ה 13 [
2 14] ל]ה [ע]ללות דברים וה[וציא [
3 [הז]את לקחתי ואקרב[ל]ה בתו[לים 15 [f.21
4 [אב]י הנער ואמה ו[הוציאו (ה above line)]אל זקנ[י [
5 16]]ל[איש הזה ל]אשה f.22
6 (17)] ל]אמר[לא מצאתי]לבתך f.23
7]]לפני זקנ[י הע]יר 18ולקח[ו]
8 (19)] כ]סף[[

The left margin of this column is preserved.

L. 2 (22:14) ע]ל֯לות. On the right, the bottom of the hook of *lamed*, with its diagonal slant, is extant. To its left, what appears to be the damaged hook of the second *lamed* is extant. It is possible that this damaged letter is in fact two letters, i.e. *yod* and *lamed*. If this is the case, then 4QDeut[f] has spelled עלילות with a *mater lectionis* for *ī, in accordance with the spelling practices of this MS.

L. 3 (22:14) הז]א֯ת. The leather is split, with the top shifted slightly to the right and down. When properly aligned, the letter before *taw* is *ʾalep*; cf. הזאת frg. 7 1.

L. 4 (22:15) הנע˹ה˺ר. The second *he* is written supralinearly.

VARIANTS

22:15 (4) הנע˹ה˺ר 𝔐q, mss ℭ𝔪𝔊] הנער 𝔐

22:15 (4) והאמה 𝔐𝔪ℭ𝔖𝔇] και η μητηρ 𝔊

22:17 (7) הע֯]יר 𝔐𝔪𝔊ℭ𝔖𝔇] +εκεινης 𝔊AC

Frgs. 24–25 Deut 23:21-26

]]∘[[

21]] למען יברכך יהוה[[

] לרשתה] *v a c*]*a t* [

22] ת]אחר לשלמו כי דרש[[

(23)] ל]נ֯דר לא יהיה בך ח]טא 24 [

] נדב]ה֯ אשר דבר֯]ת [

f.25 25] רע]ך֯ ש]בעך וא]ל [

26] בקמ]ת֯ רעך וק֯]טפת ל֯]א [

L. 3 (23:21) interval] ס 𝔐 קצה 𝔪

Frgs. 26–28 Deut 24:2-7

(3) 2]] והלכה והיתה[[

]]כריתות ונתן בידה וש]לחה [

]]ל֯]ק]חה לו לאשה 4לא יוכ]ל [

]]א֯ש֯]ר [

f.27] תחטי]א א֯ת֯ הא֯ר֯ץ֯] [

(5)] יק]ח איש אשה חדש]ה [

f.28 (6)]] יה]יה]ל֯]ביתו שנ]ה אחת וש˹מ˺ח א]ת [

]]כ֯י֯ 7כ֯]י֯ י֯מ֯צא] [

L. 7 (24:5) ושׄמח. *Mem* is written supralinearly.

VARIANTS

24:3 (2) בידה 𝔐𝔪𝔗𝔖] εις τας χειρας αυτης 𝔊

24:4 (5) [תחטי]א 4QDeut^a(תחטא)𝔐𝔗𝔖𝔙] תחטיאו 𝔪𝔊

Frgs. 29–31 Deut 25:3-9

(4,5)] לעיני]ך֯ [

] מהם֯] [

f.30]]לאשה ויבמ[ה 6 והיה הבכור א]שר תלד֯[[

] מישרא]ל 7 ואם לא יחפ֯[ץ האיש]ל֯קחת את[[

(8)]]ל[הקים לאחיו שם ב]ישראל ל[א [

f.31] וא]מר לא ח[פצתי לקח]ת֯ה 9 ונ֯ג[שה [

]]וירקה בפ֯[ניו [

Frgs. 32–35 Deut 26:18–27:10

(19)] ו]ל֯שמר א֯[ת [

] ליהו]ה אלהיך כאשר ד[בר [

(2)]27:1 את]ה֯עם לאמר ש֯[מר [

]]אשר יה֯[וה [

f.33]3]ת֯ב֯וא֯[[

f.34] ח֯לב ודב֯[ש]4 והי]ה֯ בעברכם את֯[[

] אנכ]י מצוה ה[יום את[כם או]ת֯ם בשיד [5 ו]ב֯נית שם מזבח֯[[

(7)]]ברז֯ל 6 אבנים֯[מזב]ח יהוה אלהיך והעלית עלי[ו [

f.35 [ואכ]ל֯ת֯ שם ושמח֯[ת לפני יה]ו֯ה א֯[להי]ך֯ 8 וכ֯ת֯בת על האב[נים [

]9 מ]ש֯ה וה[כהנים ה]לוים אל[כל יש]ר֯אל[[

] א]ל֯[היך 10 ושמעת ב]ק֯ו֯ל[[

L. 7 (27:4) את]כם is written supralinearly (= 𝔐𝔪).

Variants

26:18 (1) ו]לׄשמר 𝔐𝔪𝔊𝔗𝔖𝔙] +σε 𝔊*dnt*

26:18 (1) אׄ]ת כל] כל 𝔐𝔪𝔗; πασας 𝔊AO*Cdnt*; > 𝔊B; ܟܠܗܘܢ 𝔖; *omnia* 𝔙

27:1 (3) את]הׄעם 𝔐𝔪𝔊*Odnt*𝔗𝔖𝔙] > 𝔊AB*C*

27:1 (3) לאמר 𝔐𝔪𝔊AO*Cdnt*𝔗𝔙] > 𝔊B*; ܘܐܡܪ ܠܗܘܢ 𝔖

27:6 (8) יהוה אלהיך 𝔐𝔪𝔗𝔖] κυριω τω θεω σου 𝔊; *Domino Deo tuo* 𝔙

27:7 (9) ואכ]לׄתׄ שם 𝔐𝔪𝔗𝔖𝔙] και φαγη εκει και εμπλησθηση 𝔊A*O*; και φαγη και εμπλησθηση εκει 𝔊*Cdnt*; και φαγη και εμπλησθηση 𝔊B

27:9 (10) ישׂ]רׄאל[𝔐𝔪𝔊ABO*dnt*𝔗𝔖𝔙] τω λαω 𝔊*C*

Unidentified Fragments

These fragments were placed with 4QDeut[f] by the original team of editors on the basis of similarities in handwriting.

Frg. 36

1]ליׄ[

2 *vacat*

3]°ים[

Frg. 37

1]תׄיׄ °[

2]רׄים °[

3]לביׄתׄ[

Frg. 38 cols. i, ii

1]וב

2]בית

3 [בניׄ]

Frg. 39

1 ואתׄ[

2 יהו[

Frg. 40

1]°יעקבׄ[

Frg. 41

1]יׄרׄ הׄ[

2]ים הדׄ[

34. 4QDeut[g]

(PLATE XVI)

Preliminary publication: Sidnie Ann White, 'A Critical Edition', 215–40. 'Three Deuteronomy Manuscripts', *JBL* 112 (1993) 35–42. 'Special Features', *RevQ* 57–58 (1991) 165–7.

THE ELEVEN fragments of this manuscript come from four columns of text preserving portions of Deut 9:12-14; 23:18-20; 24:16-22; 25:1-5, 14–26:5; 28:21-25, 27-29. The leather of the manuscript was well-prepared, and its original colour was yellowish brown; it is now faded to grayish brown in some places, stained a darker brown in others, or so blackened that letters are no longer visible. Some shrinkage and wrinkling has occurred, so that the leather has become very thick in places, and the surface has deteriorated. Horizontal dry lines are visible on frg. 3, and the average distance between lines of script is 0.7 cm. The column-width is *c.*12.5 cm, with 52–67 letter-spaces. Frgs. 1, 3, and 11 preserve bottom margins (the last, of 5.7 cm), frgs. 2 and 9 left margins, and frg. 6 a right margin. Frgs. 2–3 come from the same column, frgs. 4–9 from the next, and frgs. 10–11 probably come two columns later.

The palaeographical study of 4QDeut[g] establishes its hand in the middle Herodian period, *c.*1–25 CE. The letter-size has become equal (cf. especially *taw*). Many letters are distinguished by *keraiai* or are thickened at the top (note particularly *ʾalep, gimel, zayin, ṭet, nun, ʿayin*). Several features of the script mark it as Herodian: the base stroke of *bet,* which is penned from left to right, breaks through slightly at the corner of the downstroke; the crossbar of *ḥet* projects to the right; *yod* is much shorter than *waw,* which is a decisive characteristic of later Herodian scripts (compare, for example, the *yod* and *waw* of 4QDeut[n]); the head of final *kap* loops into the downstroke at the right shoulder; and the usual form of medial *mem* is penned with the late Herodian technique, the left oblique being drawn upward to the right shoulder, then down into the downstroke and base, with a tick added on the left. Note especially that in one instance this tick breaks through the left oblique (ואׄמחה 1 3).

The orthographic practice of 4QDeut[g] never varies from that of the Massoretic text. Only two instances of variation from 𝔪 are preserved: 25:14 (6–9 1) ג]דולה 4QDeut[g]𝔐, גדלה 𝔪; and 25:15 (6–9 2)]יׄאריכוׄ 4QDeut[g] 𝔐, יארכון 𝔪. *Matres lectionis* are used to indicate **ay* > *ê*, e.g. שניהם 2 3 and עליך 10 4, **ū*, e.g. סרו 1 1 and תשוב 3 4, and **ī*, e.g.]ראיתי 1 2 and כי 3 2; there are no extant examples of **aw* > *ô*. A *mater lectionis* is used to mark **ā* > *ō* when accented, e.g. [א]בות 3 1 and ליתום[3 4, but not when unaccented, e.g. אנכי 3 3 and all forms of אלהים. לא is consistently spelled defectively. However, זונה 2 2 is spelled with a *waw* in 4QDeut[g], as in 𝔐 and 𝔪. The manuscript does not use *matres lectionis* to indicate any proto-semitic short vowels, i.e. **a*, **i* or **u*. It uses the short forms for all pronominal suffixes and endings (e.g. ך-, ת -, הם-).

Intervals to mark paragraph-division in 4QDeut[g] appear at the following places:

Frg. 3 5 (24:19) interval] interval 𝔐, no interval 𝔪
Frg. 3 6 (24:20) interval] ס 𝔐, no interval 𝔪
Frgs. 6–9 3 (25:16) interval] פ 𝔐, no interval 𝔪

This manuscript stands squarely in the proto-rabbinic tradition in both text and orthography. 4QDeut^{g} never differs from 𝔐 (with one possible exception: ישך 𝔐 or תשך* 𝔊 2 4, 23:20); therefore, 4QDeut^{g} is to be considered a member of the same textual family as 𝔐.

Mus. Inv. 400.

PAM 43.063; 40.967, 41.190, 41.297, 42.001, 42.636, 42.713, 42.732, 43.160.

Frg. 1 Deut 9:12-14

1 (13)] ממצרי]ם סרו[[

2 (14)]יהוה אלי לא]מר ראיתי[[

3]]וֿאֿמחה את[[

bottom margin

L. 2 (9:13) According to the space available, there is no room in the MS to accommodate the longer text of 𝔊 (see VAR.), since the reconstruction of line 1 takes up *c*.60 letter-spaces already, compared to 59 in line 2 and 52 in line 3 below. Further, the presence of לא]מר in 4QDeut^{g} indicates that it does not agree with S.

VARIANTS

9:12 (1) סרו[𝔐𝔪𝔊^{ABOdnt}𝔗𝔙] και παρεβησαν 𝔊^{C}; ܣܛܘ ܠܗܘܢ S

9:13 (2)]יהוה אלי לא]מר 𝔐𝔪𝔗𝔙] ܠܝ ܗܟܢܐ S; κυριος προς με λελαληκα σε απαξ και δις λεγων 𝔊 (see NOTE)

Frg. 2 Deut 23:18-20

1] 18ל[אֿ תהיה

2] 19]אתנן זונֿה

3] אלהי]ךֿ גם שניהם

4 20]]יֿשך

L. 2 (23:18) At the end of v 18, 𝔊 has ουκ εσται τελεσφορος απο θυγατερων Ισραηλ και ουκ εσται τελισκομενος απο υιων Ισραηλ (> 𝔐𝔪𝔗S𝔙). 4QDeut^{g} did not have space for that longer text.

L. 2 (23:19) זונֿה. This word, written in the same hand, is slightly smaller than the others, perhaps because it was first omitted, then added in the margin at the end of the line.

L. 4 (23:20)]יֿשך. There is a small trace of ink visible on the right edge of the fragment, which could be either *yod* (ישך 𝔐) or *taw* (תשך* 𝔊; see VAR.).

VARIANTS

23:18 (1) תהיה 𝔐] תחיה 𝔪

23:20 (4)]יֿשך 𝔐𝔪𝔗] εκδανεισης (+τω αδελφω σου 𝔊^{dnt}) 𝔊; ܘܪܒܐ S (see NOTE)

Frg. 3 Deut 24:16-22

1 (17)] א]בות איש בחטא[ו [
2 [בג]ד אלמנה [18]וזכרת כי ע[בד]ה[יית [
3 (19) [כ]ן אנכי מצוך לעשות את הדבר הזה[[
4 עמר בשדה לא תשוב לקחתו לגר ליתום] [
5 [יהוה]אלהיך בכל מעשה ידיך *vac* [20]כי תחבט ז[יתך [
6 [ליתו]ם ולאלמנה יהיה *vac* [21]כי תבצר כרמך לא[[
7]]יהיה [22]וזכרת כי עבד היית בארץ מצ[רים [

bottom margin

The leather of this fragment is split and shrunken; therefore some letters are split and their relative positions have become distorted. There are very short intervals before vv 20 and 21. Reconstruction suggests that there was little or no space for intervals before vv 17 and 19, both ס in 𝔐 but no interval in 𝔪 (24:18 is marked by a קצה in 𝔪).

VARIANTS

24:19 (4) בשדה 𝔐𝔪𝔊^{BO}ℭ] εν τω αγρω σου 𝔊^{ACdnt}; > 𝔖

24:19 (4) לגר ליתום] ולאלמנה יהיה 𝔐𝔪𝔊ℭ] ܐܠܐ ܬܗܘܐ ܠܥܡܘܪܐ ܘܠܝܬܡܐ ܘܠܐܪܡܠܬܐ 𝔖; *advenam et pupillum et viduam* 𝔙

24:19 (5) מעשה ידיך 𝔐𝔪𝔊^{O}ℭ^{N}𝔖𝔙] τοις εργοις των χειρων σου 𝔊^{ABC} (cf ℭ^{O})

24:20 (5) כי 𝔐𝔪ℭ𝔙] εαν δε 𝔊 (cf 𝔖)

24:20 (6) יהיה 𝔐𝔪𝔊^{O}ℭ𝔖𝔙] +και μνηθηση οτι οικετης ησθα εν γη Αιγυπτω δια τουτο εγω σοι εντελλομαι ποιειν το ρημα τουτο 𝔊^{ABC}

24:21 (6) כי 𝔐𝔪ℭ𝔙] εαν δε 𝔊𝔖

Frgs. 4–5 Deut 25:1-5

top margin?

1 [[1]]כי יהיה ר[יב [
2] והר]ש[יע]ו את הרשע] [2] [f.5
3] כדי רשעתו במספ[ר [3] [
4] ונק]לה אחיך לע[יניך [4] [
5 [5]] ומ]ת אחד מה[ם [

The space at the top of frg. 4 may possibly be the top margin. Also, כי may have been at the right margin because the new chapter probably began a new section.

VARIANT

25:3 (4) ונק]לה 𝔐⅏] ונקל ⅏^{mss}

Frgs. 6–9 Deut 25:14–26:5

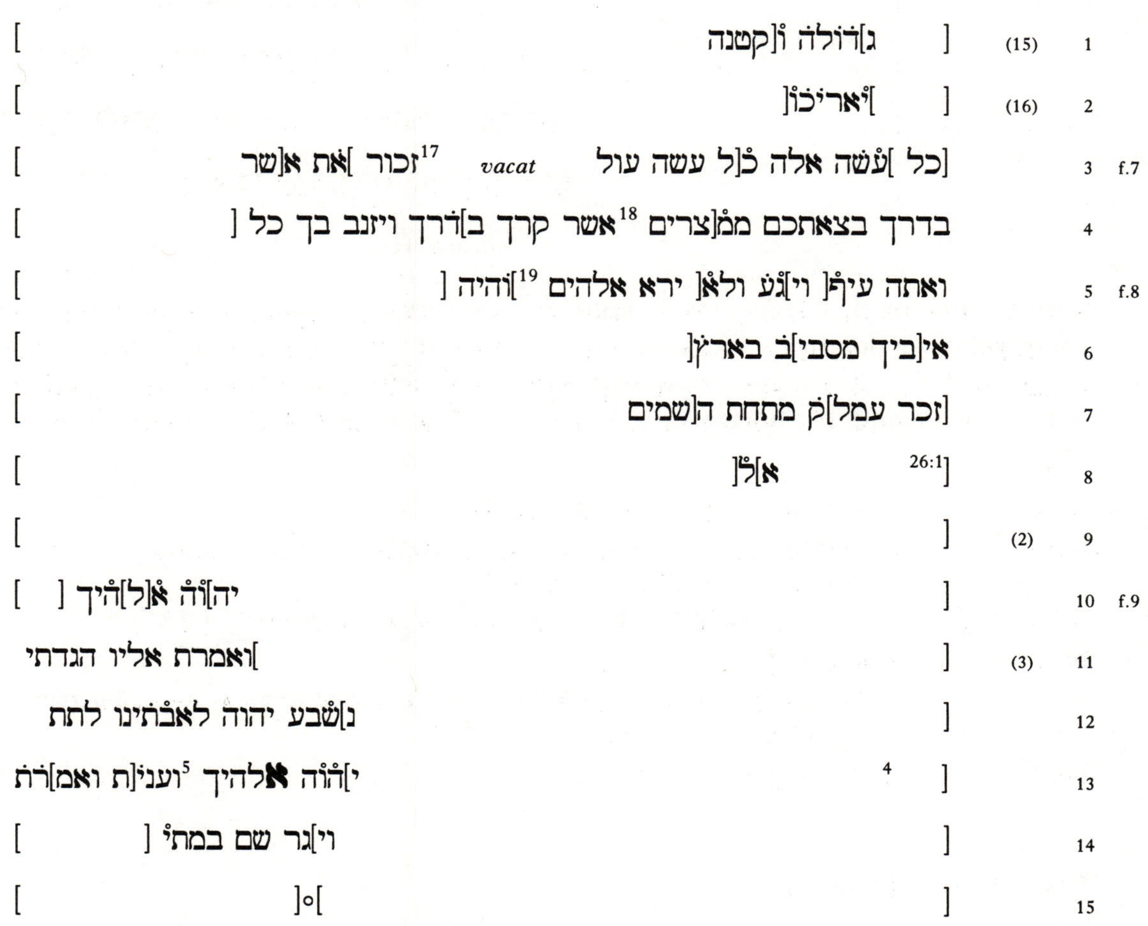

1 (15)] ג]דולה ו֯[קטנה [

2 (16)]]י֯אריכ֯ו֯[[

3 f.7 [כל]ע֯שה אלה כ֯[ל עשה עול *vacat* 17זכור]א֯ת א[שר [

4 בדרך בצאתכם ממ֯[צרים 18אשר קרך ב]דרך ויזנב בך כל] [

5 f.8 ואתה עי֯ף֯[וי]ג֯ע ולא֯] ירא אלהים 19]והיה] [

6 אי]ביך מסבי]ב בארץ֯[[

7 [זכר עמל]ק מתחת ה[שמים [

8 26:1] א[ל֯ [

9 (2)] [

10 f.9] יה[ו֯ה א֯[ל]ה֯יך] [

11 (3)]]ואמרת אליו הגדתי

12] נ]ש֯בע יהוה לא֯ב֯ת֯ינו לתת

13] 4 י]ה֯ו֯ה אלהיך 5וענ[ית ואמ]ר֯ת

14] וי]גר שם במת֯י] [

15]]◦[[

Parts of the right and left margins are preserved. The top of frg. 6 is much damaged; the reading is certain, but the leather is split and shrunken so that the letters are split and distorted.

L. 13 (26:4) אלהיך. The *ʾalep*, written by a later hand in thicker strokes, is large and bold and without *keraia*. There is a trace of ink beneath the *ʾalep* which seems to be a correction dot.

VARIANTS

25:17 (4) בצאתכם 𝔐⅏𝔊^{dnt}ℭS𝔙] εκπορευομενου σου 𝔊

25:18 (4) כל 𝔐⅏𝔊^{Odt}ℭS] > 𝔊𝔙

25:19 (6) מסבי]ב 𝔐⅏𝔊^{O}LaℭS] κυκλω σου 𝔊

Frg. 10 Deut 28:21-25

1 [ל]ר̊שת̇[ה 22]
2 (23) [ובשד]פ̊ו̊ן ובירקון ורד̇[פוך]
3 [ ]א̇שר תחתיך ברזל 24 ית̊ן[ ]
4 [ ]ע̇ליך עד השמדך̊ 25 י̊[תנך]

VARIANTS

28:22 (2) ורד̇[פוך 𝔐𝔊𝔗𝔖𝔙] ירדפוך 4QDeut[c]𝔪

28:24 (4)]ע̇ליך 𝔐𝔪𝔊𝔗𝔖𝔙] > 𝔊[B]

28:24 (4) עד השמדך̊ 𝔐𝔗𝔖] עד השמידך 𝔪; εως αν εκτριψη σε και εως αν απολεση σε (+εν ταχει 𝔊[B]) 𝔊 (cf. 4QDeut[e,f] 4QpaleoDeut[r] at 7:23; 𝔐 at 7:24[fin]; Josh 11:14).

Frg. 11 Deut 28:27-29

1 (28) [ ]ובעפלי[ם̇]
2 [ ]ו̇בתמהון [29]
3 [ ]ו̇לא תצליח את דרכיך̇[ ]

bottom margin

L. 1 (28:27)]ובעפלי[ם̇. A portion of the base of final *mem* is extant. Reconstruction suggests ובעפלים (𝔐𝔪𝔗[O]) or possibly בטחרים (cf. 𝔐[q mss]𝔪[mss]𝔗[J]; εν ταις εδραις 𝔊[AOCdnt]; την εδραν 𝔊[B]).

VARIANTS

28:29 (3) תצליח את 𝔐𝔗] תצליח 𝔪; ευοδωσει (+τοτε 𝔊[dnt]) 𝔊

28:29 (3) דרכיך̇[𝔐𝔊𝔗𝔙] דרכך 𝔪; ܐܘܪܚܬܟ ܠܘܬܟ 𝔖

35. 4QDeut^{h}

(PLATES XVII–XVIII)

Preliminary publication: Julie Ann Duncan, 'A Critical Edition', 34–50; 'New Readings for the "Blessing of Moses" from Qumran', *JBL* 114 (1995) 275–92. Esther Eshel and Michael E. Stone, 'A New Fragment of 4QDeut^{h}', *JBL* 112 (1993) 487–9.

See also F. M. Cross and D. N. Freedman, 'The Blessing of Moses,' *JBL* 67 (1948) 191–210.

4QDEUT^{h} consists of fifteen fragments which preserve material from the beginning and end of the scroll, as well as a few lines from Deuteronomy 4 and perhaps 19 (see Table 1). Frgs. 11–15 preserve parts of fourteen verses of the Blessing of Moses; the lines of the poem are not arranged stichometrically.

The leather of the fragments is stained a reddish brown colour, and the surface is glossy. Some of the pieces are discolored with both very light and very dark patches. On frgs. 11–15 horizontal dry lines are visible, and on frgs. 7, 10, and 12 vertical dry lines mark the right margin. Top margins are preserved on frgs. 5 and 7 (the latter measuring 2.0 cm). Right margins are preserved on frgs. 2, 7 (measuring 1.0 cm), 8, 9, 10 and 12. Left margins are extant at frgs. 1, 4, and 5. A bottom margin is preserved on frg. 4 (measuring 2.3 cm).

TABLE 1: *Contents of 4QDeut^{h}*

Fragment	Passage	Fragment	Passage
1	1:1-17	8	4:31-34
2–4	1:22-24, 29-39	9	19:21?
5–6	1:41, 43-46; 2:1-6	10	31:9-11
7	2:28-30	11–15	33:8-22

The letters of 4QDeut^{h} are in a small (2 mm high), precise script, and the average distance between lines of script is 0.7 cm. Most of the fragments attest a column-width of either 85–95 or 75–85 letter-spaces. Two of the fragments suggest exceptionally narrow columns: on frg. 7 the width of the reconstructed column averages 38–43 letter-spaces, and on frg. 8 it is 45–55. The occurrence of a bottom margin approximately 30 lines down from Deut 1:1 suggests either 30 or, less likely, 15 lines per column.

4QDeut^{h} is inscribed in a formal hand which may be dated to a transitional period between the late Hasmonaean and early Herodian periods, *c*.50–1 BCE. For the orthographic differences between this manuscript and 𝔐 and 𝔖, see Table 2. Archaic spelling practices are evident, particularly in the poetic material of Deuteronomy 33, although it should be noted that the practices of the scribe are not consistent.

Intervals occur on frgs. 11–15 after vv 11, 17, and 21, corresponding to paragraph-divisions in 𝔐 (ס) and 𝔖 (קצה). In addition, reconstruction of frg. 6 indicates that an interval preceded 2:2, corresponding to 𝔐 (ס) and 𝔖 (קצה). At two places (frgs. 1 9, 12 11)

TABLE 2: *Orthography*

Frg., line	Deut	4QDeut^h	𝔐	𝔐^mss	ɯ^ed	ɯ^mss
1 3	1:3	אליהם	אלהם		אליהם	
1 3	1:4	סיחון	סיחן		סיחון	סחיון
1 3	1:4	יושב	יושב		ישב	
1 4	1:4	בעשתרת	בעשתרת		בעשתרות	
1 4	1:5	הואיל	הואיל		הואל	הואיל
1 5	1:6	בחרב	בחרב		בחורב	
1 6	1:7	הגדול	הגדל		הגדול	
1 9	1:11	א]בתיכם	אבותכם		אבתיכם	אבותיכם
1 9	1:11	יוסיף	יסף		יסף	
1 10	1:13	ונבונים	ונבנים		ונבונים	
1 12	1:15	עשרות	עשרת		עשרות	
2–4 19	1:22	נבוא	נבא		נבוא	
2–4 29	1:37	תבוא	תבא		תבוא	
5–6 8	2:3	סוב	סב		סוב	
5–6 8	2:3	צפונה	צפנה		צפונה	
5–6 9	2:4	(orth. or var.?) ויראו	וייראו		וייראו	
7 1	2:28	תשבׄירני	תשברני		תשברני	תשבירני
7 3	2:29	היושבי]ם	הישבים		הישבים	היושבים
7 5	2:30	סיחו]ן	סיחן		סיחון	
8 6	4:34	ובמפת]ים	ובמופתים		ובמפתים	ובמופתים
10 2	31:10	אתׄ]ם	אותם		אתם	
11–15 2	33:9	(orth. & var.) ראיתך]	ראיתיו		ראיתי	
11–15 3	33:9	(orth. or var.?) בנו	בנו	בניו	בנו	
11–15 3	33:10	(orth. & var.) [י]שם	ישימו		ישימו	
11–15 3	33:10	קׄטורה	קטורה		קטרה	
11–15 4	33:10	וׄכלל	וכליל		וכליל	
11–15 7	33:15	גבעת	גבעות	גבעת	גבעת	
11–15 7	33:16	מלאה	ומלאה		ומלואה	
11–15 8	33:17	(orth. or var.?) קרנו	קרניו		קרניו	
11–15 10	33:19	ושפני	ושפוני		ושפוני	
11–15 10	33:19	טמני	טמוני		טמוני	
11–15 10	33:20	כלביא]	כלביא		כלביה	
11–15 11	33:21	ראשת	ראשית		ראשית	

blank spaces on the leather do not correspond to paragraphing in either 𝔐 or ɯ, but occur in the middle of phrases. In both instances the surviving physical evidence suggests that the scribe was avoiding damaged leather (see NOTES). There are three supralinear corrections, all apparently by the original scribe: הי]רדן בׄמׄדבר frg. 1 1, רב 6 8, and וב^מ^פתח]ים 8 6.

Under the VARIANTS for frgs. 11–15 (Deut 33:8-11), the evidence from the Blessing of Levi preserved in 4QTestimonia (4Q**175**) has been collated. For a discussion of the relationship between these two witnesses, see Duncan, 'New Readings'.

Mus. Inv. 389. PAM 42.711; 43.357 (frg. 8).

Frg. 1 Deut 1:1-17

היׄ]רדן בׄמׄדבר
] אׄ]לׄ כׄלׄ ישראלׄ] בע]בר בערבה מול] [
(2)]]שׄעׄיר עד קדש ברנע [3]ויהי באׄרׄ[בעים שנה בעש]תׄיׄ עׄשׄר חדש באחד לחדש
] אש]רׄ צוה יהוה א[תו] אליהם [4]אחרי הכתו את סיחון מלך האמרי אשר יושב
] יו]שב בעשתרת בׄאדרעי [5]בעבר הירדן בארץ מואב הואיל משה באר את
(6)]]אׄלינו בחרב לאמר רב לכם שבת בהר הזה [7]פנו וסעו לכם ובאו הר
] ובש]פׄלה בנגב ובחוף הים ארץ הכנעני והלבנון עׄדׄ הנהר הגדול נהר
(8)] א]תׄ הׄארׄץׄ אׄשר נשבע יהוה לאבתיכם לאברהם וליצחק וליעקב
(9)] הה]יׄא לׄאמר לא אוכל לבדי שאת אתכם [10]יהוה אלהיכם הרבה אתכם
(11)] א]בתיכם ////// יוסיף עליכם ככם אלף פעמים ויברך אתכם כאשר
(12)] וריבכ]םׄ [13]הבו לכם אׄנשים חכמים ונבונים וידעים לשבׄטׄיׄכׄםׄ וׄ[אשי]מם
(14)]]דברת לעשות [15]ואקח את ראשי שבטיכם אנשים חכמ[ים ונבונים]
]]וׄשׄריׄ מׄאות ושרי חמשים ושרי עשרות ושטרים לשבׄטׄיׄכׄ[ם]
(16)] ושפ]טׄתם צדק בין איש ובין אחיו ובין גרו [17]לא תכירו פׄנׄיׄ[ם]
] לאלה]ים הׄוׄאׄ וׄהדבר אשר יקשה מכם תקריבון אלי וׄ[שמעתיו]

The five words with which the Book of Deuteronomy begins (אלה הדברים אשר דבר משה) preceded the first extant word; the column is wider than it appears in this format. The left margin is preserved, and the line-width varies between 80 and 94 letter-spaces.

L. 1 (1:1) א]לׄ. Part of the upper stroke of *lamed* is just evident on the leather.

L. 1 (1:1) כׄלׄ. Most of the *kap* and part of the *lamed* have been destroyed by surface damage.

L. 1^{sup} (1:1) היׄ]רדן בׄמׄדבר has been inserted above the line. Although only the downstroke of *bet* is visible in the photograph, ink of the base is detectable on the leather. The phrase was probably initially lost as a result of homoioteleuton.

L. 2 (1:2)]שׄעׄיר. The left arm of *ʿayin* has been lost with the surface of the leather, as has part of the left stroke of *šin*.

L. 2 (1:3) עׄשׄר. The impression of a base-stroke on the final letter is created by a crack in the leather.

L. 3 (1:3) א[תו]. *ʾAlep* is followed by a hole in the leather.

L. 4 (1:4) בׄאדרעי. The distortion of *bet* is a result of the fact that the letter is on two pieces of leather (the piece with the cross-stroke should be raised and shifted counterclockwise slightly).

L. 6 (1:7) ובש]פׄלה. The top of the *lamed* is visible on the plate. After the photograph was taken, a small piece with the letters *pe*, the bottom of *lamed*, and *he* was joined to the fragment in the museum.

L. 7 (1:8) א]תׄ הׄארׄץׄ. The right edge of the fragment containing lines 7, 8, and 9 is made up of several small pieces which have not been joined correctly (in part a result of the loss of minute pieces around their edges, cf. line 8, *lamed* and *ʾalep* in לׄאמר). Here a small piece of leather on the right edge of the fragment has been misjoined and should be rotated clockwise (the oblique stroke to the right of *he* is actually its right leg). The small piece of leather below הׄארׄץׄ is also not a direct join (the missing part of

ṣade is seen in the stray stroke of ink to the right of the word following).

L. 9 (1:10) א]בתיכם is followed by a blank space. We would not expect a sense-division at this point in the text; the leather here is blackened, suggesting the possibility that it was unsuitable for writing.

L. 11 (1:15) A reconstruction of space for this line indicates that this MS probably read ונבונים following אנשים חכמ]ים, with 𝔊; cf. v 13 above.

L. 12 (1:15) מ̇אות. A small piece which is slightly misaligned has disorted the *mem*.

L. 12 (1:15) לשבטיכ[ם]. Surface damage has made the ink faint in some cases, but the letters are certain; see VAR.

VARIANTS

1:4	(4)	באדרעי 𝔐𝔲𝔗] ובאדרעי* 𝔊S𝔙
1:7	(6)	בנגב 𝔲𝔙] ובנגב 𝔐𝔊𝔗S
1:8	(7)	נשבע יהוה 𝔐𝔊^{dtO}S𝔙; cf דקיים יי 𝔗] נשבעתי 𝔲𝔊^{ABC}
1:15	(11)	ראשי שבטיכם 𝔐𝔲𝔗S𝔙(cf 𝔊^{Odt} τους αρχιφυλους)] εξ υμων 𝔊
1:15	(12)	ושרי 2° 𝔐] שרי 𝔲
1:15	(12)	לשבטיכ[ם] 𝔐𝔲𝔊𝔗S] לשפטיכם* 𝔊^{ABCdtO}
1:17	(13)	תכירו 𝔐𝔲𝔗S cf επιγνωσεσθε 𝔊^{AdtnO}] επιγνωση 𝔊^{BC}

Frgs. 2–4 Deut 1:22-24, 29-39

Line	Verse	Text		Frg.
18		אלי כלכם ותאמרו נשלחה אנש]ים	[	
19	(24)	הערים אשר נבוא אליהן] 23	[	
20		[ההרה ויבאו עד נח]ל	[	
21		]	[	
22		]	[	
23	(29)	]	[	
24	(30)	[תערצון ול]א תיראו]ן	[	f.3
25		[31ובמדבר]אשר רא]ית	[	
26	(33)	[המקום הזה 32]ובדבר	]לילה להראות	f.4
27	(34)	]	35אם ירא]ה איש באנשים	
28	(36)	]	[ולו אתן את	
29	(37)	]	ל]א תבוא שמה 38יהושע	
30		]	39וטפכם אשר ל]א ידע היום טוב	

bottom margin

The right, left, and bottom margins are preserved, and the line numbers are based on a format of thirty lines per column. Line-width varies between 85 and 98 letter-spaces in this column.

L. 18 (1:22) כלכם. Part of the hook of *lamed* has been rubbed away, creating the impression of a 'v'-shape on the edge of the leather.

L. 18 (1:22) אנש֯ים. Most of the *šin* has been lost as a result of surface damage.

L. 26 (1:32) ו֯בדב֯]ר[. The dark stroke above *dalet* is a stroke of ink; it appears to be accidental rather than a deliberate marking.

L. 26 (1:33) ל֯י֯לה[. *Lamed* and *yod* are small and are shifted slightly counterclockwise.

L. 30 (1:39)]וטפכם אשר ל[א ידע = 𝔊. 𝔐𝔰 have וטפכם אשר אמרתם לבז יהיה ובניכם אשר לא ידעו (cf. Num 14:31). This line is reconstructed with the shorter reading of 𝔊 on the basis of the extant reading ל[א ידע (referring to וטפכם) as opposed to לא ידעו of 𝔐𝔰 (referring to ובניכם), and on the basis of spatial requirements that preclude the longer reading (which would result in a line of 112 letter-spaces). 𝔊 may have lost the phrase through haplography (homoioteleuton), or 𝔐𝔰 may have gained the longer reading due to Num 14:31 (see VAR.).

VARIANTS

1:22 (19) אליה֯ן 𝔐] עליהן 𝔰

1:33 (26) להראות] לראתכם 𝔐; להראיכם 𝔰

1:37 (29) שמה 𝔰] שם 𝔐

1:39 (30) ידע 𝔊] ידעו 𝔐𝔰. 4QDeut^h and 𝔊 read the collective singular antecedent טפכם (τον παιδιον νεον), as opposed to 𝔐𝔰 which refer to בניכם (see NOTE).

Frgs. 5–6 Deut 1:41, 43–2:6

top margin

1] [41ותענו

2] איש]א֯ת֯

3 (42)] [

4 (43)]]ה֯הרה 44ו֯י֯]צא [f.6

5]]ב֯שעיר עד ה֯חרמה 45ו֯[[

6] בקלכ]ם֯ ולא האזין אליכם 46ותשבו בקדש ימים[[

7 (2:1)]]סוף כאשר דבר יהוה אלי ונסב את הר שעיר ימי]ם [

(supralinear: 3רב)

8] 2ויאמר יהו]ה אלי לאמר לך סוב את ההר הזה פנו לכם צפונה 4ואת[[

9] הישב]ים בשעיר ויראו מ֯]]ם֯ ונשמרתם מאד 5אל ת֯תגרו[[

10]]6אכל ת֯ש֯]ברו [

The top and left margins are preserved on frg. 5, and reconstruction indicates that one line intervened between frgs. 5 and 6. The number of letters per line on these fragments varies between 75 and 86.

L. 2 (1:41) א֯ת֯[. This identification is tentative. Unfortunately the piece with these two traces is no longer extant.

L. 4 (1:44) ו֯י֯]צא. This identification is tentative. The large head of *waw,* which is generally smaller than that of *yod* in this manuscript, may be the result of blotting of ink (cf. also ת֯תגרו[, line 9 below).

L. 8sup (2:3) רב was inadvertently omitted and then inserted above the line by the same hand.

L. 9 (2:4) The dark mark above ונשמרתם is not ink, but rather a darkened patch of leather.

VARIANTS

1:44	(5)	החרמה] חרמה 𝔐𝔪𝔊ℭ𝔖𝔙
2:3	(8)	לך] לכם 𝔐𝔪𝔊ℭ𝔖𝔙
2:4	(9)	ויראו] וייראו 𝔐𝔪 (orth. or var.?)
2:4	(9)	ונשמרתם 𝔐𝔪ℭ𝔖𝔙] και ευλαβηθησονται 𝔊 (cf ευλαβηθησεσθαι 963*)

Frg. 7 Deut 2:28-30

top margin

1 תשבׄירני ואכלתי ומים בכסף֯]

2 ר֯ק֯ אׄעברה ברגלי 29כאשר עשׂ֯]

3 בשׂ[ע]י֯ר֯ והמואבים היושבי]ם

4 (30) ◦ת הירדן אל הארץ אשׂ]ר

5 אבׄה סיחו]ן מ[ל]ך

Top and right margins are preserved. The line-length of this fragment is approximately half that of the preceding columns (38–43 letter-spaces); it is possible that this column was the last on a sheet of leather. Note that the surface is badly damaged along the right margin ruling.

L. 1 (2:28) תשבׄירני. Part of the *bet* has been eroded with the surface. The tips of the upper and lower strokes remain; see also אבׄה, line 5.

L. 4 (2:29) ◦ת. The leather preceding *taw* is badly damaged, but faint traces of ink are discernible.

Frg. 8 Deut 4:31-34

1 (32) [ישכ]ח֯ [א]ת֯]

2 אשר היו לפ]ניך

3 השמים ועד]

4 כ֯מהו 33השמע]

5 [אתה] ויחי 34או֯]

6 [באת]ת֯ ובפ(מ)ת]ים

This fragment was originally placed with 4Q**464** (see PAM 43.357) but was identified as part of 4QDeut^h by E. Eshel and M. Stone (see bibliography). The right margin of

this fragment is preserved, and the number of letters per line is 45–55. Because most columns average *c.*85 letters per line, it is possible that this column was the last on a skin.

L. 4 (4:33) Eshel and Stone suggest the possibility of reconstructing אלהים חיים with 𝔐^{mss}𝔪𝔊𝔗^{J}, as opposed to אלהים 𝔐 (Eshel and Stone, 489).

L. 6 (4:34) וב^מ^פת[ים. The original scribe inserted a supralinear *mem* after *bet*, perhaps initially omitted as a result of the graphic similarity of *bet* and *mem*.

Frg. 9 Deut 19:21?

1 נפשו̊[

2 רגל ברגל[

Frg. 9 is at a right margin. The phrase רגל ברגל occurs in 𝔐 of Deuteronomy only at 19:21. נפש בנפש does occur earlier in the verse, but it is so near that a very short line would result. There is surface damage and distortion on the edge of the fragment, but the letter following *šin* is almost certainly *waw* (or possibly *yod*) and appears to be attached to the word נפש. If the identification is correct, this would entail some variant reading.

Frg. 10 Deut 31:9-11

1 (10) הזאת ע̇ל̊[ספר

2 (11) משה את̊[ם ביום ההוא

3 כל ישראל ל̊[ראת

4]ישרא[ל[

Frg. 10 displays a right margin. The width of lines in this column varies between 66 and 82 letter-spaces, with line 2 as the shortest.

L. 2 (31:10)]ביום ההוא[has been reconstructed with 𝔊 on the basis of spatial requirements; if the line lacks this phrase (with 𝔐𝔪𝔗𝔖𝔙) it is 57 letter-spaces wide, rather than 66.

VARIANT

31:9 (1) ע̇ל̊[ספר 𝔊] > 𝔐𝔪𝔗𝔖𝔙

Frgs. 11–15 Deut 33:8-22

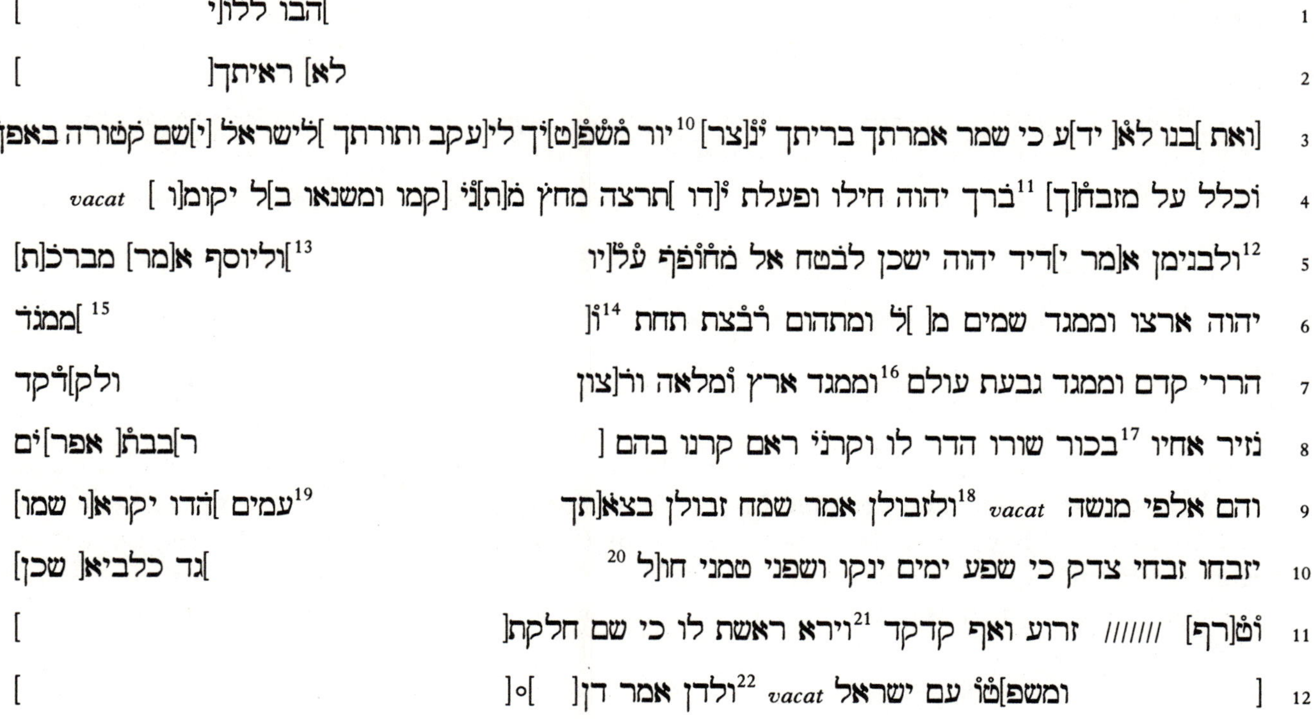
1]הבו ללו֯[י [

2]לא[ראיתך [

3 [ואת]בנו לא֯[יד]ע כי שמר אמרתך בריתך י֯נ֯[צר] 10 יור מ֯ש֯פ֯[ט]יך לי[עקב ותורתך]לישראל [י]שם ק֯טורה באפך

4 וכלל על מזבח֯[ך] 11 ב֯רך יהוה חילו ופעלת י֯[דו]תרצה מחץ מ֯[ת]נ֯י [קמו ומשנאו ב]ל יקומ[ו] *vacat*

5 12 ולבנימן א[מר י]דיד יהוה ישכן לבטח אל מ֯ח֯ו֯פ֯ף֯ ע֯ל֯[יו 13]וליוסף א[מר] מברכ֯[ת]

6 יהוה ארצו וממגד שמים מ[ ]ל ומתהום ר֯ב֯צת תחת 14 ו֯[15]ממגד

7 הררי קדם וממגד גבעת עולם 16 וממגד ארץ ו֯מלאה ור֯[צון ולק]ד֯קד

8 נזיר אחיו 17 בכור שורו הדר לו וקרנ֯י ראם קרנו בהם [ר]בבת֯[אפר]ים

9 והם אלפי מנשה *vacat* 18 ולזבולן אמר שמח זבולן בצא֯[תך 19 עמים]ה֯דו יקרא[ו שמו]

10 יזבחו זבחי צדק כי שפע ימים ינקו ושפני טמני חו[ל 20]גד כלביא[שכן]

11 ו֯ט֯[רף] ////// זרוע ואף קדקד 21 וירא ראשת לו כי שם חלקת[ ]

12 [ומשפ]ט֯ו֯ עם ישראל *vacat* 22 ולדן אמר דן[ ]◦[ ]

Part of the right margin and some of the letters along the left margin are extant. Excluding lines with intervals (lines 4, 9, 11, 12), line-width on this column varies between 77 and 84 letter-spaces.

L. 1 (33:8)]הבו. The right side of *he* appears to have been obscured by a particle at the time of photographing; it is clearly visible on the original.

L. 2 (33:9) ראיתך (for ראיתיך 𝔐). There is clearly no *yod* following *taw* in this scroll; for similar spellings in 𝔐, note, e.g., עשיתני Ezek 29:3, המציתך 2 Sam 3:8, הראיתם 2 Kgs 20:15.

L. 4 (33:10) וכלל. The lower part of *waw* has been destroyed by damage to the surface.

L. 4 (33:11)] מ֯[ת]נ֯י. The base-stroke of *nun* is barely visible under *yod*. There is a bit of blank leather following *yod*, which suggests that this MS probably read מתני (with ш) rather than מתנים (with 𝔐). However, a final *mem* slightly separated from the *yod* is not impossible.

L. 4 (33:11) ב]ל (cf. מן 𝔐ш). An alternative reconstruction is the negative particle אל, but בל is expected in this poetic context (cf. 4QTestim בל יקומו). It should be noted that the reading לא can be ruled out since at least a portion of the *ʾalep* would be evident on the leather (see VAR.).

L. 5 (33:12) לבטח. The lower part of *bet* has been lost due to surface damage.

L. 5 (33:12) מ֯ח֯ו֯פ֯ף֯. The traces for three of these five letters are virtually certain. The lower stroke of medial *pe* may be compared to that of *pe* in ופעלת, line 4 above.

L. 6 (33:13) ר֯ב֯צת. There is a split in the leather, and the pieces should be slightly separated. The right side of *reš* and a trace of the lower right corner of *bet* are discernible on the right side of the join, although the left side of *reš* and much of the *bet* are lost.

L. 7 (33:16) ארץ ו֯מלאה. As in the previous note, there is a split in the leather where the *waw* would have been, although the bottom tip of the *waw* can still be seen. This MS reads with 1QDeut^b 𝔐шℭS𝔙, whereas 𝔊 seems not to have the *waw* (cf. γης πληρωσεως).

L. 9 (33:19) עמים] ה֯דו for הודו (cf. הר 𝔐; הרי ш). The second letter could be a distorted *reš*, but *reš* and *dalet* are generally well distinguished in this script; compare, e.g., the *reš* in יקרא]ו with the *dalet* in

גד[in the line below. *Waw* and *yod* are also well distinguished in this MS (compare, e.g., the *waw* of הדו with the *yod* immediately following in יקראו); see VAR.

L. 11 (33:20) We would not expect an interval following וטׄו[רף]. The surface is scratched and blackened here, suggesting the possibility that it was unsuitable for writing.

L. 12 (33:21) ומשפ]טׄוׄ (cf. κρισιν αυτου 𝔊). The traces fit *ṭet-waw* slightly better than *yod-waw* (cf. משפטיו 𝔐ш), but the latter possibility cannot be ruled out. If this identification is correct, the variant of this MS may be orthographic, or it may read with 𝔊.

VARIANTS

33:8 (1) הבו ללו]ׄי[4QTestim 𝔊(Δοτε Λευι)] > 𝔐шℭ𝔖𝔙

33:9 (2)]לא [ראיתך 𝔊] לא ראיתיו 𝔐𝔖; לא ראיתי ш; לאׄדׄעתיכהי 4QTestim (Allegro and *BHS* err);[1] *nescio vos* 𝔙. The Targums are expansionistic here.

33:9 (3) בנו[4QTestim 𝔐ш] בניו 𝔐$^{q, mss}$ℭ; τους υιους αυτου 𝔊ℭ^{O}𝔖; וית בניהון ℭ^{J}; *filios suos* 𝔙 (orth. or var.?)

33:9 (3) שמר 4QTestim 𝔊] שמרו 𝔐шℭ𝔖𝔙. 4QDeut^{h} is consistent in reading a singular subject throughout vv 9-10 (see below, v 10), while other witnesses show some fluctuation (see Duncan, 'New Readings').

33:9 (3) בריתך] ובריתך 𝔐ш𝔊ℭ^{O}𝔖𝔙

33:10 (3) יור (for יורה?)] יורו 𝔐ш𝔊𝔖; ויאירו 4QTestim^{sup}; כשרין אלין דילפון ℭ^{O}; > 𝔙. The apocopated form of ירה (see GKC §76*f*) in 4QDeut^{h} is unexpected in this context (see 2 Kgs 13:17 and Duncan, 'New Readings').

33:10 (3) [י]שם 4QTestim*] ישימו 4QTestim^{corr}𝔐ш𝔊ℭ𝔖𝔙. 4QTestim originally read with 4QDeut^{h} (i.e. ישם); this reading was subsequently corrected to the reading as in 𝔐ш (the second *yod* was written in above the line, medial *mem* was written over final *mem*, and a *waw* was added).[2]

33:11 (4) וׄכלל 4QTestim*; וכליל 4QTestim^{corr}𝔐ш] δια παντος 𝔊. 𝔊 does not seem to have understood the sacrificial sense of כליל in this context; note also 𝔊 Deut 13:17[16], and contrast 𝔊 at 1 Sam 7:9 and Ps 51:21 [50:21] where כליל is reflected as one might expect (ολοκαυτωσιν and ολοκαυτωματα, respectively).

33:11 (4) ופעלת 4QTestim*; cf τα εργα 𝔊] ופעל 4QTestim^{corr}𝔐ш. The original reading of 4QTestim agreed with 4QDeut^{h}; the *taw* has been erased in a correction toward 𝔐ш. 4QDeut^{h} and 4QTestim read the feminine noun פעלה (either the singular construct form, or the plural construct written without a *mater lectionis*).

33:11 (4)] מׄ[ת]נׄיׄ ш] מתנים 4QTestim^{sup}𝔐

33:11 (4) ב[ל 4QTestim; cf μη 𝔊, דלא ℭ] מן 𝔐ш. For the reconstruction of בל, see NOTE; for further discussion of this variant, see Duncan, 'New Readings'.

33:11 (4) [יקומ]ו 4QTestim (יקומו) 𝔐 (יקומון) 𝔊ℭ𝔖] יקימנו ш. It is not possible to determine whether this MS included the final *nun* (= 𝔐) or not (= 4QTestim); there would be space for both *waw* and final *nun* in the lacuna.

33:12 (5) ולבנימן 𝔐^{mss}ℭ𝔊] לבנימן 𝔐; ולבנימים ш

33:12 (5) י]דיד 𝔐𝔊ℭ𝔖𝔙] יד יד ш

[1] See Strugnell, 'Notes en marge', *RevQ* 7 (1970) 226.

[2] Compare John Allegro, who judged that the correction was in the opposite direction (*DJD* V. 60). If, however, that were the case, there would have been an attempt to delete the *waw* at the end of the word; moreover, the *yod* is quite clearly a supralinear addition (see *DJD* V, Pl. XXI). See also Strugnell, 'Notes en marge', 226.

33:12 (5) אל; cf και ο θεος 𝔊] עליו 𝔐𝔗; > ⅏𝔖. This MS agrees with the tradition of 𝔊 in reading the divine name where 𝔐 appears to be corrupt;[3] see Duncan, 'New Readings'.

33:12 (5) מְחוֹפֵף] חפף 𝔐⅏; וחופף ⅏^{mss}(וחפף ⅏^{ms}). 4QDeut^{h} is unique in reading the *Polel* participle of חפף.[4]

33:13 (6) וממגד] ממגד 1QDeut^{b}𝔐⅏𝔖; απο ωρων 𝔊

33:15 (6) ממגד[1°] ומראש 𝔐⅏𝔊𝔗𝔖𝔙

33:15 (7) הררי 𝔐] הרי ⅏. 4QDeut^{h} 𝔐 represent the biform of the plural construct for geminate nouns.

33:15 (7) וממגד 2° 𝔐⅏𝔖] ומראש* 𝔊. 𝔊 repeats ומראש in the second part of the bicolon (cf. above), while 𝔐 and ⅏ alternate with וממגד. 4QDeut^{h} reads (ו)ממגד in both cola.

33:16 (7) וממגד 1QDeut^{b}𝔐⅏] και καθ' ωραν 𝔊

33:17 (8) שורו 𝔐] שׁ[ו]ר֯ 1QDeut^{b}⅏𝔊𝔖𝔙

33:17 (8) ראם 𝔐𝔊] ראמי ⅏

33:17 (8) קרנו] קרניו 𝔐⅏𝔊 (orth. or var.?)

33:19 (9) עמים]הׄדו] הר [עמים] MasDeut𝔐𝔖; עמים הרי ⅏; εθνη εξολεθρευσουσιν 𝔊 (see NOTE above). 4QDeut^{h} appears to reflect a graphic confusion of *dalet/reš* and perhaps *waw/yod* (the latter presuming a dittography of *yod* from יקראו; cf. ⅏). The proposal for 4QDeut^{h} is הדו (*defectiva* for הודו; cf. Ps 107:1). The tentative reconstruction of this line for 4QDeut^{h} is: עמים]ה(ו)דו יקרא[ו שמו] יזבחו זבחי צדק (see Duncan, 'New Readings').

33:19 (10) יזבחו 𝔐⅏𝔊^{dnt}𝔗𝔖] θυσετε 𝔊^{ABCO}

33:19 (10) ינקו 𝔐(יינקו)] יינק ⅏; θηλασει σε 𝔊

33:19 (10) חו[ל (𝔐⅏ ושפני טמני(ושפוני טמוני 𝔐⅏𝔗] και εμπορια παραλιον κατοικουντων 𝔊; ܗܐܠܦܐ ܕܡܛܫܝܢ ܒܚܠܐ 𝔖. For the reading of 𝔊 note ζαβουλων παραλιος κατοικησει / και αυτος παρ ορμον πλοιων / και παρατενει εως Ζιδωνος Gen 49:13.

33:20 (11) וטׄ[רף] 𝔐] טרף ⅏

33:20 (11) ואף] אף MasDeut𝔐; וגם ⅏; גם ⅏^{mss}; και 𝔊

33:21 (11) חלקת 𝔐⅏] εμερισθη 𝔊

[3] H. S. Nyberg first proposed the divine name for this crux (reading עַל), 'Studien zum Religionskampf im Alten Testament', *ARW* (1938) 372–7. See also Cross and Freedman (who read עֵלִי), 'Blessing', 204, n. 38 (similarly in NRSV: 'High God').

[4] Z. Ben-Ḥayyim (*Lešonenu* 22 [1958] 236–7) observes the tendency to employ the *Piʿel* conjugation for the *Qal* in late Hebrew and the Samaritan tradition. Qimron (§310.16) documents two instances at Qumran in which *Piʿel* forms have been substituted for the *Qal*: 4Q**513** 2 II 5 and 4Q**169** 3–4 II 6.

36. 4QDeut[i]

(PLATE XIX)

Preliminary publication: Sidnie Ann White, 'A Critical Edition', 241–62.

SIX IDENTIFIABLE fragments and two unidentified fragments are all that remain of this manuscript, containing portions of Deut 20:9-13; 21:23–22:9; 23:6-17, and 23:23–24:1. The leather is of medium thickness and was originally grayish to reddish brown. The surface was well-prepared, but now a certain amount of deterioration has taken place, leaving several visible cracks and some wrinkling. Frgs. 2, 3, and 5 contain the remains of pairs of columns and the margins between them average 1.3 cm. No other margins survive. Horizontal and vertical dry lines are visible on frgs. 3 and 5, and the average distance between lines of script is 0.6–0.8 cm. Frgs. 1–2 and 3 i–5 i contain 53–61 letters per line, while frgs. 3 ii–5 ii and 6 contained 41–51. Reconstruction of the amount of text between the first and the second columns on frgs. 3–5 indicates that the manuscript had *c.*39–40 lines per column.

The palaeographical study of this manuscript places it in the late Hasmonaean period, *c.*100–50 BCE. While retaining most of the characteristics of the Hasmonaean hand, it exhibits several traits that will become regular in the Herodian hand, particularly the beginning of ornamentation of the ends of letters. The latest letter types in the manuscript are *ʾalep* (the 'inverted-v' form), *bet* (the form in which the base is penned from left to right, resulting in a breakthrough at the juncture of the downstroke and the base), *ʿayin* (which is the same size as other letters and has a prominent breakthrough at the juncture of the right and left arms) and *ṣade* (where the arm is sharply bent at the 'elbow').

In orthography (see Table 1), 4QDeut[i] uses *matres lectionis* to mark **ay* > *ê* (e.g. לפניך 3–5 i 8), **ī* (e.g. כי 3–5 i 7, תשיבם 3–5 i 2), and **ū* (e.g. ועבדוך 1–2 i 3). It uses a *mater lectionis* for **u* > *o* when it is accented (e.g. קדוש 3–5 ii 12), but not when it is unaccented (e.g. כל 1–2 i 3). It usually marks **ā* > *ō* with a *waw* when it is accented and sometimes when it is unaccented (e.g. יבוא 3–5 ii 8 and וטובתם 3–5 ii 2), but this practice is not consistent (e.g. תבא 6 3, 4). The manuscript uses the short pronominal forms (e.g. ־ת, ־ך).

TABLE 1: *Orthography*

Frg., line	Deut	4QDeut[i]	𝔐	⅏[ed]	⅏[mss]
3 ii 2	23:7	וטובתם	וטבתם	וטובתם	וטובותם
5 ii 8	23:12	יבוא	יבא	יבוא	
5 ii 10	23:14	וחפרת	וחפרתה	וחפרת	
6 2	23:24	תש]מׄור	תשמר	תשמר	
6 3	23:25	תבא	תבא	תבוא	
6 4	23:26	תבא	תבא	תבוא	

Intervals to mark paragraph-divisions in 4QDeut[i] appear at 23:24 (frg. 6 3, ס 𝔐, no interval ш) and at 23:26 (frg. 6 5, ס 𝔐 קצה ш), but no intervals exist at 20:9 (frg. 1 1, ס 𝔐 קצה ш), 21:23 (frg. 3 i 2, ס 𝔐 no interval ш), and 23:25 (frg. 6 4, ס 𝔐 no interval ш).

Mus. Inv. 323. PAM 43.066; 42.006.

Frgs. 1–2 cols. i and ii Deut 20:9-13

1] צבאו]ת ב[ר]אש העם]

2]10 ל[הלחם] עליה וקרא[ת אליה ל]שלום 11והיה אם שלום]°

3]תענך ופתחה [ל]ך] והיה כל העם הנמצ[א בה יהיו]לך למס ועבדוך 12ואם ל[א]]

4] מ[ל]חמה וצרת עליה 13ו[נתנה יהוה אל[הי]ך[

Frg. 2 preserves a left margin, extending far enough to the left at line 2 to retain part of a letter in the next column.

L. 1 (20:9) no interval] ס 𝔐 קצה ш

VARIANT

20:10 (2) עליה 𝔐ш𝔊𝔗𝔖𝔙] αυτους 𝔊[B]

Frgs. 3 col. i, 4, 5 col. i Deut 21:23–22:9

1] אלהי]ך נת[ן ל]ך

2 נחלה] 22:1]השב תשיבם

3] 2 והי]ה

4] 3וכן תע]שה [לחמרו]וכן תעש]ה ולשלמת]ו f.4, 5

5] ומצאת]ה [לא תו[כ]ל] [

6]4 בדרך והתעלמת ה[קם (supralinear: מ]הם) [

7]5 גבר שלמת אשה כי ת[ו]עבת יהוה

8 (6)] צ]פור לפניך בדרך בכל עץ או על

9] ע]ל האפרחים או[על הביצים לא ת]קח

10 (7)] ל]ך

11 (8)]]תשים

12 (9)] המ[ל]אה]

Cols i and ii of frgs 3 and 5 preserve a margin of *c*.1.3 cm.

L. 6sup (22:4) מ֯]הם. The supralinear correction by the original scribe brings the MS into agreement with 𝔐⅏𝔊 and thus probably signals a small slip by the scribe, not a variant reading.

VARIANT

22:5 (7) שלמת] שמלת 4QpaleoDeut[r]𝔐⅏ (For this widespread variant, see BDB, 971)

Frgs. 3 ii–5 ii Deut 23:6-8, 12-16

1 (7) הׄקללה לברכה כי֯] [
2 (8) וטובתם [כל ימיך]ל֯[עולם [
3 לׄא] [
4] [
5] [
6] [
7] [
8 (13) השמש יבוא אׄ]ל [f.5
9 ויצאת שמה חוץ 14ו֯י֯]תד [
10 (15) חוץ וחפרת בה ו֯]שבת [
11 מתהלך בקרב] [
12 (16) קדוש ולא יר]אה [
13 תׄסׄ[גי]רׄ עׄ]בד [

L. 13 (23:16) תׄסׄ[גי]רׄ עׄ]בד. The tops of *taw* and *samek* are extant, as well as the tick of *reš* and the tips of *ʿayin*.

VARIANTS

23:6 (1) הׄקללה 𝔐⅏𝔙] τας καταρας 𝔊 (cf 𝔗𝔖)
23:6 (1) לברכה 𝔐⅏𝔊BC𝔙] εις ευλογιας 𝔊 (cf 𝔗𝔖)
23:8 (3) לׄא] 𝔐𝔊𝔗𝔙] ולא ⅏𝔖
23:12 (8) יבוא 𝔐𝔊𝔗𝔖𝔙] ואחרי כן יבוא ⅏
23:13 (9) חוץ 𝔐𝔗] הׄחו[צה] 4QpaleoDeut[r]⅏; εξω 𝔊; ܠܒܪ ܡܢ ܡܫܪܝܬܐ 𝔖
23:14 (10) חוץ 𝔐𝔗] החוצה ⅏; εξω 𝔊; ܠܒܪ ܡܢ ܡܫܪܝܬܐ 𝔖

Frg. 6 Deut 23:23–24:1

1 (24)]]ו֯כ֯י תחדל[[
2] תש]מ֯ור ועשית כאשר נדר֯ת֯[[
3]] בפיך *vacat* 25כי תבא בכרם רעך ו]אכלת [
4] כ]ל֯[י]ך֯ לא֯ ת֯ת֯[ן]26כ֯י תבא בקמת רע֯[ך [
5]]ר֯ע֯ך֯ *vacat* 24:1◦[[

L. 3 (23:24) בפיך. The tail of the *kap* has flaked off the leather.
L. 3 (23:24) interval] ס 𝔐 no interval 𝔪
L. 5 (23:26) interval] ס 𝔐 קצה 𝔪
L. 5 (24:1)]◦. The first letter can be either *kap* (cf. כי 𝔐𝔪) or *waw* (cf. °וכי 𝔊).

VARIANTS

23:25 (3) כי 4QDeut^{k2} (כא]) 𝔐 𝔪 𝔗] εαν δε 𝔊 (cf 𝔖); > 𝔙
23:25 (3) ו]אכלת 𝔐 𝔪 𝔊^{Cdt} 𝔗] φαγη 𝔊; ܬܐܟܘܠ 𝔖
23:26 (4) כ֯י[𝔐 𝔪 𝔗 𝔙] εαν δε 𝔊 (cf 𝔖)

Unidentified Fragments

These fragments were placed by the original team of editors with 4QDeut^{i} on the basis of similarities in handwriting.

Frg. 7

1]◦ה◦[
2] יהו֯ה[
3]א֯בת◦[

L. 2]יהו֯ה. Cf. יהוה in 3 i, 4, 5 i 7.
L. 3]◦א֯בת[. For the *ʾalep*, cf. that of ולא in 3 ii–5 ii 12.

Frg. 8

1]דת ה֯[
2]ל֯[ ]ל֯[

37. 4QDeut^{j}

(PLATES XX–XXIII)

Preliminary publication: Julie Ann Duncan, 'A Critical Edition', 89–114 and Pls. IV–VII.

Previous discussion: Julie Ann Duncan, 'Considerations of 4QDt^{j} in Light of the "All Souls Deuteronomy" and Cave 4 Phylactery Texts', *Madrid*, 1. 199–215 and Pls. 2–7.

J. T. Milik, 'Tefillin, Mezuzot, et Targums', (Oxford: Clarendon, 1977) 34–79.

P. W. Skehan, 'A Fragment of the "Song of Moses" (Deut. 32) from Qumran', *BASOR* 136 (1954) 12–15. 'The Qumran Manuscripts and Textual Criticism', *Volume du congrès, Strasbourg 1956* (VTSup 4; Leiden: Brill, 1957) 148–60. 'Qumran and the Present State of Old Testament Text Studies: The Masoretic Text', *JBL* 78 (1959) 21–5.

M. Weinfeld, 'Grace After Meals in Qumran', *JBL* 111 (1992) 427–40.

See also W. F. Albright, 'A Biblical Fragment from the Maccabaean Age: The Nash Papyrus', *JBL* 56 (1937) 145–76. J. Ziegler, 'Zur Septuaginta-Vorlage im Deuteronomium', *ZAW* 72 (1960) 240–6.

THIS collection of fragments from Deuteronomy and Exodus is presented as constituting a single manuscript of excerpted passages, rather than one or two biblical manuscripts. Since both the fragments of Exodus and those of Deuteronomy clearly derive from the same scribal hand (see Cross, 173–81 and Line 7 on p. 139), the relationship of these two groups of fragments may be explained by one of three possibilities: (1) the fragments represent the remnants of two different biblical manuscripts which happen to have been written by the same scribe; (2) they represent the remnants of a single biblical manuscript which contained interpolations; or (3) they derive from a single manuscript, but one which is a collection of excerpted texts, rather than a manuscript of a biblical book. With reference to the second and third possibilities, it should be noted that the two groups of fragments indeed correspond in material features and measurements. Preference for the third possibility is based on the most striking feature of these fragments, namely, that all preserve in some sense 'special use' passages (see below). Supporting evidence for the manuscript being in this genre is provided by the short column height of the manuscript, which appears to be typical of excerpted manuscripts such as 4QDeut^{n} with 12–14 lines per column and 4QDeut^{q} with 11 lines.

The leather of both the Deuteronomy and the Exodus fragments shares the same characteristics: relatively thick, medium beige, and not treated for writing on the back. Both sets of fragments are marked by small vertical folds in the leather, which have in some instances become fractures, and by surface deterioration at the edges of some of the fragments, which has resulted in loss of ink. The dry lines for ruling are no longer visible on the manuscript, though the leather has split along the right and left margins at several points due to the effects of ruling.

Top margins of *c.*1.5–1.7 cm are fully preserved on cols. I, III, IV (Deut), and X (Exod), with top margins partially preserved on cols. V and VIII (Deut) as well. Bottom margins of *c.*1.7–1.8 cm are fully preserved on cols. IX, X (Exod), and XII (Deut), with partially preserved bottom margins on cols. II and III (Deut). The only clear right margin is on frg. 34, but several fragments (1, 7, 9, and 27) have split apparently along the right marginal ruling so that the beginnings of the lines are extant. Left margins are preserved on frgs. 6, 11, 17, and 21. Only one stitched edge

survives, at the left of frg. 17, and the distance from the left marginal ruling to the stitched edge is *c*.2.3 cm.

Both those columns with text from Deuteronomy and those with text from Exodus can be reconstructed according to a format of 14 lines per column (with the exception of col. V; see NOTE). Three top margins preserved at Deut 5:1, 5:22, and 5:29, and a lower margin preserved at 5:28 indicate that there were 14 lines per column for the Deuteronomy fragments. In the Exodus material, frg. 28 preserves a top margin at Exod 12:46, and frg. 33 a bottom margin at Exod 13:1-5, again yielding 14 lines. The number of letters per line is 45–54 for most columns with Deuteronomy, though col. IV is narrower (with only 41–47) because it is the last column on its skin, and col. V has only 32–41 letters per line for that column reserved for the special passage Deut 8:5-10. Col. X, the only column with extensive text from Exodus, is slightly wider with 51–61 letters, but col. IX, with three lines of text from Exodus and one hypothetically from Deuteronomy, has the normal *c*.46 letters per line. Letters measure *c*.3 mm in height in both sets of fragments, and the average distance between lines of script is *c*.6–7 cm.

Contents of the Manuscript

The fragments preserve text from Deuteronomy 5, 6, 8, 11, and 32, and Exodus 12 and 13. On the hypothesis that these fragments all form one manuscript, Table 1 lists both the extant text and the editor's tentative view of the arrangement and contents of the original manuscript. The arrangement of Deut 8:5-10 as col. V, following the biblical order, is somewhat arbitrary, since this passage may have been placed at the beginning of the manuscript, as it is in 4QDeut[n]. Secondly, with respect to cols. VI and VII, the traditional text would not quite fill 14 lines per column if the columns were broad; but they would fit on the supposition of either narrower columns such as the preceding cols. IV and V, or a more expanded text such as 4QPhyl[K]. For further discussion of the full reconstruction of this manuscript, see Duncan, 'Considerations', 203–5.

TABLE 1: *Contents of 4QDeut[j]*

Extant Columns	Extant Text	Estimated Contents of Column
I	5:1-11	5:1-11
II	5:13-15, 21	5:11-21
III	5:22-27, 28	5:21-29
IV	5:29-33 + 6:1-3	5:29–6:3
V	8:5-10	8:5-10
VI	—	10:12-21
VII	—	10:21–11:6
VIII	11:6-10, 12, 13	11:6-13
IX	11:21? + Exod 12:43-44	11:13-21 + Exod 12:43-46
X	Exod 12:46-51 + 13:1-5	Exod 12:46–13:6
XI	—	Exod 13:6-15
XII	Deut 32:7-8	Exod 13:15-16 + Deut 32:1-9

Palaeography

The entire group of fragments is inscribed by the same classic formal hand, firm and practised, dating from the late Herodian Period, *c.*50 CE (see Cross, 173–81 and Line 7 on p. 139). The letters are broad and marked by *keraiai*; note especially the right arm of *ʾalep* (e.g. באש 11 3), the top of the right downstroke of *gimel* (e.g. ולגר 28 4), and the thickened upper arm of *lamed* (e.g. אל 1 1). Also significant are the forms of *pe* with an angular rather than rounded head, and *qop* with a prominent triangular loop at its head.

Orthography

The orthography of 4QDeut^{j} is fuller than that of 𝔐 and 𝔪 (see Table 2). Spelling patterns are fairly consistent, with the exception of suffixed forms and afformatives of the perfect, which vary somewhat, as they do also in 4QDeut^{k1}.

A *waw* is generally used to mark accented $*\bar{a} > \bar{o}$, e.g. מ]צֿוות col. V 3, לוא I 9 and 11 (but note לא I 4 and וֿזאתֿ IV 9). Unaccented $*\bar{a} > \bar{o}$ is marked with a *waw* in all instances: אלוהיך I 8; בוער III 3, אנוכי IV 5, לאבותיכם VIII 7. $*u > \bar{o}$ is written with a *waw* in both accented syllables, לאמור I 7, and unaccented syllables, כול I 1 and *passim*, החוקים I 2, הגדולים VIII 3.

For singular afformatives of the perfect, the long form is used: ושמרתה V 2, ו]עֿבדתה X 14. In the plural, the short form is used: ו]שמרתם I 3, וֿבאתם VIII 5. Pronominal suffixes, singular and plural, are written sometimes with the long form and sometimes with the short form: אלו]הֿיכֿה V 2, אלו]הֿיכה V 3, לאבו]תֿיכה X 13, אתכמה X 2; but: לך I 9bis, אלוהיך I 8, מלאכתך] II 3, בנך IV 13, לֿהם] IV 1, אלוה]יֿכם IV 10.

TABLE 2: *Orthography*

Col., line	Deut	4QDeut^{j}	𝔐	𝔐^{mss}	𝔪^{ed}	𝔪^{mss}
I 1	5:1	מושה	משה		משה	
I 1	5:1	כול	כל		כל	
I 2	5:1	החוקים	החקים		החקים	
I 2	5:1	דובר	דבר		דבר	
I 3	5:1	לעֿשותֿ]ם	לעשתם		לעשותם	
I 4	5:2	בחורב	בחרב		בחורב	
I 7	5:5	לאמור	לאמר		לאמר	
I 8	5:6	אנוכי	אנכי		אנכי	
I 8	5:6	אלוהיך	אלהיך		אלהיך	
I 9	5:7	לוא	לא		לא	
I 9	5:7	אלוהים	אלהים		אלהים	
I 11	5:9	לוֿ]א	לא		לא	
I 12	5:9	אלוהיך	אלהיך		אלהיך	
I 12	5:9	שלשֿ]ים[	שלשים		שלישים	שלשים
I 13	5:9	לשֿונאֿ]י	לשנאי		לשנאי	
I 13	5:10	וֿלשומר]י[	ולשמרי		ולשמרי	
I 14	5:11	לוא	לא		לא	
III 3	5:23	בוער[	בער		בער	
III 8	5:26	כ]וֿל	כל		כל	

TABLE 2: *Orthography (continued)*

Col., line	Deut	4QDeut[j]	𝔐	𝔐[mss]	⅏[ed]	⅏[mss]
III 9	5:26	כ]מׄונו	כמנו		כמונו	כמוני
III 14	5:28	]כולׄ[	כל		כל	
IV 1	5:29	אותׄ[י	אתי		אתי	
IV 4	5:31	כול	כל		כל	
IV 4	5:31	הׄ[ח]וׄקימׄ[	והחקים	החקים	החקים	
IV 5	5:31	אנוכיׄ[	אנכי		אנכי	
IV 5	5:31	נ]ותׄ[ן	נתן		נתן	
IV 6	5:32	[א]לוׄהׄ[יכם	אלהיכם		אלהיכם	
IV 7	5:33	בכ]ול	בכל		בכל	
IV 7	5:33	תלכ]וׄן	תלכו		תלכון	
IV 12	6:2	]כול	כל		כל	
V 1	8:5	לבב]כׄהׄ	לבבך		לבבך	
V 2	8:5	אלו]הׄיכׄה	אלהיך		אלהיך	
V 2	8:6	ושמרתה	ושמרת		ושמרת	
V 3	8:6	[מ]צׄוות	מצות		מצות	
V 3	8:6	אלו]הׄיכה	אלהיך		אלהיך	
V 4	8:6	[א]וׄתו	אתו		אתו	
V 4	8:7	אלוהיכה	אלהיך		אלהיך	
V 5	8:7	עי]נׄות	ענת		עינות	
V 8	8:9	במסכׄנות[	במסכנת		במסכנת	
V 8	8:9	ת]אׄוכל	תאכל		תאכל	
V 8	8:9	לוא	לא	ולא	לא	
V 10	8:10	ושבעתׄהׄ	ושבעת		ושבעת	
V 10	8:10	וׄ[ב]רׄכתה	וברכת		וברכת	
VIII 7	11:9	לאבותיכם	לאבתיכם		לאבתיכם	לאבותיכם
IX 12	Exod 12:43	ויוׄ[אמר	ויאמר		ויאמר	
IX 13	Exod 12:43	כול	כל		כל	
X 5	Exod 12:50	]מושׄה	משה		משה	
X 5	Exod 12:50	אהרון	אהרן		אהרן	
X 7	Exod 13:1	]מושה	משה		משה	
X 12	Exod 13:5	אלוהיכ]הׄ		אלהיך	אלהיך	
X 13	Exod 13:5	לאבו]תׄיכה	לאבתיך		לאבתיך	לאבותיך
X 14	Exod 13:5	ו]עׄבדתה	ועבדת		ועבדת	
X 14	Exod 13:5	בחוׄדׄ[ש	בחדש		בחדש	
XII 13	Deut 32:8	בהנחׄי[ל	בהנחל	בהנחיל	בהנחל	בהנחיל

Paragraphing

Two intervals are extant on the preserved fragments: one before Deut 11:13 at VIII 13 (ס 𝔐, קצה ⅏), and the other before Exod 12:43 at IX 12, which possibly follows Exod 12:42 (פ 𝔐, קצה ⅏) or more likely follows Deut 11:21 (ס 𝔐, קצה ⅏); cf. 4QPhyl[I], and see NOTES on col. IX. Reconstruction suggests that intervals also occurred before Exod 12:51 at X 6 (ס 𝔐, no interval ⅏) and before Exod 13:1 at X 7 (פ 𝔐, קצה ⅏).

Corrections

There are three corrections in this manuscript (see NOTE on each). The original scribe wrote a supralinear *yod* in מו[סׄ'פים III 7. The 2nd pl. independent pronoun has been corrected to the 2nd sing. in אתׄמׄה VIII 8. Finally, there is an apparent erasure at the left end of col. X 4.

The Character of the Manuscript

All extant clues indicate that this was a 'special use' manuscript. Selections from the *Decalogue* and its frame, from *Deuteronomy 11*, and from *Exodus 12:43–13:5* are very frequent in the twenty-one phylacteries found in Cave 4. On the basis of the passages attested in this material, J. T. Milik has characterized a 'choix maximum des péricopes': Deut 5:1–6:9, Deut 10:12–11:21, and Exod 12:43–13:16 (*DJD* VI. 38–9). With respect to the ordering of this material, while a few phylacteries from Cave 4 attest a biblical order (i.e. the Exodus passages precede those of Deuteronomy), the order most frequently attested presents passages from Deut 10:12–11:21 preceding passages from Exod 12:43–13:16; see, e.g., 4QPhyl^{A} and 4QPhyl^{I}, where the juncture between Deut 11:21 and Exod 12:43 is still preserved (*DJD* VI. 50, 63). The material evidence of 4QDeut^{j} suggests that it followed this latter sequence as well, since Exod 12:43 begins three lines from the bottom of the column and thus could not have begun the manuscript (see the proposed reconstruction at col. IX).

Deuteronomy 32 is not usually a component in this repertoire, but a portion of it has survived in one phylactery (4QPhyl^{N}), suggesting that it too was utilized in this context on occasion (see *DJD* VI. 72–3). Further evidence for the use of Deuteronomy 32 as a special selection is seen in 4QDeut^{q}; it preserves the end of Deuteronomy 32 (vv 37-43) and has a very wide left margin with no sign of stitching, suggesting that the passage was not followed by Deuteronomy 33 and 34. Talmudic references to the Levite practice of reciting Deuteronomy 32 in the temple on Sabbath day (*b. Roš Haš*. 31a; *y. Meg*. 3:6, 74b) are further indication that this chapter was a text with special significance, as recently pointed out by Moshe Weinfeld (see 'Grace').

Deuteronomy 8:5-10 is not thus far attested in phylacteries or *mezuzot*, but it is found in a similar manuscript of excerpted texts from Cave 4, 4QDeut^{n} or 'The All Souls Deuteronomy', which consists of Deut 8:5-10 followed by 5:1–6:1. Deut 8:5-10 is contained on one fully preserved column in 4QDeut^{n}; since the passage begins the column and six uninscribed lines follow it, the column was apparently intentionally reserved for it. This passage apparently constituted one full column in 4QDeut^{j} as well (see col. V). Weinfeld has discussed the possible significance of the passage for 4QDeut^{n}, pointing out its function in rabbinic tradition, as the basis for the duty of grace after meals (see *b. Ber*. 44a).

Although the survival of these passages could arguably be due to chance, the more plausible explanation of this configuration is that the fragments collectively designated as 4QDeut^{j} all derive from a single manuscript of biblical excerpts, on the order of the Nash Papyrus (see Albright), 4QDeut^{n}, and 4QDeut^{q} (see Duncan, 'Considerations').

Mus. Inv. 170, 171, 172. PAM 43.051, 43.053, 43.054, 42.720.

Col. I Deut 5:1-11

top margin

[1]ויקרא מושה אל כול ישראל[ו]יואמר [אליה]ם שמ[ע]ה ישראל את
החוקים ואת המשפטים אשר אנ[וכי] דובר ב[אז]ניכם היום הזה
ולמדתם א[ו]תם [ו]שמרתם לעשות[ם [2]י]הוה אל[והינו כ]רת עמנו ברית
בחורב [3]לא [את אבות]ינו כרת[יהוה את]הב[רית ה]זאת כי אתנו
[אנחנ]ו אל[ה פה היום כו]ל[נו חי]ים [[4]פנים בפנים דבר]יהוה עמכם
] הה]יא להגיד
[לכ]ם[את דברי]יהוה כ[י]על[ית]ם]בהר לאמור
[6]אנוכי [י]הוה אלוהיך א[שר מ]צרים מבית עבד[ים]
[7]לוא יהיה לך אלוהים [[8]לוא תע]שה לך פסל [כול]
תמונה אשר בשמ[י]ם [ו]אש[ר במים]
מתחת לארץ [9]לו[א]כי אנ[וכי יהוה]
אלוהיך אל קנ[א]שלש[ים ועל]
רבעים לשונא[י [10]]ולשומר[י מצוותי]
[11]לוא ת[שא ינ]קה[ ]

[bottom margin]

The top and left margins are visible. The words extant at the left margin show that the initial letters along the right edge are at the right margin; the straight edge (see also cols. II and IX) suggests that the fragment split along the marginal ruling. The reconstructed format of the entire scroll suggests that the letters in line 14 are in the last line of the column. The width of this column is 45–53 letter-spaces per line.

L. 1 (5:1) ו]יואמר[. Only a portion of the triangular head of *yod* is visible. Although the *waw* looks short, note that the *ʾalep* is also contracted, and cf. *waw* in אלוהיך (line 12). The piece containing יואמר must be moved slightly to the left, so that the *šin* of אשר in line 2 does not overlay the *ʾalep*. The evidence is not sufficiently clear to found any linguistic conclusions.

L. 1 (5:1) שמ[ע]ה. Note that frg. 4 should be placed slightly to the right. There has been surface loss at the top and bottom of *mem*. The tip of the final letter is on frg. 5. Its height and direction indicate that it cannot be *ʿayin* but can be the cross-stroke of *he*. The long form is especially common in biblical texts from Qumran (see Qimron, §310.13 and VAR.).

L. 4 (5:3)]הב[רית. The top of the *he* is visible. The *bet* is on a very small piece of leather which was reversed when joined to the fragment. Some of the surface seen in the photograph is not leather but hardened glue, which explains why there are no traces where we should expect to see them (e.g. just preceding the *bet*). I owe this reading to Émile Puech.

L. 4 (5:3) ה]זאת. The trace preceding *ʾalep* could be either *zayin* or *waw* (cf. col. IV 9).

L. 5 (5:3) כו]ל֯[נו חי]י֯ם֯. Final *mem* is visible below the *reš* in כרת֯[, on the line above, and part of the *yod* preceding it is barely visible on the leather. The broken line seen below *waw* of אבות]י֯נ֯ו in line 4 is perhaps the arm of *lamed* in כו]ל֯[נו.

L. 7–8 (5:5-6) This MS has no interval following v 5; ס 𝔐, קצה 𝔪.

L. 8 (5:6) עבד]ים[. *Yod* is no longer visible due to loss of surface at the edge of the leather.

VARIANTS

5:1	(1)	שמ֯[ע]ה֯ 4QDeut^{n,o}] שמע 𝔐𝔪
5:1	(2)	הזה 𝔊] > 4QDeut^{n,o}𝔐𝔪ℭ𝔖𝔙
5:2	(3)	עמנו 4QDeut^{n}𝔐𝔪ℭ𝔖𝔙] προς υμας 𝔊 (cf Ziegler, 240–6; and Wevers, *THGD,* 53)
5:3	(4)	אבות]י֯נ֯ו 4QDeut^{n}𝔐𝔪ℭ𝔖𝔙] τοις πατρασιν υμων 𝔊
5:3	(4)	אתנו 4QDeut^{n}𝔐𝔪ℭ𝔖𝔙] προς υμας 𝔊
5:5	(7)	יהו֯ה֯ 𝔐𝔪𝔊ℭ𝔙] יהוה אלוהיכם 4QDeut^{n}𝔖
5:6	(8)	אנוכי 4QDeut^{n}𝔐𝔪𝔊$^{B^{*}963}$(εγω)ℭ^{O}𝔙] εγω ειμι 𝔊$^{AB^{c}FMVOC}$ℭ^{J} Syh(ειμι sub ※); ܐܢܐ ܐܢܐ 𝔖

Col. II Deut 5:13-15, 21[18𝔪]

[top margin]

] [1

] [2

מלאכת֯ך֯] [14] [3

מלאכה] [4

בהמתך] (15) [5

כי עב֯[ד [6

חזקה֯] [7

השׁ]בת [16] [8

] [9

] [10

] [11

] [12

] [21]ולו]א ת֯ח֯מ֯[וד [13

] שור֯ו֯[∘] [14

bottom margin

Although only the bottom margin is visible, the initial letters along the straight right edge are probably at the right margin (see NOTE on col. I). Reconstruction according to 𝔐𝔪𝔊 shows that the first extant line of col. II begins at line 3. The width of this column is 48–53 letters per line.

L. 6 (5:15) עב̇[ד]. Part of the *bet* is missing due to surface loss on the edge of the fragment.

VARIANT

5:14 (5)]בהמחך 𝔐𝔪𝔊𝔗𝔖𝔙 **]** ובהמחך 4QDeut^n 𝔊^B

Col. III Deut 5:22-28 [5:19-25𝔪]

top margin

1]]ע̇נן וערפל[

2]] ויתנם

3 (23)]]בוער באש

4] [24ותאמ]ר̇ [ ]הנה הראנ̇[ו]

5]]שׁ̇מ◦נו מתוך

6] האד]ם̇ וחי [25ועת[ה]

7] מו]ס̇יפים אנחנו

8 (26)] כ]ו̇ל בשר אשר

9] כ]מ̇ונו ויחי [27]קרב

10] אלוהי]נו א̇ל̇י̇כ̇[ה]ו̇אתה̇

11]]א̇ל̇[יכה ושמענו]

12 (28)] [

13]אלי ש]מ̇עת̇[י [

14]היטיבו]כול[[

bottom margin

The top, left, and bottom margins of this column are visible, and the width of its lines is 48–52 letter-spaces.

L. 1 (5:22)]ע̇נן[ ]. The leather is split at the point where the bottom of *ʿayin* should be visible. For medial *nun* followed by final *nun*, cf. 4QDeut^b, frg. 4 (Deut 31:15).

L. 4–5 (5:24)] ותאמ]ר̇. If frg. 12 is correctly identified and placed, the top horizontal stroke looks more like *reš* than *waw* (cf. ותאמרו 𝔐).

L. 7 (5:25) מו]ס̇יפים. *Yod* has been written supralinearly above and to the left of *samek* (see VAR.).

L. 10 (5:27) אֹלׄיׄכׄ[ה וׄאׄתׄהׄ. The traces tentatively identified are the top portions of the letters. The tips of the right upper arm and the diagonal of *ʾalep* are visible before the *lamed*. Following this are the tip of *yod* and the two ticks of medial *kap*. The next traces are the tops of *waw* and *ʾalep*, the left upper portion of *taw* where it loops into the downstroke, and the right upper part of *he* where the leg loops into the cross-stroke (see VAR.).

L. 13 (5:28) שׁ[מׄעׄתׄ]י. The angular base of *taw* is not visible in the photograph because the surface of the leather is lost.

VARIANTS

5:22[19𝔖] (1) עֹנן[וערפל 4QDeut^{n}𝔖] γνοφος θυελλα 𝔊; הענן והערפל 𝔐𝔗; cf. 𝔙

5:24[21𝔖] (4) הנה] הן 4QDeut^{n}𝔐𝔖

5:24[21𝔖] (6) וחי 𝔐] ויחי 𝔖 (anticipation of 5:26[23]?)

5:25[22𝔖] (7) מו[ס]ׄיפים 4QPhyl^{B,H,J}(vid)] י]וספים 4QDeut^{n}𝔐𝔖. This MS appears to have the *Hipʿil* form of the participle, as indicated by the supralinear insertion of *yod*. On the substitution of the *Hipʿil* for *Qal* forms at Qumran, see Qimron, §310.16; cf. e.g. ומזעיקים for וזועקים in the *Temple Scroll*, 59:6.

5:27[24𝔖] (10) אׄלׄיׄכׄ[ה 𝔊^{AFN}𝔖𝔙] > 4QDeut^{n}𝔐𝔖𝔗; cf. 𝔊^{B*Bmg}(cf. the following אשר ידבר יהוה אלהינו אליך; see NOTE)

5:27[24𝔖] (10) וׄאׄתׄהׄ[4QDeut^{n}𝔐^{mss}𝔖] ואת 𝔐

Col. IV Deut 5:29-33 [5:26-30ɯ]; 6:1-3

top margin

1 ז֯[ה]ל֯הם ליראה אות[י ו]לשמ֯[ור את כול מצוותי כול]
2 [הימ]י֯ם למען ייטב להם[ו]לבני[הם לעולם 30לך אמור]
3 [להם]שובו לכם לא֯הליכם 31ואתה֯[פוה עמוד עמדי ואדבר]ה
4 [אליכה]א֯ת כול [המ]צוה ה[ח]וקים֯[והמשפטים אשר תלמ]ד֯ם
5 [ועשו]ב֯ארצ [אש]ר אנוכי[נ]ותן֯[להם לרשתה 32ושמרת]ם֯
6 [לעשות כא]שר צ֯[וה]יהוה [א]לוה֯[יכם אתכם לוא תסורו ימ]ין
7 [ושמאול 33בכ]ול הדר֯[ך]א֯שר[צוה יהוה אלוהיכם אתכם תלכ]ון
8 [למען תחיון]וטוב ל֯[כם] והא[רכתם ימים בארץ אשר]
9 [תירשון 6:1] ו֯זא֯ת֯[המצו]ה֯[החוקים והמשפטים אשר צ]ו֯ה
10 [יהוה אלוה]י֯כם ל[למד אתכם לעשות בארץ אשר אתם]
11 [עוברים שמה] לרש[תה 2למען תירא את יהוה אלוהיכה]
12 [לשמור את]כול ח[וקותיו ומצוותיו אשר אנוכי מצוך]
13 [אתה ובנך]ו֯בן בנ֯ך[כול ימי חייך ולמען יארכון ימיך]
14 [3ושמעת י]שראל[ ]

[bottom margin]

The top and left margins are visible, including a stitched edge at the left, and the last extant line is probably the final line of the column. The width of the lines is 41–47 letters-spaces.

L. 1 (5:29) ז֯[ה. The bottom of the downstroke of *zayin* and perhaps the tip of its head are visible on frg. 11, at the left edge across from וערפל of col. III.

L. 9 (5:33–6:1) The scribe probably left a small interval before chapter 6; interval 𝔐, קצה ɯ.

VARIANTS

5:31[28ɯ] (4) ה[ח]וקים֯ 𝔐mss ɯ] והחקים 𝔐𝔊

5:33[30ɯ] (7) תלכ[ון 4QPhyl^H ɯ] ת֯לכו 4QPhyl^M 𝔐 (*BHS* note 33a-a errs)

Col. V Deut 8:5-10

top margin

1 [5וידעתה עם לבב]כׄהׄ [כי כאשר]ייׄסר איש את

2 [ב]נׄו כן יהו[ה אלו]הׄיכׄה מׄיסׄ[ריכה] 6ושמרתה אׄת

3 [מ]צׄוות יהׄ[וה אלו]הׄיכה לׄ[לכת ב]כׄול דרכיו [וליראה]

4 [א]וׄתו 7כי [יהוה] אׄלוהיכה [מביאכה] אל אׄ[רץ]

5 [טו]בה ורׄ[חבה]ארץ נׄחלׄ[י מים עי]נׄות ותׄ[הומות]

6 [יוצ]אים [בב]קׄעׄה ובהר 8[ארץ חטה] ושעׄ[ורה]

7 [וגפן]וׄתׄ[אנ]ה ורמון [ארץ] זית שׄמן ודׄ[ב]שׄ 9אׄרץ

8 [אשר לוא] במסכׄנׄות[ת]אׄוכל בה לחם לוא תׄחסר

9 [כול דבר]בה אׄרׄץׄ[א]שׄר אבניה בׄרׄזל ומהריה

10 [תחצוב נחושת 10ואכלתה] ושבעתׄהׄ וׄ[ב]רׄכתה את

11 [יהוה אלוהיכה על הארץ הטובה א]שר נתן

12 [לכה *v a[c a t*

13 [*vacat*]

14 [*vacat*]

[bottom margin]

The top and left margins are visible. On the hypothesis that this is a 'special use' text, only one word is expected to follow the last extant word, נתן in line 11. Thus the vacant space below it—the dark spot on the photograph below *taw* is not ink—probably signals, not the bottom margin, but the end of this passage. Since all other clues indicate that this MS had 14 lines per column, two further blank lines may have followed, just as about 8 blank lines followed this passage in 4QDeut^{n} where the full column was reserved for this passage. The width of the column is 32–41 letter-spaces.

L. 7 (8:8) שׄמן. The surface at the right side of *šin* has been lost.

L. 9 (8:9) [דבר]. Spatial requirements suggest an additional word (or erasure) between תׄחסר at the end of line 8 and בה in line 9. For דבר, cf. מידעם 𝕿 here, and לא חסרת דבר in Deut 2:7.

L. 9 (8:9) בׄרׄזל. *Bet* and *reš* are now clearly visible on a small fragment in the museum.

L. 10 (8:10) וׄ[ב]רׄכתה. Part of the *waw* is now visible (see NOTE on line 9 above).

VARIANTS

8:5 (1) pr 6:3(vid)] pr 8:4 𝔐𝔪𝔊

8:5 (2) כן 𝔊(vid)] > 4QDeut^{n}𝔐𝔪𝕿

8:6 (3) ב]כול דרכיו 𝔊^{dnt}] בדרכיו 4QDeut^{n}𝔐⅏𝔊^{ABOC} 𝔗𝔖𝔙 (cf 10:12; 11:22; 𝔊 of 19:9; Josh 22:5)

8:7 (5) ור]חבה 4QDeut^{f,n}⅏𝔊(sub ÷ 𝔊^{G}Syh)] > 𝔐𝔗𝔖𝔙. Although this word could have been lost through parablepsis in 𝔐, it is probably expansionistic here; cf. אל ארץ טובה ורחבה in Exod 3:8.

8:7 (5) ות[הומות] 4QDeut^{n}𝔐⅏^{mss}𝔗𝔖] תהומת ⅏𝔊

8:8 (7)]ות[אנ]ה 4QDeut^{f}𝔐𝔊^{Cdt}𝔗𝔖] תאנה 4QDeut^{n}⅏𝔊

8:8 (7) ורמון 4QDeut^{n}𝔐⅏𝔊^{Cdt}] רמון 𝔊

8:9 (8) לוא 2° 𝔐⅏𝔗^{O}] ולוא 4QDeut^{f,n}𝔊𝔗^{J}𝔖

8:9 (9) ומהריה 4QDeut^{f,n}5QDeut] ומהרריה 𝔐⅏. In later Hebrew the form with the single *reš* becomes more common (Qimron, §200.14).

[Cols. VI–VII not extant]

Col. VIII Deut 11:6-13

top margin

[ו]את אהליהם ואת[כול האדם אשר לקרח]

(7) [אשר ב]רגליהם מקרב [ ]

(8) [מעשי י]הוה הגדולים אש[ר]

[החוקים] והמשפטים[אשר אנוכי מצוך היום למען תחזקו]

[ורביתם]ובאתם וירש[תם את הארץ אשר אתם עוברים את]

[הירדן]שמה לרשתה [9] ו[למען]

[יהוה] לאבותיכם לתת[ ]

[[10]כי ה]ארצ אשר אתבה [ ]

[ ]◦ משם אשר תז[רע]

[[11]והארץ אש]◦◦[ת]מה [ ]

(12) [ ]

[דורש אות]ה תמיד[ ]

[אחרית שנה] [13]וה[יה]

[אתכמה]היום [ ]

The top margin is visible, and reconstruction places the last extant word on line 14, suggesting that it is on the bottom line of this column. The line-width is 45–53 letters.

L. 1–2 (11:6) The phrase ו]אׄת אהׄליהםׄ is followed by ואת כול היקום אשר ברגליהם in all other witnesses. Since this MS has the two phrases in near vertical alignment, the first line either was partly blank or contained the additional phrase ואת כל האדם אשר לקרח attested by 𝔪4QPhyl^{A,K}.

L. 4 (11:8) The amount of space available requires the reconstruction of [החוקים] as in 4QDeut^{k1} (see also 5:31, 6:1, and 7:11), although it is lacking in 𝔐𝔪𝔊 (cf. 𝔗𝔖).

L. 4–5 (11:8) The reconstruction of the expansionistic variant [תחזקו ורביתם or תחיון ורביתם] agrees with 𝔊 where 𝔐𝔪𝔗𝔖𝔙 have תחזקו, and is based on a calculation of space between the extant portions of lines 4 and 5. 𝔊 may be influenced by למען תחיון ורבתים 8:1.

L. 5–6 (11:8) Spatial reconstruction suggests that 4QDeut^{j} read [את הירדן] with 4QDeut^{k1} and 𝔊 though it is lacking in 𝔐𝔪𝔗𝔖𝔙; cf. 30:18, 31:13 (see also 4:26 and 11:31).

L. 6 (11:8) לרשתה. The dark spot preceding the *lamed* is not ink, but rather a crack in the leather.

L. 8 (11:10) אתמׅׄה. The *mem* has been erased and dots added above and below, correcting the form to the singular. The form initially written may have included the *he* (note no crowding of letters is evident) thus attesting the long form of the independent pronoun, with final *mem* in medial position as seen below in אתכמה at col. X 2 (Exod 12:48). This passage vacillates between the 2nd sing. and 2nd pl. throughout (see VAR.).

L. 9 (11:10) The faint traces on the edge of the leather before משם favour either *he* or final *mem*, and thus the word could be the sing. יצאתה, or the longer pl. יצאתמה, or the shorter pl. יצאתם (= 4QDeut^{k1} 𝔐𝔪𝔊𝔗𝔖𝔙).

L. 13 (11:12) The interval preceding וה]יה corresponds to ס 𝔐, קצה 𝔪.

VARIANTS

11:6 (2) מקרב] בקרב 4QDeut^{k1}𝔐𝔪

11:7 (3) הגדולים 4QDeut^{k1} 4QPhyl^{K}𝔗^{N}; cf τα μεγαλα 𝔊] הגדל 𝔐𝔪𝔗^{OJ}; > 𝔊^{B}. 4QDeut^{k1} כול מעשה יהוה הגדלים seems to understand מעשה as plural (cf. Qimron §100.34 and n. 9). Though παντα τα εργα κυριου τα μεγαλα in 𝔊 might be a translation *ad sensum* of כל מעשה יהוה הגדל 𝔐, 𝔊 of Deuteronomy regularly translates כל modifying a singular noun literally (e.g. על כל מוצא פי יהוה: αλλ επι παντι ρηματι τω εκπορευομενω δια στοματος θεου Deut 8:3). The one exception is the idiom, [לשמר] את כל המצוה, which 𝔊 always translates with πασας τας εντολας, or the like (cf. 6:25; 8:1; 11:8; 15:5; 27:1). This, with the evidence of an extant Hebrew witness in the plural, indicates that 𝔊 represents a *Vorlage* like 4QDeut^{j}. With regard to the question of superiority, the reading of 𝔊^{B} is noteworthy, since it is short but without triggers for haplography. A parallel phrase occurs twice in the deuteronomic material: אשר ראו את כל מעשה יהוה הגדול אשר עשה לישראל (Judg 2:7), ואשר ידעו את כל מעשה יהוה אשר עשה לישראל (Josh 24:31). It is likely that the latter passage preserves the primitive reading of the formula, here preserved in the reading of 𝔊^{B}.

11:8 (4) [החוקים] והמשפטים 4QDeut^{k1}(החוק]ים [והׄמׄשׄ]פטים)] > 𝔐𝔪𝔊𝔗𝔖𝔙. The expansion of 4QDeut^{j} is influenced by parallel passages such as 5:31; 6:1; 7:11 (see *THGD*, 86–98, esp. 92).

11:10 (8) אתמׅׄה 𝔐(אתה)𝔗^{O}; cf (εισπορευ)η 𝔊^{Bbn}] אתם 𝔪𝔊^{AOCdt}𝔗^{NJ}𝔖 (see NOTE)

11:11 (10) ת]מה]° 𝔐𝔪(אתם 𝔐𝔪)𝔊^{Odt}𝔖𝔗] (εισπορευ)η 𝔊^{B}; συ (εισπορευ)η 𝔊^{AC}𝔙

Col. IX Deut 11:21? + Exod 12:43-44

10 °] [

11 Dt 11:21? יהוה̊] לאבותיכם לתת להם כימי השמים על הארץ *vacat?*[

12 Ex 12:43 ויו[אמר יהוה אל מושה ואהרון זאות חוקות הפסח]

13 כול בן [נכר לוא יאוכל בו 44 [

14 אז יא[וכל בו 45 46 [

bottom margin

Lines 12–14 contain Exod 12:43-46, followed by an extant bottom margin. Exod 12:46 is continued at the top of the next column with an extant top margin. Again, as in cols. I and II, the MS seems to have split along the right marginal ruling, so that the initial letters along the right edge would be at the beginnings of their lines. The width of complete lines in this column is *c*.46 letters.

This column is preceded by col. VIII containing Deut 11:6-13. It may thus be conjectured that col. IX consisted of Deut 11:14-21 followed by Exod 12:43-44, the order attested by 4QPhyl^A and 4QPhyl^I (*DJD* VI. 50, 63). A reconstruction of the text of Deut 11:14-21 supports this conjecture, since the text here would indeed require the 11 lines needed to fill out this column. Further, the extant divine name at the beginning of line 11, since it appears at the split along the right margin, must have been יהוה (Deut 11:21), not ליהוה (Exod 12:42).

The interval in line 12 would be expected whether the preceding text was from Exodus or Deuteronomy, since 𝔐 and ⅏ have intervals following both Exod 12:42 and Deut 11:21; cf. 4QPhyl^I, which preserves Deut 11:21 followed by the passage from Exodus 12, and where reconstruction indicates an interval between the passages (*DJD* VI. 63).

VARIANT

Exod 12:43 (12) pr Deut 11:21(?) **]** pr Exod 12:42 𝔐⅏

Col. X Exod 12:46–13:5

top margin

1		] הבש]ר֯ לחוץ ועצם
2	(47)	] 48וכי י]גור אתכמה
3		] והיה כאזרח]
4	(49)	] לאזר]ח֯ ולגר הגר *ras*
5	(50)	] את]מושה֯ ואת אהרון כ[ן]
6	(51)	] את]בני ישר֯אל מארץ מ֯צ֯[רים]
7		[על צבאותם 13:1וידבר יהוה אל]מושה ל֯[אמור 2]ק֯ד֯ש֯ ל֯[י]
8	(3)	] בא]ד֯ם[ ]
9		] זכ]ו֯ר֯[את היום הזה אשר יצאתם בו מארץ מצרים]
10		] בחו]ז֯ק [יד]ה֯ו֯[ציא]
11		] 4היו]ם֯ א֯[תמ]ה [יוצאים בחודש ה]אביב [5והיה]
12		] אלוהיכ]ה֯ אל ה֯[ארץ הכנעני] החתי וה֯[אמורי והפרזי]
13		[החוי והיבוסי והג]ר֯גשי כאש[ר נשבע לאבו]תיכה לת֯[ת]ל֯ה֯[ם ולזרעם]
14		] ו]ע֯בדתה את [העבודה הזא]ת בחו֯ד֯[ש]ה֯זה [6]

bottom margin

In this column the last six verses of Exodus 12 are followed directly by Exodus 13. The top, left, and bottom margins are visible. The width of the lines in this column is 51–61 letter-spaces.

L. 2 (12:48) This MS has the long form of the 2 masc. pl., with a final *mem* in medial position, אתכמה (see NOTE on col. VIII 8).

L. 4 (12:49) There appears to be an erasure after הגר; perhaps the scribe began to write the next word בתוככם but judged that there was insufficient room at the end of the line.

L. 6 (12:50-51) Reconstruction indicates that this MS may have contained an interval between the two verses; ס 𝔐, no interval 𝔪.

L. 7 (12:51[fin]) Reconstruction of the text shows that 4QDeut[j] probably contained an interval at the end of Exodus 12; פ 𝔐, קצה 𝔪.

L. 8 (13:2) This line is too short, but no longer readings are suggested by the other witnesses or the phylacteries.

L. 9 (13:3) The line has been reconstructed with the addition of בו 𝔪𝔊[BS] on the basis of spatial considerations.

L. 11 (13:4) Reconstruction suggests that an interval followed 13:4; no interval 𝔐, קצה 𝔪.

L. 11 (13:4) אׄ[תמ]ה. The *keraia* of the upper right arm of *ʾalep* is visible on the edge of the leather.

L. 12 (13:5) [אלוהיכ]הׄ with 𝔴𝔊 is reconstructed based on spatial considerations.

L. 13 (13:5) The reconstruction of לׄהׄ[ם ולזרעם] is based on the space available (cf. Deut 11:9). It also explains why the stem of final *kap* (cf. לך 𝔐𝔴𝔊𝔗𝔖𝔙) is not visible above הזה in line 14 (see VAR.).

VARIANTS

12:46 (1) לחוץ] חוצה 𝔐; החוצה 𝔴

12:48 (2) אתכמה 𝔐^{mss}𝔴(אתכם 𝔐^{mss}𝔴)𝔊𝔗𝔖𝔙] אתך 𝔐

13:4 (11) אׄ[תמ]ה 𝔐(אתם)𝔊] ואתם 𝔴

13:5 (12) אל הׄ[ארץ] אל ארץ 𝔐𝔴

13:5 (12–13) 4QDeut^{j}] הכנעני] החתי והׄ[אמורי והפרזי והחוי והיבוסי והג]רׄגשי
𝔐 הכנעני והחתי והאמרי והחוי והיבוסי
𝔴 הכנעני החתי והאמרי והפרזי והגרגשי והחוי והיבוסי
𝔊 *הכנעני והחתי והחוי והגרגשי והאמרי והפרזי והיבסי

The list of seven peoples is highly variable both in components and sequence. The partially extant והג]רׄגשי and the available space indicate that the sequence of the peoples in this MS is different from that in 𝔐𝔴𝔊. It has been restored on the basis of 4QPhyl[A,M] (see *DJD* VI. 51, 72; cf. Neh 9:8).

13:5 (13) כאשׁ[ר 𝔖] אשר 𝔐𝔴𝔗

[Col. XI Exod 13:6-16 not extant]

Col. XII Deut 32:7-8

12 בׄיׄנׄ°[
13 8בהנחי[ל
14 בני אלוהים[9

bottom margin

The right and bottom margins are visible, and the width of the lines in this column is 52–53 letters. Deut 32:7aβ begins on the third line from the bottom of the column. Although lines 12 and 13 each happen to begin a hemistich, line 14 demonstrates that the text was not arranged stichometrically. A reconstruction with Exod 13:15-16 on the first two lines, and Deut 32:1-7aα filling lines 3–11 would well fit this column, yielding the necessary fourteen lines.

L. 12 (32:7) בׄיׄנׄ°[. The lower part of *yod* is ligatured with the base-stroke of *bet*, and part of the head of *yod* is visible just before the downstroke of *nun*. Medial *nun* could have been followed either by *waw* (בינו 𝔐𝔴𝔊𝔗$^{O(ap)NJ}$), or by *he* (בינה* 𝔗^{O}𝔖𝔙; cf. שׄמׄ[ע]הׄ I 1); it is not possible to say which.

VARIANTS

32:1 (3?) pr Exod 13:16 [by reconstruction]] pr Deut 31:30 𝔐

32:8 (14) בני אלוהים[𝔊(υιων [αγγελων 𝔊^{ABOCdnt}] θεου)] בני ישראל 𝔐𝔴𝔗𝔖𝔙

Unidentified Fragments

Both the identified and the unidentified fragments of this manuscript have been arranged and numbered differently from their arrangement and numbering in 'A Critical Edition' and 'Considerations'.

Frg. 35

]מ֯י[
]◦ ל[
]◦◦ה [
]ח֯ל[

Frg. 36

]   ◦[
]   [
]ר֯וח [
]ת [

Frg. 37

] א֯[1
]ארץ [2
]◦[3
4

Frg. 38

]◦ ◦[
]נוו◦[
]◦תו[

Frg. 39

]◦◦[
]ב ◦[
]◦◦[

Frg. 40

]י֯ה◦[1
] י◦[2
]◦ [3

Frg. 41

]לך ל◦[
]ת֯◦[

Frg. 42

]ך֯   [
]ם֯ [

Frg. 43

]נה [1
]◦[2

Frg. 44

]ה֯ש[

Frg. 45

]אל֯[

Frg. 46

]ה[1

Frg. 47

]◦ זוב֯[1
]◦ה [2

38. 4QDeut^{k1}

(PLATE XXIV)

Preliminary publication: Julie Ann Duncan, 'A Critical Edition', 130–54 and Pl. VIII.

Previous discussion: Julie Ann Duncan, 'Considerations of 4QDt^{j} in Light of the "All Souls Deuteronomy" and Cave 4 Phylactery Texts', *Madrid*, 1. 199–215.

See also Sidnie A. White, '4QDeut^{n}: Biblical Manuscript or Excerpted Text?' in *Of Scribes and Scrolls: Studies on the Hebrew Bible, Intertestamental Judaism, and Christian Origins,* (ed. H. W. Attridge, J. J. Collins, T. H. Tobin; Lanham: University Press of America, 1991) 13–20; F. M. Cross, *Scrolls from the Wilderness of the Dead Sea* (Berkeley: University of California Press, 1965) 20, 31–2; J. T. Milik, 'Tefillin, Mezuzot et Targums [4Q**128**–4Q**157**]', *DJD* VI; P. W. Skehan, 'A Fragment of the "Song of Moses" (Deut 32) from Qumran', *BASOR* 136 (1954) 12–15; H. Stegemann, 'Weitere Stücke von 4QpPsalm 37, von 4Q Patriarchal Blessings und Hinweis auf eine unedierte Handschrift aus Höhle 4Q mit Exzerpten aus dem Deuteronomium', *RevQ* 6 (1967) 193–227.

THIS manuscript consists of one large fragment, and four smaller ones, preserving portions of Deuteronomy 5, 11, and 32 (see Table 1). In 'A Critical Edition', it was designated 4QDt^{k1}, being one of two manuscripts that had originally been identified as 4QDeut^{k}. While striking similarities in the hand suggest that all the fragments of 4QDeut^{k1} and 4QDeut^{k2} had been copied by the same scribe, two factors support their distinction as separate manuscripts. One is the difference in letter size, 3 mm in 4QDeut^{k1} and 2 mm in 4QDeut^{k2}. The other is that the tetragrammaton has been written in square script in 4QDeut^{k1} and in Palaeo-Hebrew in 4QDeut^{k2}. Thus far no other manuscript exhibits a discrepancy like this in the writing of the divine name. These two factors, then, support the conclusion that these fragments derive from two distinct manuscripts.

TABLE 1: *Contents of 4QDeut^{k1}*

Frg.	Deut	Frg.	Deut
1	5:28-32	4	32:22-23
2	11:6-13	5	32:25-27
3	32:17-18		

The leather of 4QDeut^{k1}, which was originally a light tan, is stained dark brown in places, and is of average thickness. Frgs. 1 and 2 have a corrugated surface. Dry lines are no longer evident on any of the fragments. The average height of a letter is 3 mm, and the space between lines measures 6 mm. A right margin of 1.5 cm has been preserved on frg. 2, and bottom margins are extant on frgs. 2 and 5, measuring 3.1 and 2 cm, respectively.

There appear to be two column-widths represented in this manuscript. On frgs. 1 and 2 it is 45–54 letter-spaces, but on frgs. 3, 4, and 5, which preserve fragmentary lines from Deuteronomy 32, it may be narrower with 36–42 spaces. The lines of this Song do not appear to be arranged stichometrically; see lines 1 and 2 on frg. 5.

The manuscript is inscribed in an Early Herodian formal hand (*c*.30–1 BCE) with strong semiformal influence seen in several instances: *ʾAlep* has an *s*-shaped axis; *gimel* has a marked curve in the axis; *he* has a heavily shaded and unusually long crossbar; the hook of *lamed* is broad; and the left downstroke of *šin* often continues past the lower right stroke, sometimes in exaggerated fashion. In addition, the *dalet* appears to be a semiformal form, drawn continuously, with the leg sometimes tending towards an *s* shape.

The orthography of 4QDeut^{k1} is generally fuller than that of 𝔐 ɯ (see Table 2). Spelling patterns are consistent, except for suffixed forms and afformatives of the perfect, which vary somewhat. The same inconsistency is found in 4QDeut^{j}. A *waw* is used to mark $*\bar{a} > \bar{o}$ both when it is accented (e.g. לוא frg. 2 9, ובקעות 2 11), and when it is unaccented (e.g. לעולם 1 3, לאבותיכם 2 7, אלוהיכה 2 12). $*u > \bar{o}$ is also marked with a *waw*, in both accented and unaccented syllables (accented, אמור 1 3; unaccented, הגדולים 2 3, כול 2 2 and *passim*). The afformative of the perfect in the singular is written in the longer form the one time it appears (והשקיתה 2 10). In the plural it is written twice in the short form (ורביתם 2 5; יצאתם 2 9), and once, with a damaged reading, in the long ויׄרשתמׄהׄ 2 5; see NOTE).

TABLE 2: *Orthography*

Frg., line	Deut	4QDeut^{k1}	𝔐	𝔐^{mss}	ɯ^{ed}	ɯ^{mss}
1 1	5:28 [25 𝔊]	ה]יׄטׄיבׄו	היטיבו		הטיבו	היטיבו ,היטבו
1 1	5:28 [25]	כׄוׄ[ל]	כל		כל	
1 2	5:29 [26]	ולש]מור	ולשמר		ולשמר	
1 3	5:29 [26]	לעׄולם	לעלם		לעלם	לעולם
1 3	5:30 [27]	אמור	אמר		אמר	
1 4	5:31 [28]	עׄמׄוד	עמד		עמד	
1 4	5:31 [28]	אליכה	אליך		אליך	
2 2	11:6	[כ]וׄלׄ	כל		כל	
2 2	11:6	כול	כל		כל	
2 3	11:7	כול	כל		כל	
2 3	11:7	(orth. & var.) הגדולים	הגדל		הגדול	
2 4	11:8	כול	כל		כל	
2 5	11:8	ויׄרשתמׄהׄ	וירשתם		וירשתם	
2 6	11:8	(orth. & var.) עוברים	עברים		באים	
2 7	11:9	לאבותיכם	לאבתיכם		לאבתיכם	לאבותיכם
2 8	11:10	כיא	כי		כי	
2 8	11:10	(morph. & var.) אתמׄה	אתה		אתם	
2 9	11:10	לוא	לא		לא	
2 9	11:10	היאה	הוא		היא	
2 10	11:10	והשקיתה	והשקית		והשקית	
2 10	11:10	(morph.; var.?) ברגליכה	ברגלך		ברגליך	
2 11	11:11	ובקעות	ובקעת	בקעות	ובקעות	
2 12	11:12	אלוהיכה	אלהיך		אלהיך	
2 12	11:12	דורש	דרש		דרש	
2 12	11:12	אוׄתׄה	אתה		אתה	

The singular pronominal suffix is written in the longer form three times (אליכה 1 4, ברגליכה 2 10, אלוהיכה 2 12) while all plural pronominal suffixes are short (ברגליהם 2 2, ולזרעם 2 7, לֹהם 1 3). The two cases of independent pronouns are in the long form: אתמה 2 8; היאה 2 9. As in 4QDeut^{k2}, כיא 2 8 is written with a double *mater lectionis* (see Qimron, §100.51).

An interval to mark a paragraph-division occurs at 2 13 (11:12-13; ס 𝔐, קצה ш), but not at 2 8 (11:9-10; ס 𝔐, קצה ш).

Two scribal corrections, apparently by the original hand, have been preserved: at frg. 2 3 (11:7) the trace above and to the left of אשר̊ may be identified as the tip of *lamed* indicating that ל̊]כם[has been inserted supralinearly (see NOTE); and similarly, at frg. 2 12 (11:12) the word עיני has been written in supralinearly.

The contents of this manuscript are excerpted from Deuteronomy 5 (the decalogue frame), 11, and 32 (the 'Song of Moses'). Portions of chapters 5 and 11 are particularly popular in the twenty-one phylactery texts surviving from Cave 4 (see Milik, 'Tefillin', *DJD* VI). Excerpts of Deuteronomy 32 appear in 4QPhyl^{N} (*DJD* VI. 72–3), 4QDeut^{q} which apparently contained only this Song (see 4QDeut^{q} in this volume), and 4QDeut^{j} (see the 4QDeut^{j} introduction in this volume and Duncan, 'Considerations'). 4QDeut^{k1} may likewise be a catena of selected passages, like the Nash Papyrus, 4QDeut^{j}, the 'All Souls Deuteronomy', and 4QDeut^{q} (see White, '4QDeut^{n}: Biblical Manuscript or Excerpted Text?'; Stegemann, 'Weitere Stücke'; and Cross, *Scrolls*).

Mus. Inv. 1090. PAM 43.056.

Frg. 1 Deut 5:28-32

1] ה]יטיבו כו̊[ל [
2 (29)] לה]ם̊[לי]ר̊אה א̊[ותי ולש]מור מצות[י [
3] ולבניה]ם̊ לעולם 30 לך אמור להם שוב̊[ו [
4 (31)] פוה]ע̊מוד עמדי ואדברה אליכה א[ת]
5] ו]ע̊שו̊ בארץ אשר̊[אנוכי]
6 (32)] א]ל̊[והיכם [

L. 2 (5:29) לה]ם̊[. Part of final *mem* may be seen in the two traces at the far right edge of the leather.

L. 2 (5:29) לי]ר̊אה. The *ʾalep* has been distorted by surface loss and peeling at the edge. Part of the right leg and the oblique axis is preserved. The left leg has been lost with the surface.

L. 2 (5:29) א̊[ותי. There are very light traces of ink here which fit *ʾalep*.

L. 3 (5:29) לבניה]ם̊. Traces of the lower stroke of final *mem* are evident at the right edge of the leather.

L. 5 (5:31) ו]ע̊שו̊. The left stem of *ʿayin* is visible, as well as the top part of *śin*. The dark area to the left of the final *waw* is discoloration and not ink.

VARIANTS

5:29 (2) ולש]מור 𝔐^{mss}] + את 𝔐ш𝔗

5:29 (2) מצות[י 𝔐^{mss}ш𝔊] pr כל 𝔐𝔊^{Ot}𝔗𝔖𝔙

5:30 (3) אמור 𝔐ш(אמר 𝔐ш)𝔊𝔗^{OJ}] ואמר 𝔗^{N}𝔊^{C}𝔙

Frg. 2 Deut 11:6-13

[ ]∘∘[ ]

[כ]וׄל [היקום] אׄשר ברגליהם בקרב כול [ישראל 7 [

[לׄ]כם

(8) את כול מעשה יהוה הגדולים אשׄר] [

כול המצוה החוק[ים]וׄהׄמׄשׄ[פטים [

למען תחזקו ורבׄיתםׄ[ובאת]םׄ ויׄרשתמׄהׄ אׄתׄ הארץׄ] [

עוברים את הירדן שמהׄ לרשתה 9 ולמׄעׄן תאריכון ימׄ[ים [

אשר נשבע יהוה לאבותיכם לתתׄ להם ולזרעם אׄ[חריהם [

זבת חלב ודבש 10 כיא הארץ אשר אתמהׄ באים] [

לוא כארץ מצרים היאה אשר יצאתם משם אשׄ[ר [

והשקיתה ברגליכה כגן היׄרׄק 11 והארץ אשר א[תמה [

(12) לרשתה ארצ הרים ובקעות למטר השמיםׄ] [

עיני

אשר יהוה אלוהיכה דורש אוׄתׄהׄ תמיד יהוה] [

שנה ועד אחרית שנה *vacat* 13 והיה אם] [

bottom margin

Right and bottom margins are preserved on this fragment.

L. 3 (11:7) [לׄ]כם היום]. The ink above and to the left of אשׄר is part of a supralinear correction, and may be identified as the top of *lamed*. The restoration is on the basis of 𝔊, υμιν σημερον.

L. 4 (11:8) וׄהׄמׄשׄ[פטים. The extant portions are on damaged pieces of leather which are misaligned. Part of the head of *waw* is apparent. A fleck of ink remains from the right side of *he*, which has been mostly destroyed by surface loss. The *mem* is small. After the *mem* the tip of the right lower arm of *šin* is visible.

L. 5 (11:8) ויׄרשתמׄהׄ. The stem of the *reš* has been entirely lost due to surface damage. At the end of the word the right leg of *he* overlapping slightly with the *mem* has created a distortion in the traces.

L. 6 (11:8) שמהׄ. The left stroke of *he* has been lost in the crack.

L. 6 (11:9) ולמׄעׄן. Distortion has been created by a misalignment in the restoration of smaller fragments; the lower piece preserving the traces of this word should be moved a millimeter to the left.

L. 7 (11:9) אׄ[חריהם. The restoration with 𝔊, μετ' αυτους, is on the basis of spatial considerations. The *ʾalep* could also be identified as part of ארץ, with 𝔐 (= 𝔪𝔗𝔖𝔙), but the shorter reading of 𝔐 has only 41 characters to correspond to this line, while the *Vorlage* of 𝔊 has 48 characters, the average length of a line in this column.

L. 8 (11:10) אתמהׄ. Misalignment in the placement of smaller fragments has created distortion. The right side of *he* has been obscured by the join (see VAR.).

L. 10 (11:10) היׄרׄק. The word is on a split and the top and bottom pieces are misaligned. The dot of ink to the far left of *reš* is actually the bottom of its stem, the ink appearing directly below the *reš* is the lower part of *yod*, and the ink below *yod* is part of the left leg of the *he*.

VARIANTS

11:6 (2) בקרב 𝔐𝔪] מקרב 4QDeut^{j}

11:6 (2) כול 𝔐𝔪𝔊𝔗^{J}] > 𝔐^{ms}𝔊^{ms}𝔗^{N}𝔙; בני 𝔗^{O}

11:7 (3) מעשה יהוה הגדולים 4QDeut^{j}(י]הוה הגדלים) 𝔊(τα εργα κυριου τα μεγαλα) cf 𝔗^{N}𝔖𝔙] מעשה יהוה הגדל 𝔐𝔪𝔗^{OJ}; τα εργα κυριου 𝔊^{B}. On the phonetic identity of מעשי/מעשה at Qumran and in BH, and on pl. forms spelled with *he*, see Qimron, §100.34.

11:8 (4) כול המצוה 𝔐𝔪𝔗^{O}] πασας τας εντολας 𝔊; cf 𝔗^{O}𝔙. 𝔊 routinely translates this idiom with the pl. form, e.g. 6:25, 8:1, 15:5, 27:1.

11:8 (4) החוק]ים ו[המשׁ]פטים 4QDeut^{j}(והמשפטים[ )] > 𝔐𝔪𝔊𝔗𝔖𝔙. A calculation of space in 4QDeut^{j} indicates that it read with 4QDeut^{k1} in the entire expansion (cf. 5:31, 6:1, and 7:11).

11:8 (5) תחזקו 𝔐𝔪𝔗𝔖𝔙] •תחיו 𝔊 (cf 4:1, 8:1, and 16:20)

11:8 (5) ורביתם 𝔊] > 𝔐𝔪𝔗𝔖𝔙. For the reading •תחיו ורביתם 𝔊, compare 8:1.

11:8 (6) עוברים 𝔐𝔊] באים 𝔪𝔙

11:8 (6) את הירדן 𝔊] > 𝔐𝔪𝔗𝔖𝔙 (cf 30:18 and 31:13, also 4:26 and 11:31)

11:9 (6) תאריכון 𝔪] תאריכו 𝔐

11:9 (7) להם 𝔐𝔊𝔗𝔖𝔙] > 𝔪

11:9 (7) ולזרעם 𝔐𝔊𝔗] לזרעם 𝔪

11:10 (8) אתמה באים 𝔪𝔊𝔗^{N}𝔖] אתה בא 𝔐𝔊^{Bn}𝔗^{OJ}

11:10 (9) היאה 4QDeut^{c}𝔪(היא)] הוא 𝔐

11:10 (10) והשקיתה 𝔐𝔪(ת- 𝔐𝔪)] και ποτιζωσιν 𝔊

11:10 (10) ברגליכה 𝔪(ך- 𝔪)] ברגלך 4QDeut^{c}(בׄרׄגׄלׄךׄ[ ) 𝔐 (orth. or var.?); τοις ποσιν (+αυτων 𝔊^{B}) 𝔊

11:12 (13) שנה 1° 𝔐^{mss}] השנה 𝔐𝔪𝔗

11:12 (13) שנה 2° 𝔐] השנה 𝔐^{mss}𝔪𝔗

Frg. 3 Deut 32:17-18

1 17יזבחו ל]שדים [

2 מקרו]ב באוׄ[

3 (18)]תׄשׁׄ[כח

Frg. 4 Deut 32:22-23

1 22כיא א]שׁ קדחה באׄפׄ[י

2 ויבו]לׄה ותלהט[

3 (23)]חׄצי[

L. 1 (32:22) באׄפׄ[י. Only a part of the vertical stroke of *pe* has been preserved; the rest of *pe* and the bottom left of *ʾalep* are lost because of surface damage.

VARIANT

32:22 (2) ותלהט[𝔐𝔪^{mss}𝔗^{FNJ}𝔙] תלהט 𝔪𝔊; שיצי 𝔗^{O}

Frg. 5 Deut 32:25-27

]שׁ֯יבה 26אמרת֯[י 1

כ]ע֯ס אויב אגור פן [(27) 2

bottom margin

VARIANTS

32:27 (2) אויב 𝔐𝔗] אׄיבי ш; εχθρων 𝔊𝔙

32:27 (2) אגור 𝔐ш] μακροχρονισωσιν 𝔊; דהיל 𝔗J; כניש 𝔗O; יתקף/תקף 𝔗FN

38a. 4QDeut^{k2}

(PLATE XXV)

Preliminary publication: Julie Ann Duncan, 'A Critical Edition', 130–54 and Pl. VIII.

THIS manuscript, designated as 4QDt^{k2} in 'A Critical Edition' (see introduction to 4QDeut^{k1}), consists of thirteen small fragments, six of which are clearly identified, and two tentatively (see Table 1). The leather is smooth and unwrinkled, of average thickness, with the back untreated for writing. It is stained a deep red-brown, but portions of the fragments are so blackened as to be illegible. Only one right margin has been preserved (frg. 2) and at frg. 2 6 a space of 0.6 cm is extant between that margin and the end of the corresponding line of the preceding column. Although no dry lines are evident, they can be presumed, since the lines of script are so uniformly spaced at *c*.0.5–0.6 cm. The average height of letters is *c*.2 mm, and reconstructed lines fluctuate from 50 to 80 letter-spaces.

TABLE 1: *Contents of 4QDeut^{k2}*

Frg.	Deut	Frg.	Deut
1	19:8-16	6–7	26:18–27:1?
2–3	20:6-19	8	21:16?
4	23:22–24:3	9–13	Unidentified
5	25:19–26:5		

The manuscript is inscribed in an Early Herodian formal hand (*c*.30–1 BCE) with strong semiformal influence seen in several instances: *ʾAlep* has an *s*-shaped axis; *he* has a heavily shaded and unusually protruding crossbar, and there is a hook on the bottom of *he* and *ḥet* (frg. 4 6); the hook of *lamed* is broad; and the left downstroke of *šin* often extends past the lower right arm, sometimes in exaggerated fashion. A medial *pe* instead of a final *pe* was written in חניפ[(4 5).

The orthography of 4QDeut^{k2} is generally more full than that of 𝔐(see Table 2). For instance כל is consistently spelled with a *waw*, and a *waw* is used to mark $*\bar{a} > \bar{o}$ both when it is accented (e.g. השלוש 1 4; ולוא 2 2), and unaccented (השופטים 2 3; נותן 5 2; אלוה]יכה 5 6). The long form of the afformative in the perfect is used in the three extant instances: והכיתה 2 8; והלכתה 5 4; ובתה 5 5. The long form of the singular pronominal suffix is used twice: עליכה 1 5; כליכה 4 4, and of the plural once: מצו]כמה 1 3 (see VAR.). Two other noteworthy orthographical variants are (1) the omission of radical *ʾalep* in a medial position in ובתה frg. 5 5 (26:3), ובאת 𝔐 (this omission is attested at Qumran, though infrequently, see Qimron, §100.61), and (2) כיא, with a double *mater lectionis*, frg. 1 10 (19:16), 2 5 (20:10), and 4 6 (24:1), but 4 3 (24:25; for digraphs in final position at Qumran, see Qimron, §100.51).

TABLE 2: *Orthography*

Frg., line	Deut	4QDeut[k2]	𝔐	𝔐[mss]	⅏[ed]	⅏[mss]
1 2	19:8	]כׄול	כל		כל	
1 4	19:9	השלוש]	השלש		השלש	
1 5	19:10	]עליכה	עליך		עליך	
1 8	19:14	בנחלתכה	בנחלתך		בנחלתך	
1 9	19:15	]לכול	לכל		לכל	
1 9	19:15	עוון	עון		עון	
1 10	19:16	]כׄיא]	כי		וכי	כי
2–3 2	20:7	ולוא	ולא		ולא	
2–3 5	20:10	כיא	כי		כי	
2–3 6	20:11	תעׄנׄכה]	תענך		תענך	
2–3 6	20:11	לכהׄ]	לך		לך	
2–3 7	20:12	לוא	לא		לא	
2–3 8	20:13	והכיתה	והכית		והכית	
2–3 9	20:14	תבוז	תבז		תבז	
2–3 10	20:15	]לכׄולׄ	לכל		לכל	
2–3 11	20:16	לכ]ה	לך		לך	
2–3 13	20:18	]כׄכול	ככל		ככל	
4 2	23:24	תשמו]ר	תשמר		תשמר	
4 3	23:24	בפיכ]ה	בפיך		בפיך	
4 3	23:25	כא	כי		כי	
4 4	23:25	כליכה	כליך		כליך	
4 6	24:1	כיא]	כי		כי	
5 2	26:1	אלוה]◦כה	אלהיך		אלהיך	
5 2	26:1	נותׄן]	נתן		נתן	
5 4	26:2	והלכתה	והלכת		והלכת	ואלכת
5 5	26:2	ש]מׄה	שם		שם	
5 5	26:3	הכוהן]	הכהן		הכהן	
5 6	26:3	אלוה[יכה]	אלהיך		אלהיך	
5 7	26:4	הכוהן	הכהן		הכהן	
6–7 1	26:18 ?	לכ]הׄ	לך	>	לך	

Intervals, or their absence, for paragraph-divisions are preserved or reconstructed in the following places:

Frg. 1 5 (19:10) no interval] ס 𝔐; no interval ⅏
Frg. 2 5 (20:9) interval] ס 𝔐; קצה ⅏
Frg. 3 13 (20:18) [interval]] ס 𝔐; קצה ⅏ (see NOTE)
Frg. 4 3 (23:24) no interval] ס 𝔐; no interval ⅏

One correction apparently by the original hand has been preserved in ת[^(א)כל frg. 3 15.

Mus. Inv. 1090. PAM 43.056.

Frg. 1 Deut 19:8-16

1] 8ו]אם ירח֯[יב [

2 (9)] את]כ֯ול הארץ אשר דב֯[ר [

3]אנוכי מצו]כמה היום לאהב[ה [

4 (10)] שלו]ש ערים על השלוש[[

5] עליכה דמים 11°[כיא [

6] מן הערים האלה֯[12 [

7 (14)] 13לוא תחו]ס֯ עינכה עליו ו֯[בערת [

8 (15)] ראשונ]ים בנחלתכה °[שר [

9] באיש]לכול עוון ולכ[ול [

10] 16]כ֯יא[[

L. 10 (19:16)]כ֯יא[. The trace visible before the head of *kap* is actually part of the letter; a crack in the surface of the leather has created the impression of two letters in the photograph.

VARIANTS

19:9 (3) מצו]כמה 𝔗^{NJ}] מצוך 𝔐⅏𝔊𝔗^{O}𝔖𝔙. 4QDeut^{k2} reads a pl. pronominal suffix. The text might also be restored as מצוה את]כמה.

19:11 (6) מן 𝔗] > 𝔐⅏

19:11 (6) האלה֯[𝔐^{mss}⅏] האל 𝔐

19:14 (8) ראשונ]ים 𝔐⅏𝔊$^{A+}$(οι προτεροι σου)𝔗𝔖] οι πατερες σου 𝔊 (for the reading of 𝔊 cf Prov 22:28: אל תסג גבול עולם . . . אשר עשו אבותיך)

Frgs. 2–3 Deut 20:6-19

1 (7) אשר נט]ע כרם [

2 (8) אשר א֯[רש אש]ה ולוא[לקחה [

3 השופטים לדבר אל הע֯[ם [

4 לבב אחיו כלבבו 9והיה[ככלות [

5 (11) העמ֯ *vacat* 10וכיא תקרב אל֯[עיר [

6 (12) שלום תע֯נכה[ופת]ח֯ה לכה֯[והיה [

7 (13) לוא תשלים ע◦[כה]ועשת[ה עמכה [

8 והכיתה את ◦[ול זכורה]ל̊[פי חרב [14] [

9 (15) [ש]ללה תבוז ל̊[כה [

10 [תעשה]לכול̊ [הערים [

f.3 11 (17) [16]] לכ]ה נ̇[חלה [

12] וה[פ̊רזי והח[וי [

13 (18)]]ככול תועב[ותם [

14 (19)] א[ל ע̇יר ימי[ם [

15] ממנו ת[א̊כל ו[אתו [

At frg. 2 6 the final letter of the corresponding line in the previous column, *he*, together with the base-line of the letter preceding it, is preserved. The space between columns here measures 6 mm.

L. 8 (20:13) את ◦[ול. A trace of perhaps the lower right corner of the *kap* in כול is extant at the edge of the leather; the rest of the letter has been destroyed by surface damage.

L. 9 (20:14) ל̊[כה. The hook of *lamed* is extant; the arm has been destroyed by surface loss.

L. 12 (20:17) וה[פ̊רזי והח[וי. הגרגשי is included by 𝔪𝔊𝔙 in the list of peoples (in differing orders), but spatial considerations indicate that it was not present in 4QDeut^{k2}.

L. 13–14 (20:18) These lines are short, possibly due to an interval after 20:18; ס 𝔐, קצה 𝔪.

L. 14 (20:19) ע̇יר. The head of *yod* is partly lost and the remnant is distorted by a crack. The dark spot just to the right of *yod* is ink, and may be the left tip of *ayin*.

L. 15 (20:19) ת[א̊כל ו[אתו. The supralinear *ʾalep*, directly above *kap*, is by the original hand. The two words תאכל ואתו are crowded together; compare עיר ימים in line 14 above.

VARIANTS

20:8 (3) השופטים] השטרים 𝔐𝔪𝔊𝔖𝔙; סרכיא 𝔗

20:10 (5) אל 𝔐] על 𝔪

20:17 (12) והח[וי 𝔐^{mss} 𝔪𝔊𝔗^{NJ}𝔖𝔙] החוי 𝔐𝔗^{O}

Frg. 4 Deut 23:22–24:3

1 (23)] ◦[והיה] בכה [

2 [24]] ◦[תשמו[ר [

3] בפיכ]ה [25]כא[תבוא [

4 (26)] וא[ל כליכה] לוא [

5 (24:1)] לוא]תניפ על ק֯[מת [
6]]ח֯ן בעיניו כיא [[
7 (3)] מב]יתו [2] ויצאה מבׄ[יתו [
8] אשר לקחה]לו לאשה וכת֯[ב [

L. 3 (23:25)]כאׄ. The scribe seems to have omitted writing the *yod* in כיא; cf. 𝔐𝔪 and the versions.

L. 4 (23:25)]ואׄ[ל֯. The tip of *lamed* is visible just below the *he* of the line above, and the bottom of its hook is visible just before the *kap*.

L. 6 (24:1)]ח֯ן[. The hook at the bottom of the leg of *ḥet* is an idiosyncracy seen in a few instances in this hand, on one or both of the legs: frg. 2 4 אחיו and unidentified frg. 8]∘ה]נ֯חילׄ[.

L. 8 (24:3) וכת֯[ב. The final extant letter is *taw*; the trace of ink on the very edge of the leather is the angle formed by the left leg, turning into the horizontal base, an angle which, on occasion, is sharp and juts back towards the right leg (cf. frg. 2 7, תשלים).

Variants

23:25 (4) כליכה 𝔐𝔪(כליך 𝔐𝔪)ℭ𝔖𝔙] > suffix 𝔊
24:2 (7) ויצאה מבׄ[יתו 𝔐𝔪𝔊^{Ot}ℭ𝔖] > 4QDeut^{a}𝔊; cf 𝔙 (*BHS* note 2^{a-a} errs)
24:3 (8) אשר לקחה] לו לאשה וכת֯[ב] וכתב 4QDeut^{q}(vid)𝔐𝔪𝔊ℭ𝔖𝔙. A calculation of space indicates that 4QDeut^{k2} read ושנאה האיש האחרון אשר לקחה]לו לאשה וכת֯[ב, in harmonization with the following clause: או כי ימות האיש חאחרון אשר לקחה לו לאשה.

Frg. 5 Deut 25:19–26:5

1] מתחת]השמׄ[ים]
2 (27:1)] אלוה]∘כה נות֯[ן [ ]
3 (2)] פר]י האדמה אׄ[שר]
4]]בׄטׄנא והלכתה אל [ ]
5] ש]מׄה [3] ובתה אל הכוהן[ ]
6] היו]ם לפני 𐤉𐤄𐤅𐤄 אלוה[יכה]
7] ו]לקח [4] הכוהן את ה[טנא]
8] [5] ואמרתה]ל[פני יהוה]

L. 6 (26:3) The scribe has written the divine name in Palaeo-Hebrew. M. D. McLean ('The Use and Development of PalaeoHebrew in the Hellenistic and Roman Periods', [Ph.D. dissertation, Harvard University, (University Microfilms) 1982] 41–7, 80–83) and J. Siegel ('The Employment of Paleo-Hebrew Characters in the Light of Tannaitic Sources', *HUCA* 42 [1971] 159–72) discuss this phenomenon as a practice which is most commonly attested in non-biblical manuscripts. Recently,

however, other biblical manuscripts have been recognized as using the Palaeo-Hebrew tetragrammaton, e.g. 2QExod[b], 4QExod[j], 4QLev[g], 4QIsa[c], in addition to 11QPs[a].

VARIANTS

26:3 (6) 𐤉𐤄𐤅𐤄 לפני] ליהוה 𝔐𝔴; κυριω 𝔊. 𝔐𝔴 have the more common BH expression (הגיד ל-); for the construction with לפני in 4QDeut[k2] compare 1 Sam 17:31 and Ps 142:3.

26:4 (7) את 𝔗[J]] > 𝔐𝔴𝔗[O]

Frgs. 6–7 Deut 26:18–27:1?

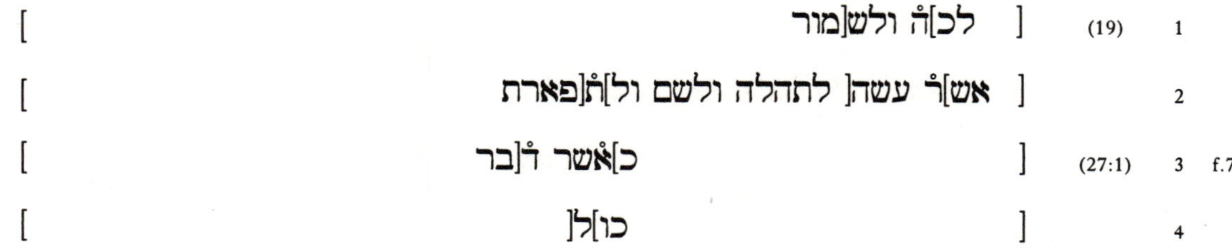

1 (19)] לכ]ה̊ ולש[מור [

2] אש]ר̊ עשה[לתהלה ולשם ול]ת̊[פארת [

f.7 3 (27:1)] כ]א̊שר ד̊[בר [

4] כו[ל] [

The identification is tentative since the lines of *c*.50 letter-spaces are somewhat short for this manuscript.

L. 1 (26:18) לכ]ה̊. What appears to be the end of the cross-stroke of *he* in לכה (cf. 𝔐𝔴 and most of the versions) might also fit the top of *reš* in דבר (cf. 𝔊[B]).

L. 2 (26:19) ול]ת̊[פארת. The trace above the *šin* of כ]אשר in line 3 could be the lower part of *taw*.

Unidentified Fragments

Frg. 8 Deut 21:16?

ביום ה]נחיל°[

The letter at the right edge of the fragment can be a perfect *nun*, displaying the slight thickening at the top of the downstroke similar to לפני frg. 5 6 (26:3). On the left edge just to the left of *lamed*, a trace of ink may be part of *waw*, in which case the fragment preserves Deut 21:16 (cf. ביום הנחילו 𝔐𝔴).

Frg. 9

1]°°[

2]ב̊כ°[

3]°[

L. 2 The trace to the right of *kap* may be identified as *bet* since the triangular shape at the edge of the leather matches the *keraia* of the topstroke of *bet*, see ובתה frg. 5 5 (26:3).

Frg. 10

] תם[

]∘∘[

Frg. 11

]בׄנ֯[

Frg. 12

]שׄבׄה֯[

Although correctly oriented on Pl. XXV, frgs. 10 and 11 are turned sideways and frg. 12 is inverted on PAM 43.056.

Frg. 13 Three lines of ink are detectable, but the leather is too blackened to be read with confidence.

38b. 4QDeut[k3]

(PLATE XXV)

Preliminary publication: Julie Ann Duncan, 'A Critical Edition', 109 and Pl. VI.

THIS manuscript, designated as part of 4QDeut[j] in 'A Critical Edition', consists of one fragment, which preserves portions of Deut 30:16-18. The surface of this blackened fragment is severely damaged, and shrinkage around the edges has resulted in distortion of the letters. Since the ink evident in the infrared photograph is often not visible on the original, in some cases it is difficult to distinguish ink from dark marks resulting from the uneven texture of the surface.

The average distance between lines is *c*.0.7 cm, while the average height of a letter is *c*.3 mm. The lines appear to be quite short, with only 25–29 letters per line. One wide right margin is preserved, measuring 2.3 cm at its fullest.

The fragment is inscribed in a classic formal hand dating from the late Herodian Period, *c*.50 CE (see Cross, 173–81 and Line 7 on p. 139).

Mus. Inv. 172.   PAM 42.720, 43.054; IAA 204.599.

Deut 30:16-18

1 (17) א֯ת֯◦]
2 לבׄב֯ך ולא תׄשמ֯]ע
3 (18) לאלהים אח֯רׄיׄםׄ]
4 היום כי אב֯דׄ]
5 יׄמ֯יׄם עׄ]ל

L. 1 (30:16) א֯ת֯◦]. The two legs of *ʾalep* are visible, as well as the right side of *taw* and the left base. There would appear to be ink following *taw*, but it is difficult to say with certainty.

L. 2 (30:17) לבׄב֯ך. The lower part of the first *bet* is distorted by the very rough surface of the leather. There is a hole where the second *bet* should be; the trace remaining, which should be part of the downstroke of the *bet*, appears to be situated too close to the final *kap*.

L. 3 (30:17) אח֯רׄיׄםׄ]. Most of the *ḥet* has been destroyed by a gouge in the leather. *Reš*, *yod* and final *mem* have shrunk.

L. 5 (30:18) יׄמ֯יׄם. Medial *mem* has been split apart; part of the right side is visible, and the strokes of the left oblique and tick are visible on the other side of the split.

39. 4QDeut[l]

(PLATE XXVI)

Preliminary publication: Julie Ann Duncan, 'A Critical Edition', 163–8 and Pl. IX.

THIS manuscript, consisting of eleven small, wrinkled fragments and preserving portions of Deut 10:12, 14-15; 28:67-68; 29:2-5; 31:12; 33:1-2; 34:4-6, 8?, is beige in colour, with some areas bleached and others blackened, so that certain letters are no longer legible.

No dry lines or *points jalons* are visible on the manuscript. One top margin of 1.5 cm has been preserved on frg. 11 and possibly a second of 1.7 cm on frgs. 8–9. Frg. 2 preserves a margin between columns, measuring 1.4 cm. Frg. 10 preserves a left margin, measuring 0.8 cm at its widest, as well as a stiched edge. Letter-height averages 0.3 cm, and the distance between lines ranges from 0.5 to 0.9 cm. Column-width varies from 43 to 63 letter-spaces, with the exception of frg. 10, which is exceptionally narrow with 32–36 letter-spaces, because it was the last column on its skin.

4QDeut[l] is written in a semicursive hand, which is best compared with 4QMMT[d] (formerly designated Sl 35b, now published in *DJD* X), a late Hasmonaean semicursive dated by Cross (p. 148, Figure 4, Line 4) to *c.*50 BCE. Some forms may also be compared with those in 4QXII[a] (see R. Fuller, 'The Minor Prophets Manuscripts from Qumran Cave IV', [Ph.D. dissertation, Harvard University, 1988]). 4QDeut[l] exhibits both a cursive and a formal or semi-formal form of *he*, *kap*, *mem*, and *taw*. 4QXII[a] and 4QMMT[d] also attest both the semicursive and the formal forms of *he* and *mem*.

א. *ʾAlep* is in the three-stroke form, אשׁ]ר 8 1 and את 11 1. The left leg is short and curves inward.

ב. There are two exemplars of *bet*, ובכׄלׄ[1 3 and וי]קברו 10 3. The strokes of the top and base are thick. In the first exemplar the new mode of penning the base from left to right is evident.

ד. *Dalet* has a thick head, which is ticked, תדעו 4 4.

ה. Two forms of *he* are evident. One is cursive in origin, a reversed *k* form with the cross-stroke and left leg drawn continuously in a crescent, the curve of which touches the right leg, היום הזה 4–5 2. The other is a formal type, with the exception that the cross-bar slants upward slightly on the left, יׄהוה 6 1, יׄהׄוׄה 5 4.

ו. *Waw* has a shaded head, often of a triangular shape. In some forms the leg of *waw* is quite short, ובכלׄ[1 3 and וכל 2 1 (cf. similar short-legged forms of *waw* in 4QXII[a]). *Waw* and *yod* are generally not sharply distinguished (e.g. היום 4 2).

כ. A cursive and a formal form of *kap* are present. The cursive type lacks a head, the downstroke is long, and the basestroke is shaded and drawn from left to right, מעליכם 4 3. This form is best compared to those in 4QPs-Enoch[a] and 6Q**8**. The formal type has a narrow head, and the downstroke curves into the basestroke; cf. 4QMMT[d].

In final *kap* the head and the right leg are drawn separately, the head a shaded stroke, the right leg beginning slightly above it, עינ]יך 3 1, and הׄרׄאׄ]ית[יך 10 1 (cf. 4QMMT[d], 4QEnoch V, and 6Q**8**, and see Cross, 185).

ל. *Lamed* has a long upper arm, slightly thickened at the top, and the hook is angular.

ם\מ. Two examples of *mem* occur: one is open on the left side, and resembles the semiformal *mem* of the early Herodian Period (compare 4QNum[b]). In two of the three instances it is ligatured to

the following letter, מעליכם 4 3 and ל]מען 4 4. The other form is a cursive *mem*, which is an oval shaped circle with a projection to the left, מעל 5 3. Both forms of medial *mem* also occur in 4QMMT[d] (Cross, 148, Figure 4, Line 4).

Final *mem* is slender, very long, and closed at the bottom left, היום 4 2 and מעליכם 4 3 (in the latter, surface damage makes it appear otherwise).

נ\ן. Medial *nun* is now shortened, ונעלך 4 3 (contrast 4QXII[a]).

Final *nun* is a simple, long straight stroke, מען 4 4, and is best compared with 4QPs-Enoch[a].

ע. *ʿAyin* has a *y*-shaped form, and in one instance it is shifted clockwise, תדעו 4 4.

ק. In the one instance of *qop*, וי]קברו 10 3, the tail is short, and the head is not entirely closed.

ר. *Reš* resembles *dalet* in that the head is a heavily shaded stroke, slightly ticked, although the right shoulder is slightly more rounded.

ש. Of the three examples of *šin*, ושׄמׄ]רו 7 1, אשׁ]ר 8 1, and משה 10 2, only one has escaped damage. The form is a cursive type: the left downstroke is drawn first, and the middle and right arms are drawn continuously, with the angle touching the downstroke in the middle of the stroke.

ת. Two types of *taw* occur in 4QDeut[l]: one is a formal type, in which the left leg does not loop into the top, but rather ends in an angular base, ללכת 1 2; the other appears to be the looped cursive type, תדעו 4 4, seen, for instance, in 4QDan[c] and 4QMMT[d] (Cross, 148, Figure 4, Lines 2 and 4).

The orthography is similar to that of 𝔐𝔪, with two exceptions:

29:4 (3) ונעלך 𝔐] ונעליכם 𝔪 (orth. and var.)
29:4 (3) לו] לא 𝔐𝔪

Mus. Inv. 390. IAA 204.599, PAM 43.052.

Frgs. 1–2 Deut 10:12-15

1 [12]ועׄתׄ]ה [
2 ללכת] [
3 ובכׄלׄ] [13] [
4 (14)] הארׄץ וכל[ה◦]
5 (15)] אׄתׄםׄ[

Frg. 1 is on the right margin, and frg. 2, containing the following line, is at the left margin. On frg. 2 letters from the adjacent column are visible.

L. 3 (10:12) ובכׄלׄ]. The top of *lamed* is visible in some photographs.

VARIANT

10:12 (2) ללכת 4QpaleoDeut[r] 𝔐𝔪𝔊𝔗[OJ]] וללכת 𝔐[mss]𝔊[B]𝔗[N] 𝔖𝔇

Frg. 3 Deut 28:67-68

עינ]יך א֯[שר 1

א]שר אמ֯[רתי 2

Frgs. 4–5 Deut 29:2-5

הגדלי]ם ההם [3]ו֯[ל]א֯[1

]עד היום הזה [4]וא֯[ול]ך[2

(5)]מעליכם ונעלך לו ב֯לת֯ה֯ מעל[3

ל]מען תדעו כי אני י֯ה֯וה[4

The surface on this fragment is badly damaged in places, which has resulted in severe distortion of some of the letters, especially ההם 4 1 and הזה 4 2, the *dalet* in עד 4 2, and the *ʾalep* in אני 5 4.

L. 2 (29:4) וא֯[ול]ך. Only the lower portion of *waw-ʾalep* is preserved. For the form of the first *waw*, see Palaeography above.

L. 3 (29:4) ב֯לת֯ה֯. The surface with the upper part of *bet* has been lost. The traces following *bet-lamed* should be *taw-he*; for the damaged *taw* see *taw* in תדעו in line 4, and for *he* see *he* in היום in line 2.

VARIANTS

29:4 (3) מעליכם 𝔐𝔪𝔊^{Odt}𝔗𝔖] > 𝔊

29:4 (3) ונעלך 𝔐 cf ומסנך 𝔗^{O}] ונעליכם 𝔪𝔊𝔗^{NJ}𝔖

29:4 (3) לו] לא 𝔐𝔪

29:4 (3) בלתה 𝔐] בלו 𝔪

Frgs. 6–7 Deut 31:12

]י֯הוה[אלהי]ה֯ם ושמ֯[רו 1

L. 1 (31:12) אלהי]ה֯ם. The trace preceding final *mem* may belong to *he* but not *kap* (cf. כם- 𝔐; see VAR.), since no base-stroke, as can be seen in מעליכם 4 3, is visible.

VARIANT

31:12 (1) אלהי]ה֯ם 𝔐^{mss}𝔪𝔊^{mss}] אלהיכם 𝔐𝔊𝔗𝔖𝔙

Frgs. 8–9 Deut 33:1-2

top margin or vacat

1 וזאת ה]ברכה אש[ר ב]ר֯ך מ֯ש֯ה֯[1
]מ֯ס֯י֯נ֯י ב֯א֯[2

L. 1 (33:1) ב]ר֯ך. The *reš* is distinguishable in PAM 43.052.

L. 1 (33:1) מ֯ש֯ה֯[. The right arm and bottom tip of *šin* are visible, as are the tips of the legs of *he*.

L. 2 (33:2) מ֯ס֯י֯נ֯י. The letters on the second line are shrunken. The left side of *mem* is visible on the edge of the leather. The head of the second *yod* has been split.

Frg. 10 Deut 34:4-6

]ה֯ר֯א֯[ית]י֯ך 1
5 וימת שם]משה 2
6 וי]קברו 3

The extant words are from the left margin. This column was the last on this skin, as shown by the stitched edge, and thus the reconstructed line-width of 32–36 letter-spaces is shorter than usual in this MS.

VARIANT

34:6 (3) וי]קברו 𝔪^{mss} 𝔊ℭ^{NF}] ויקבר MasDeut 𝔐𝔪ℭ^{O}𝔖𝔙

Frg. 11 Deut 34:8?

]◦ל את ◦◦[1

A top margin of 1.5 cm is preserved on this fragment. The ink traces could correspond to ישר]אל את מ֯ש֯[ה, and especially in light of frg. 10 containing Deut 34:4-6, identification of this fragment as Deut 34:8 is possible.

40. 4QDeut^m

(PLATE XXVII)

4QDEUT^m consists of five fragments, preserving portions of 3:18-22, 4:32-33, and 7:18-22. The leather was tan and rough; it is now brown in areas where it has suffered decay, and the surface is flaky. No paragraph-divisions or margins have been preserved, although frg. 4 may have been near the right side of its column. The average height of the letters is 2.5–3.0 mm. The distance between lines of script averages 0.7 cm, although it sometimes shrinks to *c.*0.5 cm, perhaps due to contraction of the leather.

The manuscript exhibits a formal hand which may be dated to *c.*50–1 BCE, the transitional period between the late Hasmonaean and early Herodian periods. Some semiformal influence is evident in the following: the heavily shaded crossbar of *he*, the inward curving right leg of the *ḥet* (e.g. יניח 1–3 3), and the slightly broader form of final *mem* rather than a long slender form. In addition, the leg of *dalet* sometimes tends slightly towards an *s* shape (e.g. ידעתי 1–3 2, and כדבר 4 2).

The orthography of 4QDeut^m is fuller than that of both 𝔐 and ⅏ (e.g. אלוהים and כול). The long form of pronominal suffixes is used, as well the long form of independent pronouns (see Table 1).

TABLE 1: *Orthography*

Frg., Line	Deut	4QDeut^m	𝔐	⅏
1–3 1	3:18	ל]א֯מור	לאמר	לאמר
1–3 1	3:18	אלוהי[כמה	אלהיכם	אלהיכם
1–3 2	3:18	כול	כל	כל
1–3 2	3:19	נ֯ש֯יכמה	נשיכם	ונשיכם
1–3 2	3:19	ו֯ט֯פ֯כ֯[מ]ה֯	וטפכם	טפכם
1–3 2sup	3:19	ומ]ק֯נ֯יכ֯מ֯ה֯	ומקנכם	ומקניכם
1–3 3	3:19	ל֯כ֯[מ]ה֯	לכם	לכם
1–3 3sup	3:20	אלוהיכמה	—	—
1–3 3	3:20	לאחיכמה	לאחיכם	לאחיכם
1–3 3	3:20	ככמה֯	ככם	ככם
1–3 4	3:20	ה]מ֯ה	הם	הם
1–3 4	3:20	אלוהיכמה	אלהיכם	אלהיכם
1–3 4	3:20	נותן	נתן	נתן
1–3 4	3:20	להמה	להם	להם
1–3 5	3:21	יהושוע	יהושוע	יהושע
1–3 5	3:21	ההיאה	ההוא	ההיא
4 1	4:32	לפני]כ֯ה֯	לפניך	לפניך
4 3	4:33	שמעתמה	(שמעת)	(שמעת)
5 1	7:18	אלוה]יכ֯ה֯[	אלהיך	אלהיך
5 3	7:19	אלוהיכה	אלהיך	אלהיך

TABLE 1: *Orthography (cont.)*

Frg., Line	Deut	4QDeut^m	𝔐	𝔖
5 3	7:19	לכול	לכל	לכל
5 4	7:20	במה	בם	בם
5 4	7:20	אבוד	אבד	אבד
5 5	7:21	בקרבכה	בקרבך	בקרבך
5 6	7:22	לכלותמהׄ	כלתם	כלותם

In frgs. 1–3 there are two supralinear insertions. At the end of line 2, ומ]קׄנׄיכׄמהׄ] was initially omitted and then written in between וטׄפׄכׄ[מ]הׄ and ידעתי. The omission probably occurred through *homoioteleuton*. In line 3, above יהוה and לאחיכמה, the word אלוהיכמה has been inserted (note that the word has been split between the *waw* and the *he* to accommodate the *lamed* of the word below; see VAR.). In both cases the insertions appear to have been written by the scribe who copied the manuscript.

Mus. Inv. 255. PAM 42.714.

Frgs. 1–3 Deut 3:18-22

[ל]אׄמור יהוה אלוהיׄ[כמה נתן לכמה את הארץ הזאת] לרשתה[ ] 1 f.1,2

ומ]קׄנׄיכׄמהׄ
[בני]ישראל כול ב[ני חיל *vacat?* 19רק [נׄשׄיכמה וטׄפׄכׄ[מ]הׄ ידעתי [ ] 2

אלו היכמה
[אש]רׄ נתתי לׄכׄ[מ]הׄ 20עׄדׄ אׄשׄרׄ יניח יהוה לאחיכמה ככמהׄ[ ] 3

[ה]מׄה את הא[רץ אשר יהוה]אלוהכימה נותן להמה בעבר הי[רדן ו]שׄבׄ[תמה] 4 f.3

[ ]°°[21ו]אׄתׄ יהושע צויתי בעתׄ ההׄיאה לא[מור] 5

[ ]לשני המלכים האלה כן יע[שה] 6

[ ]°[ש]םׄ 22ולׄואׄ[תי]רׄאׄוׄםׄ[ ] 7

This fragment has lines of 58 to 67 letter-spaces (except line 7, see NOTE).

L. 2 (3:19) Reconstruction suggests that there may have been an interval before v 19.

L. 2^sup (3:19) ומ]קׄנׄיכׄמהׄ] has been written supralinearly; it was probably initially lost through *homoioteleuton*. The tail of *qop* is visible, and the base of *nun* has run into the *yod* slightly, while the right side of final *he* has merged with the left side of *mem*.

L. 3 (3:19) אש]רׄ. The tick on the head of *reš* is visible; there is splitting on the leather here.

L. 3 (3:19) לׄכׄ[מ]הׄ. The small piece on which the lower parts of *lamed* and *kap* are preserved is slightly misaligned. On the other side of the break the tips of the cross-stroke and left leg of *he* are visible.

L. 3^sup (3:20) The original scribe inserted אלו היכמה above יהוה and לאחיכמה. The word has been split between the *waw* and the *he* to accommodate the *lamed* of the word below (see VAR.).

L. 4 (3:20) ו]שׁׄבׄ[תמה]. While the identification of *šin* and *bet* is tentative, it appears that the tip of the left arm of *šin* is barely visible just before the cross-stroke of *bet*.

L. 6 (3:21) המלכים. The head of the *yod* is peculiar for this hand; possibly a spill of ink has distorted it.

L. 7 (3:21) °[ש]ׄם. Cf. שמה 𝔐𝔪. The trace seen before final *mem* in the photograph is no longer on the leather, since a portion of the edge has been lost.

L. 7 (3:22) ולוׄאׄ[תי]ראׄוׄם. The identification of these traces is tentative. If it is correct, the line is only 46 letter-spaces long, or perhaps 53 letter-spaces if the MS agreed with 𝔊 in adding אלוהינו after the divine name in v 21 (see VAR. at 3:20, where this MS agrees with 𝔊 in a similar plus). There is considerable surface damage at the edge of the fragment and it appears that some ink has been lost with the surface.

VARIANTS

3:19 (2) נׄשׄיכמה וׄטׄפׄכׄ[מ]הׄ 𝔐𝔊ℭ𝔖𝔙] נׄשׁ[יכ]ם טפׄ[כם] 4QDeut^{d}𝔐^{ms}; 𝔪 טפכם ונשיכם

3:20 (3^sup) אלוהיכמה 𝔊] > 4QDeut^{d}𝔐𝔪ℭ𝔖𝔙

3:20 (4) להמה 4QDeut^{d}𝔐𝔪 (להם 𝔐𝔪)] לכם 𝔐^{mss}ℭ^{mss}

3:21 (5) ההׄיׄאה 𝔐^{q}𝔪 (ההיא 𝔐^{q}𝔪)] ההוא 𝔐

3:21 (7) °[ש]ׄם] שמה 𝔐𝔪; לתמן ℭ

3:22 (7) ולוׄאׄ] לא 4QDeut^{d}𝔐𝔪𝔊ℭ

Frg. 4 Deut 4:32-33

1		[לפני]כׄהׄ לׄמׄן[ ]	
2	(32)	[השמי]םׄ הנהיה כדבר °[ ]	
3		[כאשׁ]רׄ שמעתמה אׄ[תמה]	
4		[ ]°°[ ]	

If this identification is correct, these lines have 72 letter-spaces.

L. 1 (4:32) לפני]כׄהׄ לׄמׄן. The identification of these traces is tentative. The final *nun* is especially problematic, since in other instances in this MS it is not a simple stroke, but rather arches (see נותן 1–3 4). This variation in form, however, is also attested in 4QDeut^{h}, which is dated to approximately the same period, and in 1QM, which is dated *c.*30–1 BCE (Cross, 148, Line 4).

VARIANTS

4:32 (2) הנהיה 𝔐] הן היה 𝔪

4:33 (3) שמעתמה] שמעת 4QDeut^{o}(vid) 𝔐𝔪𝔊ℭ𝔖𝔙

Frg. 5 Deut 7:18-22

Line	Verse	Text
1	(19)	] אלוה]יכה֯[לפרעה [
2		] וה]יד החזקה ו֯[הזרע [
3	(20)	]]/// אלוהיכה לכול העמים אש֯[ר [
4	(21)	]]במה עד אבוד הנשאר[ים [
5	(22)	] אלוהיכה] בקרבכה אל גד[ול [
6		] לוא ת]ו֯כל לכלותמה֯[מהר [

The lines on this fragment have 56–68 letter-spaces (but see NOTE on L. 1–2).

L. 1–2 (7:19) The inclusion of הגדלים ההמה with 𝔊 after והמפתים would yield a slightly long line, with 74 letter-spaces as compared to 56–68 in the other lines on this fragment.

L. 3 (7:19) The smudge preceding אלוהיכה may be an erasure.

L. 4 (7:20) אבוד appears to have been written over an erasure.

VARIANTS

7:19 (3) אלוהיכה 5QDeut 𝔐𝔪𝔊^{mss}𝔗^{OJ}] ο θεος ημων 𝔊

7:22 (6) לכלותמה֯[ ] כלותם 4QDeut^{e} 5QDeut 𝔐𝔪

41. 4QDeut[n]

(PLATES XXVIII–XXIX)

Preliminary publication: Sidnie Ann White, 'A Critical Edition', 268–99.

Previous discussion: Sidnie Ann White, 'The All Souls Deuteronomy and the Decalogue', *JBL* 109 (1990) 193–206. '4QDt[n]: Biblical Manuscript or Excerpted Text?', *Of Scribes and Scrolls* (ed. H. W. Attridge, J. J. Collins, and T. H. Tobin; College Theology Society Resources in Religion 5; Lanham, MD: University Press of America, 1990) 13–20.

Frank Moore Cross, Jr., *Scrolls from the Wilderness of the Dead Sea* (San Francisco: Lawton & Alfred Kennedy, 1969) 18, 29–30 [the manuscript was captioned as 4QDeut[m]].

Esther Eshel, '4QDeut[n]—A Text that has Undergone Harmonistic Editing', *HUCA* 62 (1991) 117–54.

H. Stegemann, 'Weitere Stücke von 4QpPsalm 37, von 4Q Patriarchal Blessings und Hinweis auf eine unedierte Handschrift aus Höhle 4Q mit Exzerpten aus dem Deuteronomium', *RevQ* 6 (1967) 193–227.

M. Weinfeld, 'Grace after Meals in Qumran', *JBL* 111 (1992) 427–40.

See also W. F. Albright, 'A Biblical Fragment from the Maccabaean Age: The Nash Papyrus', *JBL* 56 (1937) 145–76.

THIS manuscript, designated the 'All Souls Deuteronomy' manuscript thanks to its purchase by the All Souls Unitarian Church in New York City, is exceptionally well-preserved. 4QDeut[n] is not a manuscript of the complete book of Deuteronomy but contains excerpts: almost all of Deut 8:5-10 and 5:1–6:1, in that order, on four complete columns and two partially damaged columns. Cols. II–VI form one continuous sheet of leather, with a sewn right edge on col. II. Col. I has sewn edges on both sides; it was originally attached on the left to the right side of col. II and was separated only in the process of restoration. Another Cave 4 manuscript of excerpted texts, 4QDeut[j], also contains these passages, but in 4QDeut[j] their order cannot be determined with certainty.

The leather of 4QDeut[n] is thin, almost transparent in places, and reddish brown in colour. The surface was well-prepared but had several patches that were unsuitable for writing (marked by ///// in the transcription), and thus the scribe passed over them when copying the manuscript. Horizontal dry lines are visible on cols. I–IV and vertical dry lines on col. I. Guiding dots mark the dry lines on col. II.

The measurements of the manuscript vary from column to column. The average distance between lines of script for cols. I–VI is 0.4 cm. The margin between columns averages 1.2–1.4 cm. The height of the sheet containing cols. II–VI is 7.1 cm, while the height of the inscribed column is 5.5 cm. Col. I is 9.5 cm wide, and has between 40 and 65 letters per line; it has 7 inscribed lines, but 15 dry lines. Col. II is 5.3 cm wide and has 27–38 letters per line; it has 12 inscribed lines, but 14 dry lines. Col. III is 6.0 cm wide and has 34–50 letters per line. Col. IV is 6.4 cm wide and has 42–51 letters per line. Col. V is 7.1 cm wide and has 46–53 letters per line; cols. III–V contain 12 inscribed lines each. Col. VI, the damaged column, has 11 extant lines (though it probably contained a twelfth), and its width can be estimated at between 42 and 56 letters per line.

Palaeographical study places this manuscript in the early Herodian period, *c.*30–1 BCE. The letters are mostly of standard size (although final *mem* can be quite large) and are distinguished by thickening and *keraiai*. They are quite squat and characterized by a

thick ductus. The latest letter-forms present in this manuscript are *ʾalep* (the 'inverted-v' form); *bet* (the base stroke is penned from left to right, resulting in a slight break-through at the juncture of the downstroke and the base stroke); *waw* and *yod* (which are indistinguishable, a sure sign of an early Herodian hand); *ṭet* (which is made in two movements); *ʿayin* (the right arm is thickened or bent at the tip, a characteristic of the Herodian period); and medial and final *ṣade*.

The orthography of 4QDeut^{n} is full. It consistently uses *matres lectionis* to mark **aw* > *ô* (e.g. שורו IV 12), except for *Hipʿil* verbs (e.g. ויציאך IV 2), **ay* > *ê* (e.g. אליהם II 2, וביניכם II 9, and מבית III 1), **ī* (e.g. אנוכי II 3, כי I 1), **ū* (e.g. אנחנו II 7, יאריכון IV 8). It usually uses a *mater lectionis* for both accented and unaccented **ā* > *ō* (e.g. אבות III 5, עינות I 3, לוא I 6, participles, and all forms of אלוהים, but cf. לא II 5). The manuscript also uses a *waw* to mark **u* > *o* (e.g. החושך V 3, כול I 6, גודלו V 5, but cf. משה II 1 and כל II 1, III 11). It does not use a *mater lectionis* to mark **a* and **i*, but it sometimes marks the *ā* vowel of the 2nd masc. sing. perfect verb with *he*, e.g. וזכרתה IV 2, but e.g. וידעת I 1. The *ʾalep* has quiesced in pronunciation; its position in spelling is uncertain in places (cf. הזות II 6 and הזואת V 7). It uses the long form of a pronoun three times (אתה V 10bis, III 12) and the long form of a pronominal suffix only once (להמה VI 3), but normally uses the short forms (ך-, ת-, etc.).

Listed in Table 1 are the orthographical variants of 4QDeut^{n}, as compared with 𝔐𝔪 and the Nash Papyrus where extant. Since לוא and כול are consistently marked with *matres lectionis* (see the exceptions noted in the discussion of orthography) they are not included in this table.

TABLE 1: *Orthography*

Col., Line	Deut	4QDeut^{n}	𝔐	𝔪	𝔪^{mss}	PapNash
I 1	8:5	אלוהיך	אלהיך	אלהיך		
I 1	8:6	ושמרתה	ושמרת	ושמרת		
I 2	8:6	אלוהיך	אלהיך	אלהיך		
I 2	8:6	אותו	אתו	אתו		
I 3	8:7	אלוהיך	אלהיך	אלהיך		
I 3	8:7	עינות	עינת	עינות		
I 3	8:7	(orth. & var.) ותהומות	ותהמת	תהומת	תהומות, ותהומת, תומת ותתהומת, ותהומות	
I 4	8:8	ושעורה	ושערה	ושערה		
I 6	8:9	במסכנות	במסכנת	במסכנת		
I 7	8:9	תחצוב	תחצב	תחצב		
I 7	8:9	נחושת	נחשת	נחשת		
I 7	8:10	ושבעתה	ושבעת	ושבעת		
I 8	8:10	וברכתה	וברכת	וברכת		
I 8	8:10	אלוהיך	אלהיך	אלהיך		
I 8	8:10	הטובה	הטבה	הטובה		
II 2	5:1	אליהם	אלהם	אליהם		
II 2	5:1	החוקים	החקים	החקים		
II 3	5:1	אנוכי	אנכי	אנכי		
II 3	5:1	דובר	דבר	דבר		

TABLE 1: *Orthography (cont.)*

Col., Line	Deut	4QDeut^{n}	𝔐	⅏	⅏^{mss}	PapNash
II 3	5:1	באוזניכם	באזניכם	באזניכם		
II 4	5:1	אותם	אתם	אתם		
II 4	5:1	לעשותם	לעשתם	לעשותם		
II 5	5:2	אלוהינו	אלהינו	אלהינו		
II 5	5:2	בחורב	בחרב	בחורב		
II 6	5:3	אבותינו	אבתינו	אבתינו		
II 6	5:3	הזות	הזאת	הזאת		
II 7	5:3	כולנו	כלנו	כלנו		
II 9	5:5	ואנוכי (orth. & var.)	אנכי	ואנכי		
II 9	5:5	עומד	עמד	עמד		
II 9	5:5	וביניכם	וביניכם	ובינכם		
II 12	5:6	אנוכי	אנכי	אנכי		
II 12	5:6	אלוהיך	אלהיך	אלהיך		אלהיך
III 2	5:7	אלוהים	אלהים	אלהים		אלהים
III 4	5:9	תעובדם	תעבדם	תעבדם		
III 5	5:9	אנוכי	אנכי	אנכי		אנכי
III 5	5:9	אלוהיך	אלהיך	אלהיך		אלהיך
III 5	5:9	קנא	קנא	קנא		קנוא
III 5	5:9	פוקד	פקד	פקד		פק]ד
III 5	5:9	עוון	עון	עון		
III 6	5:9	שלשים	שלשים	שלישים		שלשים
III 6	5:9	רבעים	רבעים	רבעים	^{Sad}רביעים	רבעים
III 6	5:10	עושה (orth. & var.)	ועשה	ועשה		
III 7	5:10	לאוהבי	לאהבי	לאהבי		לאהבי
III 7	5:10	ולשומרי	ולשמרי	ולשמרי		ולשמרי
III 7	5:10	מצוותי (orth. & var.)	מצותו	מצותי		מצותי
III 7	5:11	אלוהיך	אלהיך	אלהיך		א]להיך
III 8	5:11	שמו	שמו	שמו		ש]מה
III 10	5:12	אלוהיך	אלהיך	אלהיך		
III 10	5:13	תעבוד	תעבד	תעבד		תעבוד
III 11	5:14	אלוהיך	אלהיך	אלהיך		אלהיך
III 11	5:14	בו		בו		בה
III 12	5:14	וחמורך	וחמרך	וחמרך	וחמורך	וחמרך
IV 1	5:14	גריך (orth. & var.)	וגרך	וגרך		
IV 2	5:15	וזכרתה	וזכרת	וזכרת		
IV 2	5:15	ויציאך	ויצאך	ויוצאך	^{Sad}ויוציאך	
IV 3	5:15	אלוהיך	אלהיך	אלהיך		
IV 3	5:15	ובזרוע	ובזרע	ובזרע	ובזרוע	
IV 4	5:15	אלוהיך	אלהיך	אלהיך		
IV 6	Exod 20:11	וינוח	וינח	וינח		
IV 8	5:16	אלוהיך	אלהיך	אלהיך		
IV 8	5:16	יאריכון	יאריכן	יארכון	^{Sad}יאריכון	יאריכון

TABLE 1: *Orthography (cont.)*

Col., Line	Deut	4QDeut^{n}	𝔐	⅏	⅏^{mss}	PapNash
IV 9	5:16	אלוהיך	אלהיך	אלהיך		אלהיך
IV 9	5:16	נותן	נתן	נתן		נתן
IV 10	5:19	תגנוב	תגנב	תגנב		תג]נב
IV 10	5:20	ברעיך	ברעך	ברעך		ברעך
IV 10	5:21	תחמוד	תחמד	תחמד		תחמוד
IV 11	5:21	רעיך	רעך	רעך		
IV 11	5:21	תחמוד		תחמד		
IV 11	5:21	רעיך 2°	רעך	רעך		רעך
IV 12	5:21	חמורו (orth. & var.)	וחמרו	וחמרו	וחמורו	וחמרו
IV 12	5:21	לרעיך	לרעך	לרעך		לרעך
V 2	5:22	חושך		חשך		
V 2	5:22	ויכותבם (orth. or var.?)	ויכתבם	ויכתבם		
V 2	5:22	לוחות	לחת	לוחת	לוחות, לחות	
V 3	5:23	החושך	החשך	החשך		
V 4	5:23	בוער	בער	בער		
V 4	5:23	וזקניכם	וזקניכם	וזקניכם	וזקיניכם^{Sad}	
V 5	5:24	אלוהינו	אלהינו	אלהינו		
V 5	5:24	כבודו	כבדו	כבודו		
V 5	5:24	גודלו	גדלו	גדלו		
V 5	5:24	קׄולׄו]	קלו	קולו		
V 7	5:25	הגדולה	הגדלה	הגדלה		
V 7	5:25	הזואת	הזאת	הזאת		
V 8	5:25	לשמוע	לשמע	לשמע		
V 8	5:25	אלוהינו	אלהינו	אלהינו		
V 9	5:26	אלוהים	אלהים	אלהים		
V 9	5:26	כמונו	כמנו	כמונו		
V 10	5:27	אלוהינו	אלהינו	אלהינו		
V 11	5:27	אלוהינו	אלהינו	אלהינו		
VI 3	5:29	להׄמה	להם	להם		
VI 3	5:29	אׄותׄ]י	אתי	אתי		
VI 4	5:29	לעולם	לעלם	לעלם	לעולם	
VI 5	5:31	עמוד	עמד	עמד		
VI 8	5:32	תסורו	תסרו	תסורו		
VI 9	5:33	אלוהיכם	אלהיכם	אלהיכם		

Intervals to mark paragraph-divisions in 4QDeut^n appear at the places listed in Table 2.

TABLE 2: *Intervals*

Col., Line	Deut	4QDeut^n	𝔐	𝔪
I 2	8:6	interval	—	—
I 5	8:8	interval	—	—
I 7	8:9	interval	—	—
I 9	8:10	interval	—	קצה
II 12	5:5	—	—	קצה
III 2	5:7	—	interval	—
III 7	5:10	—	ס	—
III 8	5:11	end of line	ס	קצה
IV 7	5:15	/////	ס	קצה
IV 9	5:16	—	ס	=·:
IV 9	5:17	—	ס	=·:
IV 10	5:18	—	ס	=·:
IV 10	5:19	—	ס	=·:
IV 10	5:20	—	ס	=·:
IV 11	5:21 (1° רעיך)	—	ס	—
IV 12	5:21	interval	ס	קצה
V 3	5:22	—	interval	—
V 12	5:28 (אל]י)	—	—	קצה

Under the VARIANTS for cols. II–IV, which contain the Decalogue, the evidence has been collated from the Massoretic, Samaritan and Greek witnesses of Exodus, as well as the Nash Papyrus; the sigla used are 𝔐^{Ex}, 𝔪^{Ex}, 𝔊^{Ex}, and PapNash respectively. Owing to the complexity of the textual evidence in the Decalogue, usually only the main witnesses are cited, and variations within the versions can be found in the apparatus of the critical editions.

For discussions of the textual character of 4QDeut^n, essentially a harmonistic text, see the articles by White and Eshel (different readings from the latter are corrected in the NOTES below).

Mus. Inv. 981. PAM 42.642.

Col. I Deut 8:5-10

top margin

[5]וידעת עם לבבך כי כאשר ייסר איש את בנו יהוה אלוהיך מיסרך [6]ושמרתה את
מצות יהוה אלוהיך ללכת בדרכיו ולאהבה אותו *vacat*
[7]כי יהוה אלוהיך מביאך אל ארץ טובה ורחבה ארץ נחלי מים עינות ותהומות
יצאים בבקעה ובהר [8]ארץ חטה ושעורה וגפן תאנה ורמון ארץ זית שמן ודבש

vacat

[9]ארץ אשר לוא במסכנות תאכל בה לחם ולוא תחסר כול בה ארץ אשר
אבניה ברזל ומהריה תחצוב נחושת *vac* [10]ואכלת ושבעתה
וברכתה את יהוה אלוהיך על הארץ הטובה אשר נתן לך

vacat

bottom margin

L. 1 (8:6) ושמרתה] ושמרת (Eshel)
L. 2 (8:6) interval] > 𝔐 𝔪
L. 5 (8:8) interval] > 𝔐 𝔪
L. 7 (8:9) interval] > 𝔐𝔪 (Eshel)
L. 9 (8:10) interval 𝔪] > 𝔐

Variants

8:5 (1) בנו 𝔐𝔪𝔗] +כן 4QDeut^{j}𝔊(vid)
8:6 (2) בדרכיו 𝔐𝔪𝔊^{ABOC}𝔗𝔖𝔙 (cf 10:12, 11:22; 𝔊 of 19:9; Josh 22:5)] ב]כ̇ול דרכיו 4QDeut^{j}𝔊^{dnt}
8:6 (2) ולאהבה (cf 11:13, 22, 19:9; 30:6, 16, 20)] וליראה 4QDeut^{f}𝔐𝔪𝔊𝔗𝔖𝔙
8:7 (3) ארץ טובה ורחבה 4QDeut^{f,j}𝔪𝔊] ארץ טובה 𝔐𝔗𝔖𝔙
8:7 (3) ותהומות 4QDeut^{j}𝔐𝔪^{mss}𝔗𝔖] תהומות 𝔪^{Sad}(תהומת 𝔪^{vGall})𝔊
8:7 (4) בבקעה ובהר 4QDeut^{j}𝔐𝔪] δια των πεδιων και δια των ορεων 𝔊 (cf 𝔗𝔖)
8:8 (4) חטה ושעורה וגפן תאנה ורמון]
4QDeut^{f}; חטה ושערה גפן̊ ות̊[אנה] \ [ ]
4QDeut^{j}; ושע̊[ורה] [וגפן]ות̊[אנ]ה ורמון
5QDeut;] ורמון[
𝔐𝔗𝔖; חטה ושערה וגפן ותאנה ורמון
𝔊; חטה* ושערה גפן תאנה רמון
𝔪 חטה ושערה גפן תאנה ורמון
8:9 (6) תאכל בה לחם 4QDeut^{f,j}𝔐𝔪𝔗𝔖] φαγη τον αρτον σου 𝔊 (cf 𝔙)
8:9 (6) ולוא 4QDeut^{f}𝔊𝔗^{J}𝔖] לא 4QDeut^{j}(לוא)𝔐𝔪𝔗^{O}
8:9 (7) אבניה 4QDeut^{j}𝔐𝔪𝔊𝔗𝔖] λιθοι 𝔊^{BCn}(cf La)
8:9 (7) ומהריה 4QDeut^{f,j} 5QDeut] ומהרריה 𝔐𝔪. In later Hebrew the form with single *reš* becomes more common (Qimron, 26).

Col. II Deut 5:1-6

top margin

[1]ויקרא משה אל כל ישראל ויאמר
אליהם שמעה ישראל את החוקים ואת
המשפטים אשר אנוכי דובר באוזניכם
היום ולמדתם אותם ושמרתם לעשותם
[2]יהוה אלוהינו כרת עמנו ברית בחורב [3]לא
את אבותינו כרת יהוה את הברית הזות כי
אתנו אנחנו אלה פה היום כולנו חיים היום
[4]פנים בפנים דבר' יהוה עמכם בהר מתוך
האש [5]ואנוכי עומד בין יהוה וביניכם בעת
ההיא /////// להגיד לכם את דברי יהוה
אלוהיכם כי יראתם מפני האש ולוא עליתם
בהר ///// לאמר [6]אנוכי יהוה אלוהיך אשר

bottom margin

L. 10 There is a large splotch of ink in the blemished space.

VARIANTS

5:1 (2) שמעה 4QDeut^{j,o}] שמע 𝔐𝔪
5:1 (4) היום 4QDeut^{o}𝔐𝔪ℭ𝔖𝔙] היום הזה 4QDeut^{j}; εν τη ημερα ταυτη 𝔊
5:2 (5) אלוהינו 𝔐𝔪ℭ𝔖𝔙] ο θεος υμων 𝔊
5:2 (5) עמנו 4QDeut^{j}𝔐𝔪ℭ𝔖𝔙] προς υμας 𝔊
5:3 (6) אבותינו 4QDeut^{j}𝔐𝔪ℭ𝔖𝔙] τοις πατρασιν υμων 𝔊
5:3 (7) אתנו 4QDeut^{j}𝔐𝔪ℭ𝔖𝔙] προς υμας 𝔊
5:3 (7) אנחנו 4QDeut^{o}𝔐𝔪ℭ𝔖𝔙] υμεις 𝔊
5:3 (7) כולנו 𝔐𝔪ℭ𝔙] παντες 𝔊; ܟܠܢ 𝔖
5:3 (7) היום 1° 𝔐𝔪ℭ] > 𝔊
5:3 (7) חיים היום 𝔊] חיים 𝔐𝔪ℭ; ܚܝܝܢ ܚܢܢ 𝔖; *et vivimus* 𝔙
5:5 (9) ואנוכי 𝔪𝔊𝔖] אנכי 𝔐ℭ𝔙
5:5 (10–11) דברי יהוה אלוהיכם 𝔖] יהוה[4QDeut^{j}; דבר יהוה 𝔐; דברי יהוה 𝔪𝔊ℭ𝔙
5:6 (12) אנוכי 4QDeut^{j}𝔐𝔪𝔊^{B*963}(εγω) Laℭ^{O}𝔙𝔐^{Ex}𝔪^{Ex}] εγω ειμι 𝔊$^{AB^{c}FMVOC\mathfrak{C}J}$ Syh(ειμι sub ※)𝔊^{Ex};
ܐܢܐ ܐܢܐ 𝔖

Col. III Deut 5:6-14

top margin

1 הוצאתיך מארץ מצרים מבית עבדים [7]לוא יהיה
2 לך אלוהים אחרים על פני [8]לא תעשה לך פסל וכול
3 תמונה אשר בשמים ממעל ואשר בארץ מתחת ואשר
4 במים מתחת לארץ [9]לוא תשתחוה להם ולוא תעובדם
5 כי אנוכי יהוה אלוהיך אל קנא פוקד עוון אבות על
6 בנים על שלשים ועל רבעים לשנאי [10]עושה חסד לאלפים
7 לאוהבי ולשומרי מצוותי [11]לוא תשא את שם יהוה אלוהיך
8 לשוא כי לוא ינקה יהוה את אשר ישא את שמו לשוא
9 [12]שמור ///////// את יום השבת לקדשו כאשר צוך יהוה
10 אלוהיך [13]ששת ימים תעבוד ועשית את כול מלאכתך
11 [14]וביום השביעי שבת ליהוה אלוהיך לוא תעשה בו כל מלאכה
12 אתה בנך בתך עבדך ואמתך שורך וחמורך

bottom margin

L. 1 (5:6) מבית] ומבית (Eshel)
L. 11 (5:14) כל מלאכה was written by the original scribe, but in the margin, probably as a correction.

VARIANTS

5:6 (1) מבית עבדים 4QDeut^{j}𝔐𝔪𝔊ℭ𝔖𝔙𝔐^{Ex}𝔪^{Ex}𝔊^{Ex}] > PapNash
5:7 (1) יהיה 4QDeut^{j}𝔐𝔪ℭ𝔖𝔙𝔐^{Ex}𝔪^{Ex}] εσονται 𝔊𝔊^{Ex}
5:8 (2) פסל 4QDeut^{j}𝔐𝔪ℭ𝔙𝔐^{Ex}𝔪^{Ex}] γλυπτον 𝔊; ειδωλον 𝔊^{B}𝔊^{Ex}; ܟܠ ܨܠܡܐ 𝔖
5:8 (2) וכול 𝔪𝔊𝔖𝔙𝔐^{Ex}𝔪^{Ex}𝔊^{Ex}] כל 𝔐ℭ
5:9 (4) תעובדם] תעבדם 𝔐𝔪
5:9 (5) אנוכי 𝔐𝔪ℭ𝔙𝔐^{Ex}𝔪^{Ex}] εγω ειμι 𝔊; εγω γαρ ειμι 𝔊^{Ex}; ܐܢܐ ܐܢܐ 𝔖
5:9 (6) על שלשים 𝔪𝔊PapNash𝔖𝔙𝔐^{Ex}𝔪^{Ex}] ועל שלשים 𝔐 (cf ℭ)
5:9 (6) ועל רבעים 4QDeut^{j}𝔐𝔪PapNash𝔐^{Ex}𝔪^{Ex}] + γενεαν 𝔊 = ℭ𝔖𝔙; + γενεας 𝔊^{Ex}
5:10 (6) עושה] ועשה 𝔐𝔪𝔊ℭ𝔖𝔙𝔐^{Ex}𝔪^{Ex}𝔊^{Ex}
5:10 (7) מצוותי 𝔪𝔊PapNashℭ𝔖𝔙𝔐^{Ex}𝔪^{Ex}] מצותו 𝔐. *Waw* and *yod* are indistinguishable in this script, therefore the 4QDeut^{n} reading is materially uncertain.
5:11 (8) יהוה 2° 𝔐𝔪𝔊ℭ𝔖𝔙𝔐^{Ex}𝔪^{Ex}] κυριος ο θεος σου 𝔊^{Ex}
5:12 (9) שמור 𝔐𝔪𝔊ℭ𝔖𝔙𝔪^{Ex}] זכור 𝔐^{Ex}𝔊^{A}𝔊^{Ex}PapNash
5:12 (9) לקדשו 𝔐] לקדשהו 𝔪

5:12 (9–10) כאשר צוך יהוה \ אלוהיך 𝔐𝔪𝔊𝔗𝔖𝔙] > 𝔐^{Ex}𝔪^{Ex}𝔊^{Ex}PapNash

5:13 (10) ועשית את כול] ועשית כל 𝔐𝔪 PapNash𝔐^{Ex}𝔪^{Ex}

5:14 (11) וביום השביעי 𝔊𝔊^{Ex}PapNash] ויום השביעי 𝔐𝔪𝔗𝔖𝔐^{Ex}𝔪^{Ex}; *septimus dies* 𝔙

5:14 (11) תעשה בו כל 𝔪𝔊 PapNash𝔖𝔙𝔊^{Ex}] תעשה כל 𝔐𝔗𝔐^{Ex}𝔪^{Ex}

5:14 (III12–IV1)

גריך	ובהמתך \		וחמורך	שורך	ואמתך	עבדך	בתך	בנך	אתה	𝔊^{B}]
וגרך	בהמתך	וכל	וחמרך	שורך	ואמתך	ועבדך	ובתך	ובנך	אתה	𝔐𝔗𝔖;
וגרך	בהמתך	וכל	וחמרך	שורך	ואמתך	עבדך	ובתך	ובנך	אתה	𝔪𝔊PapNash𝔊^{Ex};
וגרך	בהמתך	וכל	וחמרך	ושורך	ואמתך	עבדך	ובתך	ובנך	אתה	𝔙;
וגרך	בהמתך				ואמתך	עבדך	ובתך	ובנך	אתה	𝔐^{Ex};
וגרך	בהמתך				ואמתך	עבדך	ובתך	ובנך	אתה	𝔪^{Ex}.

Col. IV Deut 5:14-21

top margin

ובהמתך גריך אשר בשעריך //// למען ינוח עבדך ואמתך 1

כמוך [15]וזכרתה כי עבד היית ////// בארץ מצרים ויציאך 2

יהוה אלוהיך משם ביד ///////////// חזקה ובזרוע נטויה 3

על כן צוך יהוה אלוהיך ////////// לשמור את יום השבת 4

לקדשו כי ששת ימים עשה יהוה את השמים ואת הארץ 5

את הים וכול אשר בם וינוח ביום השביעי על כן ברך יהוה 6

את יום השבת לקדשו ///// [16]כבד את אביך ואת אמך כאשר 7

צוך יהוה אלוהיך ///////// למען יאריכון ימיך ולמען ייטב 8

לך על האדמה אשר יהוה אלוהיך נותן לך [17]לוא תרצח [18]לוא 9

תנאף [19]לוא תגנוב [20]לוא תענה ברעיך עד שוא [21]לוא תחמוד 10

אשת רעיך לוא תחמוד בית רעיך שדהו עבדו אמתו 11

שורו חמורו וכול אשר לרעיך *vacat* 12

bottom margin

L. 2 (5:15) //////] > (Eshel)
L. 12 (5:21) interval] ס 𝔐, קצה 𝔪

VARIANTS

5:14 (1) אשר בשעריך 𝔐𝔪𝔊𝔗𝔖𝔙𝔐^{Ex}] ο παροικων εν σοι 𝔊^{B}𝔊^{Ex}

5:14 (1–2) למען ינוח עבדך ואמתך כמוך 𝔐𝔪𝔊𝔗𝔖𝔙] > 𝔐^{Ex}𝔪^{Ex}𝔊^{Ex}PapNash

5:14 (1) ואמתך 𝔐𝔪𝔊𝔗𝔖𝔙] +ο βους σου και το υποζυγιον σου 𝔊$^{C(-529)\ 127}$; +το υποζυγιον σου 𝔊^{mss}

5:15 (2–4) וזכרתה כי עבד היית בארץ מצרים ויציאך יהוה אלוהיך משם ביד חזקה ובזרוע נטויה על כן צוך יהוה אלוהיך לשמור את יום השבת 𝔐𝔪𝔊ℭ𝔖𝔙] > 𝔐^{Ex}𝔪^{Ex}𝔊^{Ex}PapNash

5:15 (4) לשמור 𝔊ℭ𝔖𝔙] לעשות 𝔐𝔪

5:15 (5–7) לקדשו כי ששת ימים עשה יהוה את השמים ואת הארץ (+και 𝔊^{Ex}) את הים וכול אשר בם וינוח ביום השביעי על כן ברך יהוה את יום השבת לקדשו(𝔐^{Ex}𝔪^{Ex}𝔊^{Ex} ויקדשהו) 𝔐^{Ex}𝔪^{Ex}𝔊^{Ex}] > 𝔐𝔪ℭ𝔖𝔙; και αγιαζειν αυτην 𝔊. 4QDeut^{n} has added the reason for the Sabbath observance from the Exodus version of the fourth commandment. The Nash Papyrus also has both reasons, but in the reverse order.

5:15 (6) וינוח] וינח 𝔐^{Ex}𝔪^{Ex}

5:16 (7–8) כאשר \ צוך יהוה אלוהיך 𝔐𝔪𝔊ℭ𝔖𝔙] > 𝔐^{Ex}𝔪^{Ex}𝔊^{Ex}PapNash

5:16 (8–9) למען יאריכון ימיך ולמען ייטב \ לך 𝔐𝔪ℭ𝔖𝔙] [למען] \ ייטב לך ולמען יאריכון ימיך PapNash𝔊𝔊^{Ex} (μακροχρονιος γενη 𝔊𝔊^{Ex}; μακροχρονιοι ητε 𝔊^{B}); למען יארכון ימיך 𝔐^{Ex}𝔪^{Ex}

5:16 (9) על האדמה 𝔐𝔪𝔊PapNashℭ𝔙𝔐^{Ex}𝔪^{Ex}] επι της γης της αγαθης 𝔊^{Ex}; ܒܐܪܥܐ ܛܒܬܐ 𝔖

5:17-19 (9–10) לוא תרצח לוא(𝔐ℭ𝔙 ולא) \ תנאף לוא(𝔐ℭ𝔙 ולא) תגנוב 𝔐𝔪𝔊ℭ𝔖𝔙𝔐^{Ex}𝔪^{Ex}𝔖^{Ex} 4QPhyl^{a} XQPhyl^{3} 1QPhyl] לוא תנאף לוא תרצח לו[א \ תג]נב PapNash𝔊; *לא תנאף לא תגנב לא תרצח 𝔊^{Ex}

5:20 (10) שוא 𝔐𝔪𝔖PapNash] שקר ℭ𝔐^{Ex}𝔪^{Ex}; ψευδη 𝔊𝔊^{Ex}

5:21 (10–11)

Witness	Text
𝔊𝔊^{Ex}]	לוא תחמוד \ אשת רעיך לוא תחמוד בית רעיך
𝔐ℭ;	ולא תחמד אשת רעך ולא תתאוה בית רעך
𝔪𝔪^{Ex};	לא תחמד בית רעך ולא תחמד אשת רעך
𝔖;	לא* תחמד אשת רעך ולא תחמד בית רעך
𝔐^{Ex};	לא תחמד בית רעך לא תחמד אשת רעך
PapNash	לוא תחמוד [את אשת רעך לו]א תתאוה את ב[י]ת רעך

5:21 (11–12)

Witness	Text
]	שדהו עבדו אמתו \ שורו חמורו וכול אשר לרעיך
𝔐ℭ;	שדהו ועבדו ואמתו שורו וחמרו וכל אשר לרעך
𝔊𝔊^{Ex};	ושדהו* ועבדו ואמתו ושורו וחמרו וכל בהמתו וכל אשר לרעך
𝔪;	שדהו עבדו ואמתו שורו וחמרו וכל אשר לרעך
𝔪^{Ex};	שדהו עבדו ואמתו ושורו וחמרו וכל אשר לרעך
𝔖;	ושדהו וכרם עבדו אמתו ושורו וחמרו וכל אשר לרעך
𝔙;	ושדהו ועבדו ואמתו ושורו וחמרו וכל אשר לרעך
𝔐^{Ex};	ועבדו ואמתו ושורו וחמרו וכל אשר לרעך
PapNash	שד]הו ועבדו ואמתו וש]ורו וחמרו וכל אשר לרעך

Col. V Deut 5:22-28

top margin

1 [22]את הדברים האלה דבר יהוה אל כול קהלכם בהר מתוך האש

2 חושך ענן וערפל קול ג[ד]וֹל ולוא יסף ויכותבם על שני לוחות

3 אבנים ויתנם אלי [23]ויהיׄ [כשו]מעכם את הקול מתוך החׄושך וההר

4 בוער באש ותקרבון אלי כול ראשי שבטיכם וזקניכם [24]ותא[מרו]

5 הן הראנו יהוה אלוהינו את כבודו ואת גודלו ואת קולו[שמ]ענו

6 מתוך האש ביום הזה ראינו כי ידבר יהוה את ה[אדם וחי]

7 [25]ועתה למה נמות כי תאכלנו האש הגדולה הזואת אם י[וספים]

8 אנחנו לשמוע את קול יהוה אלוהינו עוד ומתנו [26]כי מי כ[ול בשר]

9 אשר שמע קול אלוהים חי מדבר מתוך האש כמונו ויחי

10 [27]קרב אתה ושמע את כול אשר ידבר יהוה אלוהינו ואתה

11 תדבר אלינו את כול אשר ידבר יהוה אלוהינו אליך ושמע[נו]

12 ועשינו [28]וישמע יהוה את קול דבריכם בדברכם א[לי]

bottom margin

L. 2 (5:22) ג[ד]ול] גדול (Eshel)
L. 3 (5:23) [כשו]מעכם] כשומעכם (Eshel)
L. 10 (5:27) ידבר] דבר (Eshel)
L. 11 (5:27) ידבר. *Yod* is written above the line by the original scribe.

VARIANTS

5:22 (2) חושך ענן וערפל 𝔪] ענן וערפל[4QDeut^{j}; σκοτος γνοφος θυελλα 𝔊; הענן והערפל 𝔐ℭ; ܒܚܫܘܟܐ ܥܢܢܐ ܘܥܪܦܠܐ 𝔖; *et nubis et caliginis* 𝔙
5:22 (2) ויכותבם] ויכתבם 𝔐𝔪 (cf Qimron, §311.13d)
5:22 (3) ויתנם 4QDeut^{j}𝔐𝔪ℭ𝔖𝔙] και εδωκεν 𝔊
5:23 (3) הקול 𝔐𝔪𝔊ℭ𝔖𝔙] της φωνης κυριου 𝔊^{C}
5:23 (3) החושך 𝔐𝔪ℭ𝔖𝔙] του πυρος 𝔊
5:24 (5) הן 𝔐𝔪] הנה 4QDeut^{j}
5:24 (5) הראנו 𝔐𝔪𝔊ℭ𝔖𝔙] εδειξεν 𝔊^{B}
5:24 (5) ואת גודלו 𝔐ℭ𝔖𝔙] את גודלו 𝔪; > 𝔊
5:24 (6) ביום הזה 𝔊] היום הזה 𝔐𝔪ℭ𝔖
5:24 (6) יהוה ℭ] אלהים 𝔐𝔪𝔊𝔖
5:26 (8) כול 4QDeut^{j}𝔐𝔪ℭ] > 𝔊𝔖
5:26 (9) חי] חיים 𝔐𝔪ℭ
5:27 (10) ידבר] יאמר 𝔐𝔪ℭ
5:27 (10) אלוהינו 𝔐𝔪𝔊ℭ𝔖] + אליכ[ה 4QDeut^{j}𝔙
5:27 (10) ואתה 4QDeut^{j}𝔐^{mss}𝔪] ואת 𝔐

Col. VI Deut 5:28–6:1

top margin

1 ויאמר י[הוה]

2 (29) דברו אלי֯ך֯[ ]

3 לה֯מה ליראה או֯ת֯[י]

4 (31) להם ולבניהם לעולם[30]

5 פה עמוד עמדי ואדבר[ה]

6 והמשפטים אשר תלמ֯[דם]

7 להם לרשתה 32ושמרתם[ ]

8 (33) אתכם לוא תסורו י[מין]

אתכם
9 //// אלוהיכם תלכו[ ]

10 בארצ אשר֯[תי]ר֯[שון 6:1]

11 א֯[שר]

L. 9 (5:33) interval] > (Eshel)

L. 9 (5:33) אתכם is written supralinearly by the original scribe.

L. 10 (5:33) בארצ. A medial *ṣade* appears in a final position.

VARIANTS

5:32 (8) אתכם 𝔐𝔪𝔗] > 𝔊S

5:32 (8) תסורו 𝔐𝔪𝔊B𝔗S] εκκλινεις 𝔊

5:33 (9sup) אתכם 𝔐𝔪𝔗𝔇] > 𝔊S

42. 4QDeut^{o}

(PLATE XXX)

FIFTEEN fragments from the beginning and end of this Deuteronomy scroll preserve portions of Deut 2:8; 4:30-34; 5:1-5, 8-9; 28:15-18, 33-36, 47-52, 58-62; and 29:22-25. The leather, of medium thickness, is medium to dark brown in colour, with a somewhat worn surface. Horizontal and vertical dry lines are visible on frgs. 2 and 14, while the right margins of frgs. 3 and 14 show guiding dots. Left margins are preserved on frgs. 2 (measuring 0.9 cm and displaying the remains of sewing) and 5, right margins on frgs. 3 and 14, and a possible top margin on frg. 6. The column-width varies, with frgs. 1–7 from the beginning of the scroll containing 46–56 letter-spaces per column, and frgs. 8–15 from the end of the scroll having 60–86. The average distance between lines of script is 0.7 cm.

Palaeographical study of 4QDeut^{o} places its hand in the late Hasmonaean period, *c.*75–50 BCE. The size of the letters has become equal (cf. especially *taw*), and there is no ornamentation. The latest forms are *ʿayin*, which has rotated vertically and has a prominent breakthrough at the juncture of the right and left arms, and final *mem*, in which the left downstroke begins above the head and reaches down to close the bottom of the letter. The base-strokes of all relevant letters are straight (cf. especially medial *ṣade*).

The orthographic practice of 4QDeut^{o} is generally similar to 𝔐 and ⅏, all three of which show minor inconsistencies (see Table 1). It marks the following vowels with *matres lectionis*: **aw* > *ô* (או 2–4 5), **ū* (אנחנו 5 4), **ī* (ראשנים 2–4 3), and **ā* > *ō* when accented (באתות 2–4 8, but never לא, and not when unaccented, אנכי 7 2). There are no extant examples of **ay* > *ê*. The proto-semitic short vowels **a*, **i*, and **u* are not marked with *matres lectionis*. The short forms of the pronominal suffixes and endings are used (e.g. ך-, כם-, and הן- except אתה 2–4 7).

One interval marks a paragraph-division at frg. 7 3 (5:9) which 𝔐⅏ lack.

TABLE 1: *Orthography*

Frg., line	Deut	4QDeut^{o}	𝔊	𝔐	𝔐^{mss}	⅏^{ed}	⅏^{mss}
2–4 3	4:32	]ר̊אשנים		ראשנים	הראשנים	הראישונים	
2–4 8	4:34	באתות]		באתת		באתות	באותות^{Sad}
2–4 8	4:34	ובזרע̊]		ובזרוע		ובזרוע	
5 3	5:2	בחרב	בחורב 4QDeut^{j,n}	בחרב		בחורב	
5 5	5:5	עמד	עומד 4QDeut^{n}	עמד		עמד	
9–11 3	28:36	אותך̇]		אתך		אתך	
12–14 2	28:48	ובערום]		ובעירם		ובערום	ובחרום
12–14 5	28:51	ועש]ת̇רות		ועשתרת		ועשתרות	

Mus. Inv. 1091. PAM 43.055; 41.423, 42.003, 42.006, 42.632, 42.712.

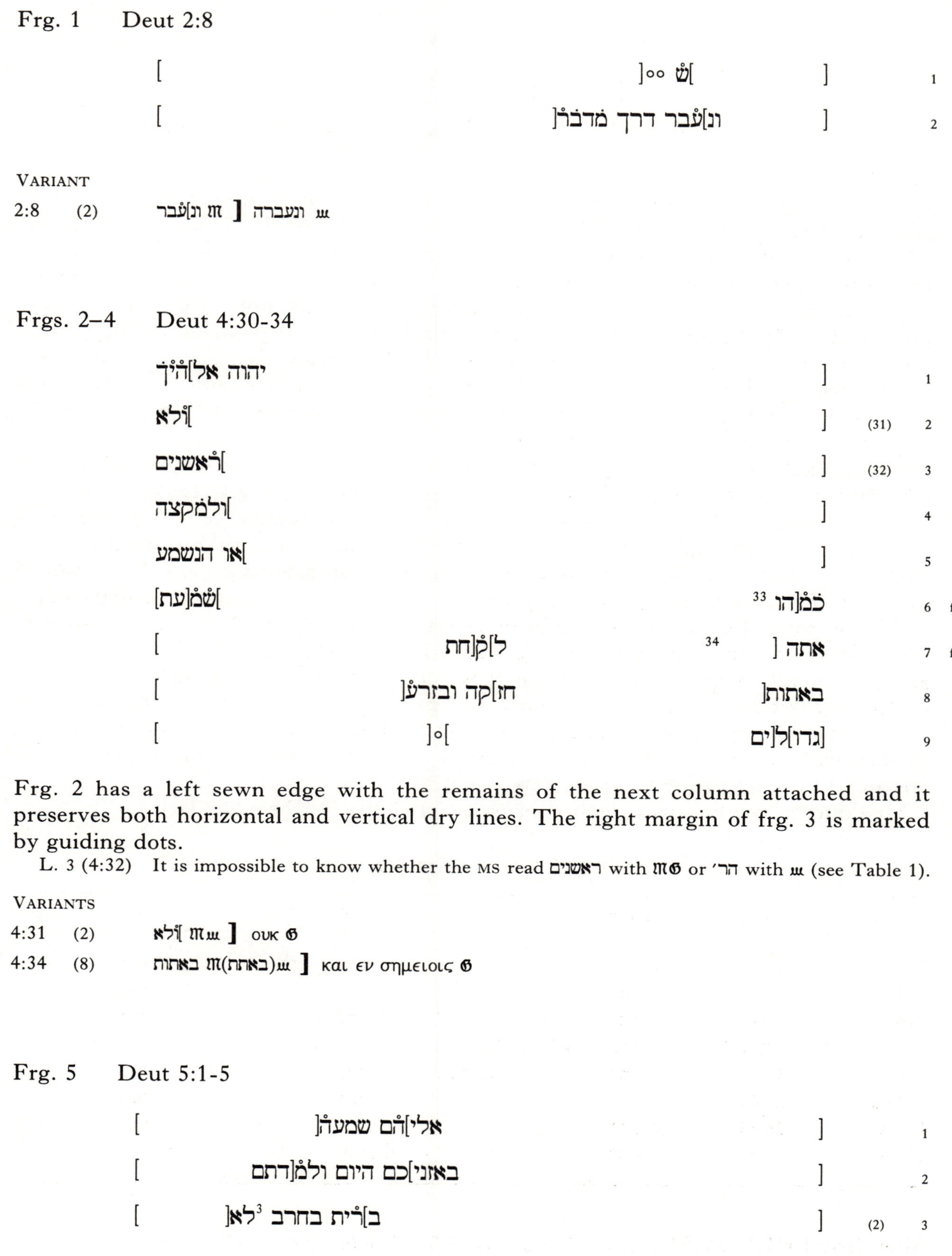

Frg. 1 Deut 2:8

1]]שׁ °°[[
2] ונ]ע̇בר דרך מ̇דב̇ר̇[[

VARIANT

2:8 (2) ונ]ע̇בר 𝔐] ונעברה 𝔪

Frgs. 2–4 Deut 4:30-34

1] יהוה אל]ה̇י̇ך
2 (31)]]ו̇לא
3 (32)]]ר̇אשנים
4]]ולמ̇קצה
5]]או הנשמע
6 f.3 כמ̇]הו [33]]שׁמ̇[עת]
7 f.4 אתה] [34] ל]ק̇[חת [
8 באתות[חז]קה ובזרע̇[[
9 [גדו]ל[ים]°[[

Frg. 2 has a left sewn edge with the remains of the next column attached and it preserves both horizontal and vertical dry lines. The right margin of frg. 3 is marked by guiding dots.

L. 3 (4:32) It is impossible to know whether the MS read ראשנים with 𝔐𝔊 or הר' with 𝔪 (see Table 1).

VARIANTS

4:31 (2)]ו̇לא 𝔐𝔪] ουκ 𝔊
4:34 (8) באתות 𝔐(באתת)𝔪] και εν σημειοις 𝔊

Frg. 5 Deut 5:1-5

1] אלי]ה̇ם שמעה̇[[
2] באזני]כם היום ולמ̇[דתם [
3 (2)] ב]ר̇ית בחרב [3] לא[[

]אנחנו אלה פה ה֯[יום]] 4

5 אנ[כ֯י עמד] (4) 5

]יראתם] 6

L. 5 This MS may have read אנכי with 𝔐 or ואנכי with 𝔰𝔪 (von Gall errs with ראנכי). Over the *ʿayin* and *mem* of עמד there are two random dots of ink.

VARIANTS

5:1 (1) שמעה֯ 4QDeut^{j,n}] שמע 𝔐𝔰𝔪

5:1 (2) היום 4QDeut^{n}𝔐𝔰𝔪] היום הזה 4QDeut^{j}; εν τη ημερα ταυτη 𝔊

5:3 (4) אנחנו 4QDeut^{j,n}𝔐𝔰𝔪] υμεις 𝔊

5:3 (4-5) אלה פה ה֯[יום כלנו חיים 4QDeut^{n}𝔐𝔰𝔪] ωδε παντες ζωντες σημερον 𝔊

Frgs. 6–7 Deut 5:8-9

These fragments are difficult to position relative to each other. If they are arranged together, the top line of frg. 6 must come before, but on the same line as, the top line of frg. 7. In that case, the top of the *lamed* which appears in the second line of frg. 6 cannot be properly placed, since it does not fit any of the other witnesses (𝔐𝔰𝔪𝔊) to this passage. *Lamed* occurs in three words in v 9, each so close that traces of a second *lamed* at the bottom of frg. 6 should be visible. Therefore, the word להם has been reconstructed at the appropriate point in the text (see VAR.), which allows for a reasonable (although short: 37 letter-spaces) reconstruction of line 1. The second problem is the patch of uninscribed leather at the bottom of frg. 7, underneath which two traces of a fourth line of text can be seen. If it is an interval to mark a paragraph division, according to the reconstruction it falls in the middle of v 9. It may, however, be scribal avoidance of an area unsuitable for writing, but there is too little evidence to be certain. The reconstruction of frgs. 6–7 arranged together follows:

top margin?

ואשר במים מ֯תחת [לארץ 9 לא תשתחוה להם ולא] 1 f.6,7

[תעבד]ל֯[הם כ]י֯ אנכי יהו֯ה֯[אלהיך אל קנא פקד עון] 2

[ ] *vacat* [ ] 3

[ ]∘ ∘[ ] 4

VARIANT

5:9 (2) תעבד]ל֯[הם] תעבדם 𝔐𝔰𝔪; λατρευσης αυτοις 𝔊

If, however, one of these fragments does not belong to 4QDeut°, they should be reconstructed individually, as follows:

Frg. 6 *Deut 5:8-9*

top margin?

ואשר במים] מתחת לארץ 9לא תשתחוה להם ולא תעבדם כי אנכי[1

[יהוה א]ל֯[היך אל קנא פקד עון אבות על בנים ועל שלשים ועל] 2

Frg. 7 *Deut 5:8-9*

]]מ֯תחת [ואשר במים מתחת לארץ 9לא] 1

[תשתחוה להם ולא תעבדם כ]י֯ אנכי יהו֯ה[אלהיך אל קנא פקד עון אבות] 2

] *vacat* [ ] [3

]]∘∘[[4

This reconstruction, which assumes an interval for paragraph-division at the end of v 9 (no interval 𝔐𝔰), may suggest that frg. 7 belongs to a different manuscript.

Frg. 8 Deut 28:15-18

]]∘[[1

]]בקול יהוה א֯[להיך [(15) 2

] ה]ק֯ללות האלה והשיג֯ו֯ך[16 [3

] [אדמתך שגר אלפי]ך [(17,18) 4

L. 4 (28:18) There are traces of ink below שגר, but they are too high to belong to the next line.

VARIANT

28:18 (4) אדמתך 𝔐𝔊] +ופרי בהמתך 𝔐ms𝔰

Frgs. 9–11 Deut 28:33-36

[יגיעך י]א֯כל עם אשר[ ]ה֯י֯מ֯[ים 34 [1 f.9,10

] 35י]כ֯כ֯[ה י]הוה [ ] לא ת]וכל [2

[36יולך יהו]ה֯ אותך[ ] לא֯[[3

[אלהים אח]רים ע֯[ץ ואבן [4

Frgs. 12–14 Deut 28:47-52, 58-62

1 (48)] י]הׄוה אלהיךׄ[[

2 (49)] ו]בצמא ובערום[[

3 (50)]]מקׄצׄה הׄאׄרׄ[ץ [

4 f.13] 51ואכל פרי] בהמׄ[תך [

5 (52)] ועש]תׄרות צאנ[ך [

6]]בהן בכלׄ[[

7]]°°°[[

[lines 8–11 missing]

12 f.14 לׄאׄ תׄשׄ]מר [

13 (59) הזה את] [

14 (61) ונאמנים] 60 [

15 (62) אשר לׄאׄ] [

16 הייתםׄ] [

Frg. 12 cannot be located in the Rockefeller Museum. The right margin of frg. 14 shows horizontal and vertical dry lines and guiding dots.

VARIANT

28:48 (2) ו]בצמא ובערום 𝔐𝔪𝔊ℭ𝔖𝔇] > $𝔊^B$

Frg. 15 Deut 29:22-25

1] באפו ו]בׄחׄמׄתׄו 23ואמרו כׄ[ל [

2] 24]ו֯אמרו על אשר עזבו] את [

3]]מׄארץ מצרים 25[וי]לׄ[כו [

4] ח]לׄקׄ[לׄהם [

L. 2 (29:24) עזבו. What appears to be a dot of ink above the *bet* is merely dirt.

VARIANT

29:22 (1) ו]בׄחׄמׄתׄו 𝔐𝔪] και οργη 𝔊

43. 4QDeut^{p}

(PLATE XXXI)

THIS manuscript consists of three fragments preserving portions of Deut 6:4-11. The leather, of medium thickness, is yellowish brown in colour and has a damaged surface. Frg. 2 preserves a margin between two columns as well as a bottom margin. Horizontal ruling is also extant on frg. 2. The column-width is 55–69 letter-spaces, and the distance between lines of script is 0.8–0.9 cm.

Palaeographical study of 4QDeut^{p} establishes its hand in the late Hasmonaean period, *c.*75–50 BCE. The letter-size has become equal, and there is no ornamentation. The latest forms are *ʿayin*, which has rotated vertically and has a prominent breakthrough at the juncture of the right and left arms, and *he*, where the head is made in a 'v-shaped' stroke. *Yod* has a late Hasmonaean form, with a large, angular head, distinguishing it from *waw*, which has a thin, curled head.

The orthographic evidence for 4QDeut^{p} is sparse. The manuscript marks *$\bar{u}$ with a *waw* (והיו 1 2), and *$\bar{a}$ > $\bar{o}$ in the fem. pl. ending (ל֯טוטפות[3 4), but not לא (2 7). There are no other *matres lectionis* preserved. The manuscript uses the short pronominal suffix form ך-. The only orthographic variant preserved is located at frgs. 1–3 4 (6:8) ל֯טוטפות, לטטפות ⅏ vGall, לטטפת 𝔐⅏ Sad.

An interval marks a paragraph-division at frgs. 1–3 5 (6:9); ס 𝔐, קצה ⅏.

On the basis of the extant evidence, it is impossible to assign 4QDeut^{p} to a textual tradition.

Mus. Inv. 1091. PAM 43.055; 42.712.

Frgs. 1, 2 col. i, 3 Deut 6:4-11

1 f.2] אלה]י֯נו יהוה א֯[חד 5ואהבת את י]ה֯וה

2] 6]ו֯היו הדברי֯[ם א]ש֯ר

3 (7)] ובש]כ֯בך

4 f.3 (9) [ובקומך 8]ו֯ה֯י֯ו֯ ל֯טוטפות[ ]ב֯ית֯ך

5 [ובשעריך *va[cat*] [

6 10] א]ל֯ה֯יך אל[ ]ו֯ליעקב

7 (11)] גד]ל֯[ות]לא מ֯ל֯[א]ת֯

bottom margin

L. 3 (6:6-7) If the text is restored according to the other extant witnesses (𝔐⅏𝔊) it is too long for the space available. Many opportunities exist within the line for loss of text through haplography.

VARIANTS

6:7 (3) ובש[כ֯בך 𝔐 𝔪 (בשכבך)] και κοιταζομενος 𝔊

6:9 (4) ב֯ית֯ך[𝔐] בתיך 𝔪; των οικων υμων 𝔊

Frg. 2 col. ii

7 והב֯ ֯]

Col. ii has not been identified.

L. 7 For the bottom right corner of *bet* cf. ובש[כ֯בך 2 i 3 (as opposed to *bet* in וליעקב 2 i 6).

44. 4QDeut^{q}

(PLATE XXXI)

Preliminary publication: P. W. Skehan, 'A Fragment of the "Song of Moses" (Deut. 32) from Qumran', *BASOR* 136 (1954) 12–15. See also 'The Qumran Manuscripts and Textual Criticism', *Volume du congrès, Strasbourg 1956* (VTSup 4; Leiden: Brill, 1957) 148–60, esp. 149–50 and n. 1 on p. 150.

P. M. Bogaert, 'Les trois rédactions conservés et la forme originale de l'envoi du Cantique de Moïse (Dt 32,43)', *Das Deuteronomium, Entstehung, Gestalt und Botschaft* (ed. N. Lohfink; BETL 68; Leuven: Leuven University Press, 1985) 329–40. A. van der Kooij, 'The Ending of the Song of Moses: On the Pre-Masoretic Version of Deut 32:43', *Studies in Deuteronomy: In Honour of C. J. Labuschagne on the Occasion of His 65th Birthday* (ed. F. García Martínez et al.; Leiden: Brill, 1994) 93–100.

THIS manuscript, surviving only in a few fragments with text from Deut 32:37-43 and 32:9-10(?), perhaps originally contained only the Song of Moses (Deut 32:1-43); see the introduction to 4QDeut^{j}. The edition presented here supersedes the preliminary edition published in 1954, since a new fragment (frg. 3) has been added, giving new light on the arrangement of the reconstruction. Note in addition that the fragment containing *bhnḥy[l] . . . bny ʾl[whym]*, mentioned in the second paragraph of 'A Fragment', belongs to 4QDeut^{j} (frg. 34), and that the fragment containing Deut 4:30-32, mentioned in the third paragraph, belongs to 4QDeut^{o} (frg. 2).

The leather of the manuscript was very thin, carefully prepared on the inscribed (hair) side, and smooth on the back. Its colour was light tan with grey tones, although some parts, especially to the left of the stitching, now display honey tones, probably as a result of moisture. Some darkening at the edges of the leather also causes confusion due to the illusion of ink.

The left and bottom margins of col. I and all four margins of col. II are preserved; there are traces of stitching and thread preserved at points between the two columns. The first line extant in col. I is probably the original top line of that column, but see the general NOTE on that column. The full height of the original manuscript, measuring 11.4 cm, is preserved on the left side, although moisture has caused some darkening, contraction, and splitting along the top edge. The distance from the first ruled line to the top edge of the manuscript is *c.*0.7 cm, and that from the last ruled line to the bottom edge is 2.8–2.9 cm. Each column originally contained eleven lines, which were lightly ruled with a dry point. The distance between the lines of script is 0.7–0.9 cm, and the height of the letters averages 0.3 cm.

The extant text ends at Deut 32:43, without the final verses of chapter 32 and without chapters 33–34, and there are indications that the manuscript was intended to end at that point. Col. II is written on a separate piece of leather; its left margin is broad with no stitching along the left side; and, presented stichometrically, it is intentionally arranged to end at the bottom of its column.

In contrast to the format of col. II which is very neat and symmetrical with all lines containing only one hemistich, col. I presents a problem. Its lines appear asymmetrical, the right margin seems unusually irregular, lines 5–8 and 11 contain more than one

hemistich, and the remaining clues allow for two possible textual reconstructions of the column (see the general NOTE on col. I).

The two extant columns of the scroll, ending at Deut 32:43, are most likely not just the final columns from a larger manuscript of the Book of Deuteronomy which ended with this Song. The limited height of the scroll, the arrangement of the lines, the small number of words per column, and the absence of the final verses of chapter 32 strongly suggest that 4QDeut^{q} probably contained only the Song of Moses (Deut 32:1-43). It would thus join the category of 'special use' manuscripts (see the introduction to 4QDeut^{j}), and the appearance of Deuteronomy 32 in 4QDeut^{j} and 4QPhyl^{N} support this hypothesis.

The manuscript is inscribed in a formal hand of the late Hasmonaean or early Herodian period, dating from the second half of the first century BCE or perhaps the beginning of the first century CE. The distinction between *waw* and *yod* is maintained fairly consistently, and thus איֹוב is transcribed in II 5 (איוב 𝔪^{mss}; אויב 𝔐𝔪 32:42).

The orthography is similar to that of 𝔐 and 𝔪 and their slightly varying manuscripts; only four orthographic differences are preserved:

32:38 (I 5) ו]יעזרכם 𝔐𝔪^{mss}] ויעזרוכם 𝔐^{mss}𝔪
32:41 (I 10) שנתי 𝔪𝔐^{mss}] שנותי 𝔐
32:42 (II 5) פ[ר]עות 𝔐] פרעת 𝔪; פרחת 𝔪^{ms}
32:43 (II 8) יקום 𝔐] יקם 𝔪

The possible transposition איֹוב at 32:42 mentioned above would constitute an error, but the dot seen above the *ʾalep* of אׄל in I 8 (Deut 32:40) is probably not intentional. No other errors, corrections, or insertions, however, whether by the original scribe or by a later hand, are preserved in the manuscript, although if the dark spots above col. I line 1 form a supralinear insertion, this would be an exception. The remains of a large ink smear or marginal flourish, *c.*2.0 cm long and *c.*0.5 cm wide, are visible in the damaged section about 1.5 cm to the left of line 5 of col. II, as are possible impressions of letters from the previous revolution of the scroll there and to the left of line 7.

The surviving clues reveal a manuscript that was probably a 'special use' manuscript, containing only the Song of Moses (Deut 32:1-43), excerpted from a bibilical manuscript circulating in Jewish circles around the middle of the first century BCE. 4QDeut^{q} and the Massoretic *textus receptus* display distinctly variant forms of the text—more than one variant for every pair of the scroll's short lines. 4QDeut^{q}, or its *Vorlage*, however, should not be naïvely dismissed as a so-called 'vulgar text' for a number of reasons. Virtually all of its readings are documented in other biblical manuscripts; some readings (שמים 32:43) are more ancient than those preserved in 𝔐, which revised polytheistic terms secondarily for theological purposes; and other readings (אדמת 32:43) appear superior to unusual forms in 𝔐.

Though not identical to 𝔊, 4QDeut^{q} shares several unique readings with the Septuagint version of Deuteronomy and bears witness to the existence of the variant Hebrew *Vorlage* used by the Septuagint translator, at least for this section of Deuteronomy (cf. Skehan, 'A Fragment', 12, 14). 4QDeut^{q} and 𝔊 agree in seven readings against 𝔐, including all of the significant readings (the hemistichs 32:43b and e, שמים, בניו; see NOTE and VARIANTS).

The question whether the longer form of the poem found in 4QDeut^{q} and 𝔊 or the shorter form found in 𝔐 is preferable is more complicated and requires extensive

analysis, since there are literary and theological forces at work (see the bibliography above and the commentaries).

Mus. Inv. 676. PAM 42.164; 41.350.

Frg. 1 Deut 32:9-10(?)

1] נח]לתו

2 10] ישמ]ן֯

Thus Skehan transcribed this fragment and tentatively placed it as Deut 32:9-10. Ulrich would read לתי[for the first line and א֯[for the second line (contrast the stroke here, slanting toward the left as it descends, with the final *nun* in יין I 4), but has no identification to offer. If Skehan's reconstruction is correct, a column earlier than the extant col. I was stichometric by the full line. The reading נחלתו would agree with 𝔐𝔗𝔖𝔙 against 𝔪𝔊 which add ישראל as the end of the line. ישמן would agree with 𝔐𝔊𝔖𝔙 against ישמנהו 𝔪 (ישימנהו 𝔪^{mss}).

Col. I: Frgs. 2–5 i Deut 32:37-41c

[top margin]

]◦◦◦◦[

1 [וא]מר יהו֯ה֯[איה אלהימו]

2]]◦◦[ ]אשר֯[חסיו בו]

3 38[אשר]חל֯[ב]י֯ זבח֯[ימו יאכלו]

4 [ישתו] יין [נסיכם]

5 [יקומו ו]יעזורכם [יהי עליכם סתרה]

6 39[ראו עתה]כי אני א֯[ני הוא ואין אלהים עמדי]

7 [אני אמית ואחיה מחצתי ואני ארפא]

8 [ואין מידי] מצי֯[ל 40כי א]ש֯א אל֯[שמים י]ד֯י f.3–5

9 [ואמרתי חי]א֯נכי [לעולם]

10 [41א]ם֯ שנתי ב֯[ר]ק֯ ח֯ר֯בי [ ]

11 [ותאחז]במשפט יד֯[י] אשיב נק֯[ם]ל֯צ֯רי

bottom margin

Parts of the left and bottom margins are preserved, but the format of the column is problematic. Since col. II clearly contains 11 lines as well as the top and bottom margins, and since lines 8 and 11 of col. I are aligned with the corresponding lines of col. II, col. I also must be reconstructed with 11 lines. There appears, however, to be ink above the words presented as line 1. These words either are a supralinear insertion above the suggested line 1 or themselves constitute a mostly lost line 1. In this latter case, the current line numbers 1–6 would become 2–7, and current line 7 (for which nothing is extant) would disappear. This could plausibly be explained by a parablepsis from ואין in line 6 to ואין in line 8 (note that line 6 is the longest line). Both options are governed by the 11-line format, and the option presented above presumes a supralinear insertion and no parablepsis.

An additional problem is the vertical alignment. In contrast to col. II which is very neat and symmetrical with all lines containing only one hemistich, the lines of col. I are asymmetrical, and lines 5–8 and 11 contain additional hemistichs. The odd arrangement of the transcription as presented (note the right margin) reflects a reconstruction based on the vertical clues preserved in extant fragments.

L. 1sup (32:37)]○○○○[. There appears to be writing above ואמר יהוה in line 1; see general NOTE above.

L. 2 (32:37)]○○[ ]. For this part of the fragment it is difficult to determine whether some of the dark spots are ink or damage, whether the small piece is actually attached to the larger fragment, and, if not, whether it is properly oriented. 𝔐𝔪 have צור at this point, 𝔊 lacks צור but appears to have אשר (ἐφ' οἷς) as in this MS. Moreover, to judge from line 1, the space available before אשר seems to require another word in addition to צור. Either אי (𝔐 in 37a) or איה (𝔪) might be repeated, and in view of אשר, one could expect the article on הצור. Thus some form of אי(ה) (ה)צור may be suggested.

L. 3 (32:38) The last stroke in חל̊[ב]י̊[cannot be part of the *bet*, but must follow it as *yod*, as in ℭ (see VAR.).

L. 4 (32:38) In this short hemistich there is a wide space after יין, perhaps due to a defect in the leather (see also the space following [ו]יעוזרכם in the line below). At the left edge of the leather there is a dark spot caught in cellulose tape; it is difficult to discern whether it is ink, and if so, what its original position was.

L. 8 (32:40) An ink dot is clearly visible above the *ʾalep* of אל̊, but it does not seem to have been made intentionally.

VARIANTS

32:37 (1)]ו[א]מר יה̊ו̊ה̊[𝔊Syh(sub ÷)] ואמר 𝔐ℭ𝔖𝔙; ואמרו 𝔪𝔙mss

32:37 (2)]○○[ ]אשר̊[[ ]] צור 𝔐𝔪α′ θ′ ℭ; אשר* 𝔊𝔙 (see NOTE)

32:38 (3) חל̊[ב]י̊[ℭ cf 𝔙] חלב 𝔐𝔪𝔊ℭ𝔖. For the plural form, cf. 1QS IX 4 (ומחלבי זבח); there are four instances in 4Q nonbiblical texts (see NOTE and the 'Preliminary Concordance').

Col. II: Frg. 5 ii Deut 32:41d-43

𝔊	𝔐	4QDeut^q	
		top margin	
=	ולמשנאי אשלם	[ולמשנ]אי אשלם	1
=	42אשכיר חצי מדם	[42אשכיר]ה חצי מדם	2
=	וחרבי תאכל בשר	[וחרבי תא]כל בשר	3
=	מדם חלל ושביה	[מדם חלל ו]שביה	4
= 𝔐	מראש פרעות אויב	וׄמׄרׄאׄשׄ פׄ[ר]עׄוׄת איׄוׄב	5
= 𝔔 + 𝔐	43הרנינו גוים עמו	43הרנינו שמים עמו	6
= 𝔔 (see note)		והשתחוו לו כל אלהים	7
=	כי דם עבדיו יקום	כי דם בניו יקום	8
=	ונקם ישיב לצריו	ונקם ישיב לצריו	9
= 𝔔		ולמשנאיו ישלם	10
= 𝔔	וכפר אדמתו עמו	ויכפר אדמת עמו	11
		bottom margin	

At least part of all four margins are preserved for this column which was evidently the last in this manuscript.

L. 5 (32:42) The *waw* in וׄמׄרׄאׄשׄ is mostly preserved at the margin before *mem* (see VAR.). The tops of *waw* and *taw* in פרעות are pulled too far to the left as they appear in the photograph.

L. 5 (32:42) איׄוׄב(vid). The *waw* and *yod* in this hand are often well distinguished, and thus the transcription. It should be noted that some 𝔪^mss have איוב (see VAR.).

L. 6–7 (32:43) The 𝔊 tradition has a double rendering of these two lines:

εὐφράνθητε, οὐρανοί, ἅμα αὐτῷ,
καὶ προσκυνησάτωσαν αὐτῷ πάντες (> πάντες B) υἱοὶ θεοῦ·
εὐφράνθητε, ἔθνη, μετὰ τοῦ λαοῦ αὐτοῦ,
καὶ ἐνισχυσάτωσαν αὐτῷ πάντες ἄγγελοι θεοῦ·

The 𝔊 manuscripts and the daughter versions interchange υἱοὶ and ἄγγελοι in these lines with no family pattern discernible; the alternation is very old (cf. Heb 1:6). The reading ἄγγελοι appears to be the older 𝔊 form elsewhere for בני אלהים (cf., v.g., D. Barthélemy, *Les devanciers d'Aquila* [VTSup 10; Leiden: Brill, 1963] 299), and stands in 𝔊 of Ps 96[97]:7 for the present Hebrew line. Without prejudicing the original form of the Hebrew, it can perhaps be posited that καὶ ἐνισχυσάτωσαν αὐτῷ πάντες ἄγγελοι θεοῦ with BAFM La Arm Boh Sa, plus R in the Odes, represents the oldest form of this text in Greek (cf. 32:8 where ἄγγελοι θεοῦ is the original reading of 𝔊), and that the introduction of προσκυνησάτωσαν and of υἱοὶ θεοῦ is the result of recensional activity dating back to about the turn of the era.

The double rendering shows that 𝔊 knew two Hebrew forms of the text. The first agrees with 4QDeut^q and the first line of the second happens to agree with 𝔐. The agreement of ἔθνη with 𝔐 is neutralized, however, since the second Hebrew tradition with ἔθνη also included the second hemistich which 𝔐 lacks.

VARIANTS

32:42 (2) ה[אשכיר]] אשכיר 𝔐𝔴

32:42 (5) ומׄר֯א֯ש֯ 𝔴ms𝔊mss 𝔖] מראש 𝔐𝔴𝔊ℭ𝔙

32:42 (5) אי̈ו̇ב(vid) 𝔴mss] אויב 𝔐𝔴

32:43a,b (6–7) הרנינו—אלהים] The 𝔊 tradition preserves a double rendering of these lines.

32:43 (6) שמים 𝔊(1°)] גוים 𝔐𝔴𝔊(2°) Rom 15:10 ϵβρ′ α′ ℭ𝔖𝔙

32:43 (7) והשתחוו לו כל אלהים (cf Ps 97:7) 𝔊(και προσκυνησατωσαν αυτω παντες [> παντες 𝔊B] υιοι θϵου; see NOTE)] > 𝔐𝔴 ϵβρ′ ℭ𝔖𝔙

32:43 (8) בניו 𝔊] עבדיו 𝔐𝔴 ϵβρ′ ℭ𝔖𝔙

32:43 (10) ולמשנאיו ישלם 𝔊] > 𝔐𝔴 ϵβρ′ ℭ𝔖𝔙 (cf 32:41d [II 1] in 1st sing)

32:43 (11) ויכפר] וכפר 𝔐𝔴; + κυριος 𝔊

32:43 (11) אדמת 𝔴𝔊𝔙] אדמתו 𝔐 ϵβρ′ α′ ℭ𝔖(ℭ𝔖 as though ו′ אדמתו)

47. 4QJosh[a]

(PLATES XXXII–XXXIV)

Preliminary publication: Eugene Ulrich, '4QJoshua[a] and Joshua's First Altar in the Promised Land', *New Qumran Texts and Studies* (STDJ 15; ed. George J. Brooke with Florentino García Martínez; Leiden: Brill, 1994) 89–104. Leonard J. Greenspoon, 'The Qumran Fragments of Joshua: Which Puzzle are They Part of and Where Do They Fit?', *Septuagint, Scrolls and Cognate Writings. Papers Presented to the International Symposium on the Septuagint and Its Relations to the Dead Sea Scrolls and Other Writings (Manchester, 1990)* (SBLSCS 33; ed. G. J. Brooke and B. Lindars; Atlanta: Scholars Press, 1992) 159–94.

Alexander Rofé, 'The Editing of the Book of Joshua in the Light of 4QJosh[a]', *New Qumran Texts and Studies*, 73–80. Lea Mazor, 'The Septuagint Translation of the Book of Joshua', *BIOSCS* 27 (1994) 29–38. Klaus Bieberstein, *Lukian und Theodotion im Josuabuch, Mit einem Beitrag zu den Josuarollen von Ḫirbet Qumrān* (Biblische Notizen Beiheft 7; München, 1994) 85–93.

THIS manuscript is inscribed in a formal book hand classified by F. M. Cross as Hasmonaean, and thus dated in the second half of the second century or the first half of the first century BCE. It is the oldest extant witness to the Book of Joshua in any language. 4QJosh[b], the only other manuscript found at Qumran clearly containing the Book of Joshua, is to be dated around the middle of the first century BCE, and unfortunately there is no text extant that is common to both.

4QJosh[a], as interpreted below, is significant in that it preserves a sequence of the narrative that is at variance with, and probably prior to, that found in the received text of Joshua. If correctly assessed, this manuscript narrates that the first altar built by Joshua in the newly-entered land was built at Gilgal immediately after the crossing of the Jordan (after Joshua 4), not later on Mt. Ebal (cf. 8:30-35 𝔐 and 9:3-8 𝔊).

Assuming correct analysis of frg. 1, the contents of columns I–V can be reconstructed with reasonable confidence (see Table 1), although the text in col. V is shorter than that in 𝔊 or in 𝔐. In contrast, the distribution of the contents of cols. VI–VIII is uncertain. Col. VI contained roughly 8:25-29 followed by 9:1-13, on the assumption that 8:30-35 was absent. Frgs. 17–18 (Josh 10:2-5) and frgs. 19–22 (Josh 10:8-11) were probably either at the bottom of col. VII or at the top of col. VIII.

TABLE 1: *Contents of 4QJosh[a]*

Extant Columns	Fragments	Extant Text	Estimated Contents of Column
I	1–2	8:34-35; 5:X*, 2-7	8:34-35; 5:X*, 2–6:5
II	3–8	6:5-10	6:5-22
III	—	—	[6:22–7:12]
IV	9 i–12	7:12-17	7:12–8:3
V	9 ii, 13–16	8:3-14, 18?	8:3-25?
VI	—	—	[8:25-29?; 9:1-13?]
VII or VIII	17–22	10:2-5, 8-11	?

* X designates some editorial text not found in 𝔐𝔊.

The leather of the manuscript is light tan, thin, polished on the recto and also well-prepared on the verso. The pores are unusually large especially on cols. IV–V. Top margins are generously preserved on frgs. 1, 3, 4, 6, 9, and possibly 20; in fact, all of the extant fragments come from the top half of the scroll, with the possible exception of frgs. 15–21. It is possible that frgs. 15 and 21 preserve bottom margins, but there are also reasons to doubt this. Right margins are preserved on frgs. 3, 9 ii, 17, and probably 21, and left margins on frgs. 1, 9 i, and 15.

The number of letters per line is *c*.62–72 for col. I, *c*.50–65 for col. II, *c*.47–56 for col. IV, *c*.49 for col. V, and *c*.56–65 for col. VII/VIII. The number of lines per column can be estimated as *c*.27–30. The width of the columns, though never preserved entirely for any column, can be estimated as *c*.13.5 cm for col. I, *c*.11.3 cm for col. II, *c*.12 cm for col. IV, *c*.11 cm for col. V, and 10 cm for col. VII/VIII.

The orthography (see Table 2) displays a slightly fuller use of *matres lectionis* than that in 𝔐. Though the words כל and לא are consistently spelled so, the scroll's orthography is not generally consistent, just as the orthography of 𝔐 is not consistent (cf. לעבר 3:17 in 𝔐 but לעבור 4:1; אליהם 4:12 but אלהם 6:6; וילנו 3:1 but תלינו 4:3). The non-systematic nature of the scroll's orthography is evident in the name 'Joshua', which is spelled in three ways: יהשע in frg. 1 1, 5; יהושע in frg. 3 2; and יהושוע in frgs. 1 1 (vid), 3 4, 8 8, and 9 ii 1. Although 𝔐 is consistent in using יהושע within the Book of Joshua, the spelling יהושוע also occurs in other books in 𝔐 (e.g. Deut 3:21; Judg 2:7). Note also the two forms for 'trumpets' in col. II of this manuscript: שופ֯ר[ות] (7 5), and הׄשפ֯ר֯ות (8 7).

TABLE 2: *Orthography of 4QJosh*[a]

Col., Line	(Frg.)	Joshua	4QJosh[a]	𝔐
I 1	(1)	8:35	יהשע	יהושע
I 2	(1)	8:35	ההולך	ההלך
I 4	(1)	5:2	יהש]ע	יהושע
I 5	(1)	5:3	י]הׄשע	יהושע
II 1	(3)	6:5	חמ]ת	חומת
II 6	(7)	6:8	הולך	הלך
II 7	(8)	6:9	הׄשפ֯ר֯ות	השופרות
II 7	(7)	6:9	הולך	הלך
II 8	(8)	6:10	יה]ושוע	יהושע
IV 2	(9 i)	7:13	קום	קם
IV 4	(9 i)	7:13	אויביכם	איביך
V 1	(9 ii)	8:3	יהושוע	יהושע
?	(17–18 4)	10:4	ׄ[הו]שׁוע	יהושע
?	(19 2)	10:9	ויבוא (corr)	ויבא

Only two intervals where the evidence is clear have been preserved. At 7:13 there is a short interval in the middle of the 'verse' where 𝔐 has none; and before 7:16 there is a major interval mirrored in 𝔐. See also frgs. 19–22 and the general NOTE there.

The scribe may have written *ʾalep* over *ʿayin* in אל at 6:6, and at 10:9 he wrote the required *ʾalep* supralinearly (see NOTES). Perhaps a larger error occurred at 7:14 where the scribe apparently omitted about six words due to parablepsis. One addition, probably from 8:18, was inserted by a later hand.

With respect to individual textual variants, the scroll agrees with 𝔐 against 𝔊 in only two insignificant readings, but agrees with 𝔊 against 𝔐 at least six times, again in relatively insignificant readings. The predominant pattern is that the scroll frequently goes its own way, disagreeing with both 𝔐 and 𝔊 in significant readings. In particular, the text of frg. 15 needs to be studied for its variants and affiliations, since it is noticeably shorter than the text in either 𝔐 or 𝔊, though 𝔊 is already shorter than 𝔐 (see Mazor, 'The Septuagint Translation').

The correct assessment of the significance of this manuscript hinges primarily on the order of the text in frg. 1 and the relationship between frg. 1 and frg. 3. First, a sure starting-point is that on a single fragment (frg. 1), the account of Joshua's reading of the Torah (8:34-35 in 𝔐, 9:7-8 in 𝔊) is followed by text that cannot be 9:1 or 9:9 but is a transitional temporal clause (about a line and a half not in 𝔐 or 𝔊), and then is followed by what appears to be the beginning of the account of the circumcision (5:2 in 𝔐𝔊; note the similarity between 5:1 and 9:1). Secondly, examination in the museum of the torn edges of the skin at the left of frg. 1 and the right of frg. 3 strongly suggests that the two were originally connected at the top edge of the manuscript for *c*.1.0 cm. The contours of the two edges of the skin correspond to each other so closely that they appear to have been torn one from the other (for further details, see Ulrich, '4QJoshua[a]'). Furthermore, an enhanced digital image of the two edges produced by G. Bearman and B. and K. Zuckerman confirms that the two edges of these fragments align perfectly.

In so far as the present arrangement is correct, the sequence of the narrative in this manuscript would place the building of the first altar in the newly-entered land immediately after the crossing of the Jordan at Gilgal. It should be noted, however, that, although the first two lines of frg. 1 correspond to Josh 8:34-35 (the reading of the Torah), it is not certain that 8:30-31 (the building of the altar) preceded, since that would occur at the unpreserved bottom of the preceding column. The building of the altar, however, is linked with the reading of the Torah in both 𝔐 and 𝔊[B], despite the fact that the combined passage is placed at different points in those two texts. Moreover, the two elements are linked in the earlier passage (Deut 27:1-8) where Moses issues the command that this altar be built: all the words of the Torah are to be written on the altar.

With regard to logic and coherence, the sequence in 𝔐𝔊 is puzzling. First, the building of the altar is curiously delayed in 𝔐𝔊 from the entry into the land in chapter 4 until after chapter 8. Moreover, there is a militarily incomprehensible trip to build the altar in unprotected territory, followed by immediate abandonment of it. Finally, whereas Gilgal was an ancient sacrificial shrine (cf., e.g., 1 Sam 10:8; 11:14-15; 15:21; Amos 4:4; 5:5), Mt. Ebal is never mentioned again as the place for the altar but only as the place of the curse (Deut 11:29; 27:13); indeed, it seems to make sense only as a countermove to the Samaritans' claim for Mt. Gerizim.

In contrast, the sequence which 4QJosh[a] apparently presents is simple and unproblematic, since one would expect from Deut 27:2-3 that the altar would be built

at Gilgal, 'when you cross over the Jordan into the land'. The mention of a specific mountain (בהר גריזין/בהר עיבל) does not come until Deut 27:4 and could well be an insertion, since the verse reads perfectly well without it. The Samaritan Deuteronomy has בהר גריזין at Deut 27:4, which makes sense either as an ancient northern claim or as a late Samaritan claim, and the Old Latin—surely reflecting an ancient form of 𝔊—has *Garzin*. בהר עיבל in 𝔐 at Deut 27:4 best makes sense as a Judaean replacement for or counterclaim to the Samaritans' בהר גריזין. The inclusion of either mountain in Deut 27:4 would require transposing the account about Joshua's building of the altar.

The relatively simple sequence in 4QJosh^{a}, uncomplicated by a specific local claim, finds textual support in Josephus. He follows the account of the crossing of the Jordan (*Ant*. V.16 –19) with Joshua's building of an altar and sacrificing upon it (βωμὸν . . . ἔθυεν ἐπ' αὐτοῦ, *Ant*. V.20), exactly where it appears to be placed in 4QJosh^{a}. It could be argued that Josephus is adding an 'unscriptural' embellishment, describing the stones taken from the Jordan not merely as a monument but also as an altar for sacrifice. But later in the narrative, between the conquest of Ai (*Ant*. V.45–48; 8:1-29 in 𝔐) and the Gibeonites' ruse (*Ant*. V.49–57; 9:3-27 in 𝔐), he makes no mention of an altar or a journey to Mt. Ebal (as in 8:30-35 in 𝔐). He does, however, eventually recount the building of the altar at Shechem, explicitly mentioning that it was commanded by Moses and that half the people were stationed on Mt. Gerizim and half on Mt. Ebal (*Ant*. V.69); but this is not until after all the warfare, and not until after the tabernacle was set up at Shiloh (= Josh 13:1/18:1). Pseudo-Philo (*Bib. Ant*. 21.7) seems to know and link both traditions (I am grateful to Prof. Chr. Begg for bringing this text to my attention).

Thus it may be conjectured that the witnesses display three stages in the history of the text. First, 4QJosh^{a} and Josephus present an early form of the narrative which places the building of the altar at Gilgal at the end of chapter 4, in accord with the command as read in Deut 27:2-3 and Deut 27:4 without the insertion of a place-name. Secondly, the Samaritan tradition includes בהר גריזין at Deut 27:4, constituting a Samaritan claim. A tertiary sequence is preserved in 𝔐𝔊, with בהר עיבל in 𝔐 at Deut 27:4 as a Judaean counterclaim to בהר גריזין. According to this hypothesis then, the narrative about the building of the altar, which originally followed the crossing of the Jordan and preceded the circumcision account, was subsequently transposed in accordance with Moses' revised command in 𝔐 to its present, curious position at Josh 8:30-35.

Mus. Inv. 1092, 1093. PAM 43.060, 43.057; IAA 329.237.

Col. I: Frgs. 1–2 Josh 8:34-35; 5:X, 2-7

top margin

1 [בספר]התׄורה 35לא היה דבר מכל צוה מׄשה[את יה]ושוע אשר לא קרא יהשע נגד כל
2 [ישראל בעברו]את הירדׄ[ן]וׄהנשים והטף והג[ר] ההולך בקרבם 5:Xאחר אשר נתקוׄ[ ]
3 [ ]לׄ[ ]אׄת ספר התורה אחר כׄן [ ]לׄ° נושאי הארׄון[ ]
4 [5:2בעת]הׄהיא אמר יהוה אליהש[ע ע]שׄ[ה לך חרבות צרים]
5 [ושוב מל את בני ישראל 5:3ויעש]ל[ו י]הׄשע ח[רבות צ]רׄ[ים וימל את בני ישראל אל]
6 [גבעת הערלות 4וזה הדבר אשר מל יהושע כ]ל[ ]הׄעׄםׄ הׄיׄצׄ[א ממצרים הזכרים כל] f.2
7 [אנשי המלחמה מתו במדבר בדרך בצאתם]מׄמׄצׄרׄים 5כׄיׄ[מלים היו כל העם היצאים]
8 [וכל העם הילדים במדבר בדרך בצ]אׄתם ממצׄ[רים לא מלו 6כי ארבעים שנה הלכו]
9 [בני ישראל במדבר עד תם כל הגוי]אׄנׄשי המלחׄ[מה היצאים ממצרים אשר לא שמעו]
10 [בקול יהוה אשר נשבע יהוה להם לב]לׄתי ראות את הׄ[ארץ אשר נשבע יהוה לאבותם]
11 [לתת לנו ארץ זבת חלב ודבש 7ואת בני]הׄם הקׄ[ים]

The top and left margins of this column are preserved, and examination of the torn edges of this fragment and those of frg. 3 makes it virtually certain that the right edge of frg. 3 originally followed directly to the left of frg. 1. The text in this manuscript is different from that in either 𝔐 or 𝔊. Here the passage numbered as 8:34-35 in 𝔐 is followed by an editorial transition, then 5:2-7; whereas in 𝔐 it is followed by 9:1, and in 𝔊 by 9:3.

L. 2–3 (5:X) Following בקרבם (8:35^fin), the scroll has a transition apparently between the reading of the Torah (which ends with 8:35) and the circumcision ritual (which begins with 5:2).

L. 2 (5:X) נתקוׄ[. The final letter can be a perfect *waw*. The dark spot 0.1 cm to the left is not ink but a shadow at the edge of the photograph; if the letter were *dalet* (e.g. as in נתקד[שו), the top left tip and perhaps even the cross-bar should still be visible on the leather.

L. 3 (5:X) כׄן [ ]לׄ°. There is clear leather inside the *kap* and after the *nun*; it is כן not ק. Professor A. Rofé (p. 78) suggests עלו following; I gratefully acknowledge his suggestion for this and several other improved reconstructions. In this case, however, the head of the final letter appears to be too broad for *waw*.

L. 5 (5:2) The length of the line suggests that this MS, like 𝔊, probably lacked שנית (𝔐) after ישראל.

VARIANTS

8:34	(1)	בספר] התׄורה 𝔐] εν τω νομω Μωυση 𝔊
8:35	(1)	מכל] + אשר 𝔐𝔊
8:35	(1)	את יה]ושוע 𝔊] > 𝔐
8:35	(2)	בעברו]את הירדׄ[ן] > 𝔐𝔊
8:35	(2)	בקרבם 𝔐] τω Ισραηλ 𝔊
8:35	(2–4)	8:35 + X + 5:2] 8:35 + 9:1 𝔐; 8:35 + 9:3 𝔊
5:X	(2–3)	אחר °1—הארׄון[ ] cf 5:1 𝔐𝔊
5:6	(10)	ראות 𝔊(ιδειν αυτους)] הראותם 𝔐

Col. II: Frgs. 3–8 Josh 6:5-10

top margin

1 f.3-6 גדולה ונפלה חמתׄ[ ]ועלה העםׄ[א]יש [נ]גדו [6]

2 יהושע בן נון אל הכׄ[הנים ויאמ]רׄ אל֯[יהם] שאו א[ת]

3 ושבעה כהנים ישא[ו יוב]ל֯ים לפני אׄ[רון יהוה 7ויאמר]

4 f.7 יהושע אל העם[והח]ל֯[וץ יעבר לפ]נׄי֯[ארו]ן֯[יהוה]

5 [8ויהי כ]אׄמׄר י[הושע שב]עׄה שופרׄ[ות]

6 f.8 [ ]ל֯[פני בשופרו]תׄ וארׄון בׄרית יהׄוׄה הולך[ ]

7 (9) [ ] השׄפׄרׄות והמאׄ[ס]ף הולך [ ]

8 (10) [יה]ושוע לא[מר]ל֯[א]

9 [ ]עד י[ום]

The top and right margins of this column are preserved and were originally joined to the left of frg. 1 (see NOTE on col. I).

L. 2 (6:6) אׄל. The ʾalep may have been written over ʿayin.

L. 3–4 (6:7) The MS includes יהושע, and thus the verb is reconstructed as ויאמר (= 𝔐^{q,mss}𝔗𝔖𝔙^{edd}) and not ויאמרו (= 𝔐).

L. 7 (6:9) השׄפׄרׄות. The dark diagonal line below רׄו is not ink on the surface of the leather.

VARIANTS

6:5	(1)	ו]עלה] ועלו 𝔐; και εισελευσεται 𝔊
6:7-10	(3–9)	𝔊 aliter
6:7	(4)	יהושע] > 𝔐𝔊(vid)

Col. IV: Frgs. 9 col. i –12 Josh 7:12-17

top margin

1 [יפנו לפ[נ]י] איביו ולא פנים כי היו לחרם ולא אוסיף להיות

2 [עמכם אם] לא תשמידו החרם מקרבכם 13קום קדש את העם ואמרת

3 [התקדשו]למחר   כי כה אמר יהוה אלהי ישראל חרם בקרבכם

4 [ישראל ל]א תוכל לקום לפני אויביכם עד הסירכם החרם מקרבכם

5 [14ונקרבתם]בבקר לשבט[יכם ו]היה השבט אשר ילכדנו יהוה תקריבו

6 [ל]בתים [והבית]אש[ר ילכדנו יהו]ה יקרב לגברים 15והיה הנלכד בהם f.10

7 ישר[   ]עבר את ברית יהוה כי עשה

8 [נבלה בישראל   *va[cat*

9 [ ] 16וישכם יהושע בבקר ויקרב את ישראל ל]שבטיו וילכד את[שבט]

10 [יהודה 17וי]קרב[את משפחות יהודה וילכד את]משפח[ת הזרחי ויקרב את] f.11,12

11 [משפחת]הזר[חי לגברים וילכד זבדי 18   [

The top and left margins of this column are preserved, continuing over to the next column. The word at the right margin is preserved in line 7.

L. 3 (7:13) There is a short interval before כי; no interval 𝔐.

L. 5 (7:14) It appears that the scribe read יהוה תקריבו and skipped to יהוה תקריבו 𝔊* / יהוה תקרב 𝔐 later in the verse due to parablepsis (see VAR.).

L. 8–9 (7:15-16) Most of line 8 was left blank, and there may have been a short indentation in line 9, before v 16; interval 𝔐 (cf. *BHS*).

L. 11 (7:17) הזר[חי]. The top of *he* is clearly visible on the leather.

VARIANTS

7:12 (1) איביו] איביהם 𝔐𝔊

7:12 (1) ולא פנים] > 𝔐𝔊

7:12 (1) ולא 2°] לא 𝔐𝔊

7:13 (3) בקרבכם 𝔊] בקרבך 𝔐

7:13 (4) אויביכם 𝔊] איביך 𝔐

7:14 (5) יהוה תקריבו] יהוה תקריבו(יקרב 𝔐) למשפחות והמשפחה אשר ילכדנה יהוה תקריבו(תקרב 𝔐) 𝔐𝔊

7:15 (6) בהם] בחרם 𝔐𝔊[mss]; > 𝔊

7:15 (7) כי] וכי 𝔐𝔊

7:16 (9) את[שבט] שבט 𝔐

Col. V: Frgs. 9 col. ii, 13–16 Joshua 8:3-14, 18?

top margin

Text		Verse	Line	Frg.
יהושוע וכל עם המלחמה֯]			1	
גבורי החיל וישל֯ח֯ם ל֯[ילה [4]			2	
אל העיר מא֯ח֯[רי העיר			3	
[5]ואני וכל[העם			4	
ב֯ר֯א֯ש֯[נה ונסנו לפניהם [6]ויצאו]א֯ח֯ר֯ינו ע֯ד֯[התיקנו			5	f.13
]		(7)	6	
[והורשתם]א֯ת הע[יר [8]			7	f.14
[את הע]י֯ר באש֯]		(9)	8	
[ויל]כו א֯ל֯]			9	
[10]]	ויעל הוא ו]ה֯זקנים		10	f.15
]	א]ת֯ו וישובו	(11)	11	
] נגד] הע֯י֯ר	[14]ויהי] כראות	(12)	12	f.16
[מלך העי]י֯מהר֯[ו	לק]ר֯אתם		13	
[[18?]ויאמר יהוה אל יהושע נטה בכידון אשר ב]ידך אלהעי			14?	

vacat? (or bottom margin?)

The top, right, and left margins are partly preserved. It is possible that the bottom margin is also preserved, but that is unlikely: other columns indicate *c*.27–30 lines per column, so that a bottom margin here would require an additional 13 or so lines between frgs. 14 and 15. In contrast, the fixed relative position of the extant words in lines 7–9 and 10–13 appears to require a shorter text similar to that in 𝔊, rather than a longer text as in 𝔐.

L. 1 (8:3) המלחמ֯ה֯]. The top of *he* 1° is reasonably clear, although the leather is split and separated.

L. 7–9 (8:7-9) The relative position of the words in these three lines appears to require a shorter text similar to that in 𝔊.

L. 13 (8:14) There seems to be ink on the surface of the leather above the line after י֯מהר֯[ו. It is probably either a random ink dot or a supralinear letter. It could possibly be the top of a *lamed* but cannot be the bottom of a descending letter from the line above.

L. 14? (8:18?) Beneath line 13 a later scribe added words similar to the text of v 18 in what appears to be an interval or the bottom margin. The addition is in larger letters, in different ink, and lacks a space between the two words אל העי. The form of the final *kap* in ב]ידך was not common prior to the early Herodian period.

VARIANTS

8:10 (10) ו[ה]זקנים 𝔊 La] וזקני ישראל 𝔐𝔊^{mss}

8:11 (11–12) [ ] \ וישובו] עלו ויגשו ויבאו 𝔐𝔊(ανεβησαν και πορευομενοι ηλθον)

8:14 (13) לק]ר[אתם 𝔊] לקראת ישראל 𝔐

8:18? (14?) 8:14^{fin}] + ב[י]דך אלהעי 4QJosh^{a} $^{(corr)}$ 2°m.; cf. בידך אל העי 𝔐; εν τη χειρι σου επι την πολιν = בידך על העיר (see NOTE)

Frgs. 17–18 Joshua 10:2-5

1 (3) עׄרׄיׄ המׄ]מלכה

2 צדק מלך [ירושלם אל הוהם]מׄלׄךׄ ח]בׄרׄ[ו]ןׄ[f.18

3 מלך לכיש ואל ד[ביר] מׄ[ל]ךׄ עגלון לאמר 4 עלו אלי ועזׄ[רני

4 [כ]יׄ השלימה את יׄ[הו]שוע ואת ישראל 5 ויאספו ויעׄלׄ[ו

5 [ירושלם מ]לׄ[ך חברו]ןׄ[מ]לׄךׄ יׄרמות מ]ל[ך]לכיׄ[ש

The right margin is preserved and its ruling is visible.

L. 4 (10:4) יׄ[הו]שוע. The *yod* is under the *dalet* of ד[ביר (line 3) and the *ʿayin* is under the *mem* of מׄ[ל]ךׄ. The required distance between the letters on line 3 of frgs. 17 and 18 suggests that the full spelling of the name occurred on line 4 (cf. the orthography in Table 2).

VARIANT

10:4 (4) ואת ישראל] ואת בני ישראל 𝔐𝔊

Frgs. 19–22 Joshua 10:8-11

0 [*v ac*]*a t* / *top* [*margin?*] f.19,2

1 [8 ויאמר י]הׄוׄה אׄל יׄ[הושע אל תירא מה]םׄ כי בידך נתתי[ם לא יעמד איש]

2 [מ]הׄםׄ בפניךׄ 9 ויבואׄלׄ[יהם יהושע פתאם] כל הלילה הׄלׄ[ך מן הגלגל 10 ויהמם]

3 [י]הוה לפנ[י] ישראל ויכׄ[ם מכה גדולה בגבעון וירדפם דרך מעלה בית חורן ויכם]

4 עׄ[ד עזקה ועד] מקדה 11 ויה[י ב]נׄסם [מפני ישראל הם נמורד בית חורן] f.21,2

5 ויהוה השליך עליהם אבניםׄ מן השמׄ[ים עד עזקה וימתו רבים אשר מתו]

6 באבני הברד מאשר הרגו [בני ישראל בחרב *vacat?* [

7? [ ] *vacat/bottom margin?*

The format of this column is difficult to determine. The space at the top of frg. 20 could be the top margin of col. VIII or simply an interval (פ 𝔐). Similarly, the space at

the bottom of frg. 21 could be the bottom margin of col. VII or simply an interval (ס 𝔐). Finally, frg. 21 appears to contain the words at the right margin of this column, but there are ink traces to the right of them. As in the Temple Scroll (11QT[a]), it is possible that these traces are due to ink seeping through from the words in the next revolution of the scroll.

L. 2 (10:9) ויבוא. The ink is thick and smudged here, but it appears that the scribe wrote ויבו, and (since the following word [אלידהם] begins with *ʾalep*) at first omitted the *ʾalep* of ויבוא and proceeded to the next word, then perhaps intended to write *ʾalep* in the space between the words but wrote an incorrect letter, and wrote *ʾalep* thickly over it.

VARIANTS

10:9	(2)	ויבו*] ויבוא 4QJosh[a (corr)]; ויבא 𝔐 (see NOTE)
10:9	(2)	הֹלֹך] עלה 𝔐; εισεπορευθη 𝔊[BG]; εξεπορευθη 𝔊[N]; επορευθη Ιησους 𝔊[A]
10:11	(5)	אבניֹם] + גדלות 𝔐; λιθους χιλαζης 𝔊; λιθους μεγαλους 𝔊[mss]

48. 4QJosh^{b}

(PLATE XXXV)

Preliminary publication: E. Tov, '4QJosh^{b}', *Intertestamental Essays in Honour of Józef Tadeusz Milik* (ed. Z. J. Kapera; Qumranica Mogilanensia 6; Kraków, 1992) 1. 205–12.

See also K. Bieberstein, *Lukian und Theodotion im Josuabuch, Mit einem Beitrag zu den Josuarollen von Ḫirbet Qumrān* (Biblische Notizen Beiheft 7; München, 1994) 85–93.

THIS manuscript preserves portions of Josh 2:11-12 and 3:15–4:3 on frgs. 1–3 and Josh 17:1-5, 11-15 on frgs. 4–5; the text on frg. 6 cannot be identified. Frgs. 1–3 are medium brown, and frgs. 4–6 are light brown with large patches of leather peeled off, showing the lower layer. There are slight signs of horizontal and vertical dry ruling on frgs. 1 and 2. Frg. 4 shows shrinkage and is darkened at the right edges. Cross in unpublished notes describes the hand as late Hasmonaean and thus dates the manuscript to the middle of the first century BCE.

The preserved sections are too fragmentary to provide complete measurements, but some details can be reported. A complete top margin on frg. 5 measures 1.6 cm, while incomplete top margins are preserved on frg. 1 (measuring 0.9 cm), frg. 2 (0.6 cm), and frg. 6 (1.3 cm). Frg. 2 preserves a right margin of 1.5 cm, which may have constituted the beginning of a sheet. Frg. 5, with a left margin of *c*.1.2 cm, is the end of a sheet, for it contains signs of stitching. Between the two columns of frg. 6 there is a margin of 1.5 cm.

The distance between lines of script is 0.7–0.8 cm on frgs. 1–3, but 0.5–0.6 cm on frgs. 4–6, and the length of lines on frg. 2 is reconstructed to be 8.7–9.2 cm, but on frg. 5, 7.5–8.0 cm (see Table 1).

TABLE 1: *Length of Lines*

Frg., line	Extant	Reconstructed	Total
2 2	5.3 cm	3.4 cm	8.7 cm
2 3	5.0 cm	4.2 cm	9.2 cm
5 5	5.5 cm	2.0 cm	7.5 cm
5 7	5.5 cm	2.5 cm	8.0 cm

Frgs. 4 and 5 come from tops of adjacent columns, and given the intervening text of 𝔐, the columns in this portion of the scroll are estimated to have contained 16 lines, with an inscribed height of 8.0 cm and, with the inclusion of top and bottom margins, a total height of 12.0–12.5 cm. Frgs. 1–3, written with a greater distance between the lines, then, probably come from columns of 11 lines (see NOTES to frgs. 1 and 4). All the fragments, however, have been written by the same scribe, and they probably belong to the same scroll. If this assumption and the preceding calculations are correct, the scroll would be relatively long because it has shorter columns than most of the other Qumran scrolls.

This text reflects the same orthography as 𝔐. The *plene* spelling of נתתה in 17:14, which reflects the majority spelling also elsewhere in 𝔐, further underlines the close connection with 𝔐.

Supralinear insertions occur in three places: חטים 2 2, יהוש]ע 2 6, and *he* of ובׄ[נתׄ]ה 5 1. On frgs. 2–3 the insertions are probably *secunda manu*.

The text of 4QJosh^b agrees usually with 𝔐 against 𝔊 (see especially frgs. 4–5). At the same time 4QJosh^b agrees twice with 𝔊: the omission of מזה in 4:3 and the supralinear addition of חטים in 3:15. Of significance is the agreement of the reconstructed text of 4QJosh^b with 𝔊 in 4:1-3, but since it goes against the general character of the scroll, it is very tentative.

4QJosh^b contains several readings not known from other sources: בימי in 3:15, אשר כׄה in 17:14, the sequence of elements in 17:11, הנפות in 17:11 and probably also ותאמ]רׄ] in 2:12. Likewise, the text of frg. 2 6 differs from that of 𝔐 and 𝔊, but its reconstruction remains dubious. See further 17:13 הורישהו (הורישו 𝔐).

In the following, the siglum 𝔊* denotes the unrevised text of 𝔊 (usually 𝔊^B). In the VARIANTS, if 𝔊* disagrees with 𝔐, then it is assumed that some 𝔊^{mss} agree with 𝔐.

Mus. Inv. 392. PAM 42.274, 43.061 (41.302).

Frg. 1 Josh 2:11-12

top margin

1 [לסיחון ולעוג אשר החרמתם אותם 11 ונשמע וימס לבבנו ו]לאׄ קמה עוד רוח באיש

2 [מפניכם כי יהוה אלהיכם הוא אלהים בשמים ממעל ועל הארץ מתחת 12 ותאמ]רׄ השבעו

Both frgs. 1 and 2 preserve the top margin of a column. It is difficult, however, to calculate the distance between these two fragments in the scroll. Between frg. 1 1 (2:10) and frg. 2 1 (3:15) 32 lines of *c.*67 letter-spaces (excluding intervals) are reconstructed, based on the width of line 2 of frg. 1 and the text of 𝔐. The height of the scroll is estimated to be 12–12.5 cm (see the 4QJosh^b introduction and NOTE on frg. 4). According to these calculations three columns would have intervened between the top margin of frg. 1 and that of frg. 2.

VARIANTS

2:11 (1) באיש 𝔐] + ὑμῶν 𝔊* (= S)

2:12 (2) ותאמ]רׄ] ועתה 𝔐𝔊. The remnant of the first preserved letter on this line appears to be *reš*, certainly not *he* as required by 𝔐. For the reconstruction cf. Gen 25:33, 47:31; Judg 15:12; 1 Sam 30:15.

Frgs. 2–3 Josh 3:15–4:3

top margin

1 נשאי הארון נטבלו בק֯צׄ[ה המי]ׄם וׄהׄ[ירדן]

חטים
2 בימי קציר ^{16}ויעמדו המים הירדים מלׄ[מעלה]

3 מאד<מׄ֯א[ד]>מׄאדם העיר אשׄר מצד צ[רתן]

4 (17) [י]ׄם המלח תמו נכרת[ו]

5 [בר]ית יהוה ב[חרבה]

יהוש[ע
6 (4:1) [ ]תׄ[מו]

7 (2) [ ]אׄל יהוש[ע]

8 (8) [ ]לכם מתוך הׄ[ירדן]

9 [ע]מׄכם והנ[ח]תׄם אׄ[ותם]

L. 1 (3:15) The final *mem* of ׄם[המי] is only partially preserved, and it is not a perfect example of that letter, which is usually closed. But the position of the remnants of ink points to a final rather than a medial *mem*, since the two marks are too close together to be a medial *mem*. Alternatively the marks could be the bottoms of *mem* and *yod*, which could be reconstructed as [...בק֯צׄ[ה מי]מׄיׄ הׄ[ירדן והירדן as in 𝔊 (cf. τοῦ ὕδατος τοῦ Ἰορδάνου. ὁ δὲ Ἰορδάνης...𝔊). However, such a reading would yield too long a line if the remainder of the reconstruction is correct.

L. 2 (3:15-16) חטים has been inserted supralinearly, possibly by a different hand (note the *ḥet* and *mem* and the different shade of ink).

L. 3 (3:16) There is no certainty regarding מאד<מׄ֯א[ד]>מׄאדם at the beginning of this line. After the first word, *mem* and *ʾalep* have been erased, probably by the original scribe who recognized the dittography (duplicating either the preceding or the next word, completely or partially). What is now a hole just before מׄאדם may have been inscribed with a *dalet*, which may have been subsequently erased, creating the hole in the leather, in other words: מאד<מׄ֯א[ד]>מׄאדם. Alternatively, the space which is now the hole may have been uninscribed, and the first letter of the next word, which looks like a final *mem* but differs in shape from the final *mem* of the same word and of other words, may have been reshaped from another letter (*bet*?). Note that the letter lacks the tick on the left top and that it is larger than the final *mem* of the same word and of other instances of *mem* on the same fragment. However, because of the *ketib/qere* variation here and the text of 𝔊 (see VAR.), other explanations are possible as well. For example, it is possible that the first letter of מׄאדם had a double function. Initially, perhaps it belonged to מׄ֯א[ד]ׄם, which was repeated by way of dittography. But then that word was partially erased. Possibly the scribe, who realized that the erasing of one letter created a hole, did not wish to create another hole, and hence left the final letter unchanged, reusing it as the first letter of the next word (מׄאדם), even though the use of final letters in non-final positions is very rare.

L. 6 (3:17) [יהוש[ע is written in small letters and its position relative to line 5 and the letter below it suggests that it is written as a supralinear insertion to line 6. The additions both here and in line 2 were added *secunda manu* (note the different *waw* and the different shade of ink). The remnant of *taw* under the *yod* is the proper distance from the letters of line 5 to be on line 6, as is reflected in the reconstruction. Alternatively, if that remnant is taken as the second line of the addition, there would be no room in the reconstruction for the end of 3:17. For the addition of יהושע, cf. 4:10 𝔐 and 4:5, where 𝔐 adds יהושע, which is lacking in 𝔊.

L. 7–9 (4:1-3) The reconstruction of the text for these lines is problematic. Frgs. 2 and 3 must belong to the same column because frg. 2 preserves a top margin, the text on frg. 3 follows immediately that on frg. 2, and the column with frg. 2 would have only 6 lines if frg. 3 were on the next column (note that frg. 5 contains at least 10 lines). The length of the lines in frg. 2 is consistently *c*.50 letter-spaces (the fact that frg. 1 has lines of a different length is irrelevant, since it belonged to a different column). Accordingly a reconstruction primarily based on 𝔊 seems best (see below).

RECONSTRUCTION OF FRG. 2

top margin

1 נשאי הארון נטבלו בקׄצ̊[ה המי]ם̇ ו̊ה̇[ירדן מלא על כל גדותיו]

חטים

2 בימי קציר [16]ויעמדו המים הירדים מל̊[מעלה קמו נד אחד הרחק]

3 מאד<מ̇א̊[ד]>מ̇אדם העיר אשׁר מצד צ̇[רתן והירדים על ים הערבה]

4 [י]ם̇ המלח תמו נכרת[ו והעם עברו נגד יריחו [17]ויעמדו הכהנים נשאי]

5 [הארון בר]ית יהוה ב[חרבה בתוך הירדן הכן וכל ישראל עברים]

יהוש]ע

6 [בחרבה עד אשר]ת̇[מו וכל הגוי לעבר את הירדן [4:1]ויהי כאשר תמו]

RECONSTRUCTION OF FRG. 3 ACCORDING TO 𝔐

7 [כל הגוי לעבור את הירדן ויאמר יהוה] א̇ל יהוש[ע לאמר [2]קחו לכם מן העם שנים עשר אנשים איש]

8 [אחד איש אחד משבט [3]וצוו אותם לאמר שאו]ל̇כם מתוך ה̇[ירדן ממצב רגלי הכהנים]

9 [הכין שתים עשרה אבנים והעברתם אותם ע]מ̇כם והנ̇[ח]ת̊ם א̇[ותם במלון אשר תלינו]

This reconstruction of lines 7–9, based on 𝔐, seems impossible, because frgs. 2 and 3 must belong to the same column, but the lines of frg. 3 are noticeably longer that those of frg. 2, while on frg. 3 line 7 would be yet much longer than lines 8–9. In this reconstruction, as in the next, the beginning of 4:1 would be in line 6.

RECONSTRUCTION OF FRG. 3 ACCORDING TO 𝔊

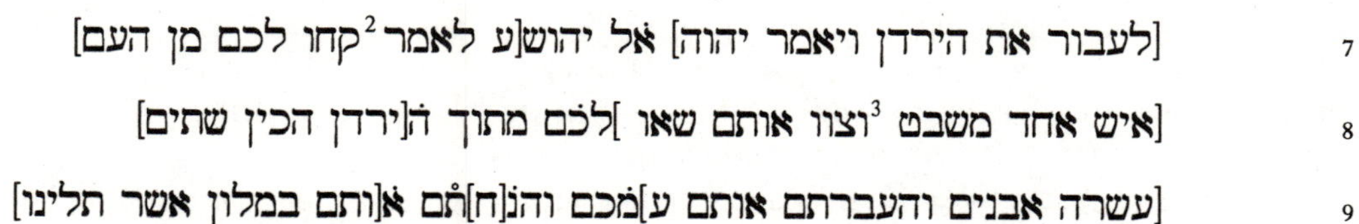

7 [לעבור את הירדן ויאמר יהוה] א̇ל יהוש[ע לאמר [2]קחו לכם מן העם]

8 [איש אחד משבט [3]וצוו אותם שאו]ל̇כם מתוך ה̇[ירדן הכין שתים]

9 [עשרה אבנים והעברתם אותם ע]מ̇כם והנ̇[ח]ת̊ם א̇[ותם במלון אשר תלינו]

Reconstructing lines 7–9 according to the shorter text of 𝔊 (with two additional minuses) is legitimate, even though as a rule 4QJosh[b] agrees with 𝔐 against 𝔊, and even though frg. 2 contains only one reading which is significantly close to 𝔊 (the supralinear חטים). This reconstruction seems to be the best one, since the lines are similar in length to those in frg. 2.

This reconstruction does not include the following elements of 𝔐:

4:1 כל הגוי (not reconstructed here, although it could have appeared supralinearly in either line 6 or 7, or like 3:17 it may not have been present);

4:2 שנים עשר אנשים;

4:2 איש אחד (one of the two occurrences of this phrase, creating a text like 𝔐 of Deut 1:23);

4:3 לאמר (extant in 𝔊);

4:3 ממצב רגלי הכהנים.

VARIANTS

3:15 (1) הארון 𝔐] τὴν κιβωτὸν τῆς διαθήκης κυρίου 𝔊*

3:15 (1) ה̇מי[ם̇] 𝔐] τοῦ ὕδατος τοῦ Ἰορδάνου 𝔊* (see NOTE)

3:15 (2) בימי] כל ימי 𝔐; ὡσεὶ ἡμέραι 𝔊* (= כימי?)

3:15 (2^{sup}) חטים 𝔊*(πυρῶν)] > 𝔐 (see NOTE; cf. the paraphrase in 4Q**379** [4QapocrJosh[b]] frg. 12 7; cf also Gen 30:14, Judg 15:1, 2 Sam 24:15 𝔊, and Judith 8:2)

3:16 (3) מׄאדם<מׄא̊[ד]> $𝔐^{q}$(מאדם)ℭSטּ] באדם 𝔐; σφοδρῶς 𝔊*(= מאד or במאד; see NOTE). To seek a connection between what was written in 4QJosh[b] and the textual corruption evident in 𝔐 and 𝔊 (באדם/מאדם 𝔐, [ב]מאד 𝔊) would be merely speculative. The first word in all witnesses is מאד; the second word is באדם/מאדם in 𝔐, מׄאדם in 4QJosh[b], and מאד* again in 𝔊. 4QJosh[b], however, has a third element, the word or letters which have been erased; but that word or those letters cannot be taken as a base for the second word in 𝔊, since it is an addition to the other two elements. For the same reason neither can what was written in 4QJosh[b] be connected with the *ketib/qere* variation of 𝔐.

The witnesses for the whole context are as follows (see NOTES):

]	[הרחק] מאד<מׄא̊[ד]>מׄאדם העיר אשׁר מצד צ[רתן]
$𝔐^{k}$	הרחק מאד באדם העיר אשר מצד צרתן
$𝔐^{q}$	הרחק מאד מאדם העיר אשר מצד צרתן
$𝔊^{B}$	הרחק* מאד מאד עד צד צרתן

3:16 (3) העיר 𝔐] ἕως 𝔊 (= עד?). The fact that this construction is not possible in Hebrew is irrelevant for the discussion. An alternative explanation of the Greek evidence would be that it lacks the phrase העיר אשר as a whole, and that ἕως μέρους reflects מצד.

3:16 (3) אשׁר 𝔐] > 𝔊*

3:16 (3) מצד 𝔐] (ἕως) μέρους 𝔊*; the equivalence is not certain; see above on העיר.

3:16 (3) צ[רתן] 𝔐] Καριαθιαρ(ε)ιμ $𝔊^{AFMNrell}$; Καθιαιρειν $𝔊^{B}$. Since only the first letter of the word of 4QJosh[b] has been preserved, the exact reconstruction of 𝔊 is less relevant, but it seems that 𝔊 reflects a *qop* instead of the *ṣade* of 4QJosh[b]𝔐.

3:16 (3) [והירדים] 𝔐] +κατέβη 𝔊*. 4QJosh[b] could have had here an additional word, like 𝔊 (ירדו according to Margolis).

3:16 (4) תמו 𝔐] εἰς τὸ τέλος 𝔊 (cf similar translations in 8:24, 10:20)

3:17 (6^{sup}) יהוש[ע]] > 𝔐𝔊. Since line 7 contains part of Josh 4:1, line 6 must have contained the beginning of 4:1 preceded by the end of 3:17, which began in line 4. Even though the reconstruction of line 6 remains dubious, the minimal conclusion is that the text of this MS differed from that of both 𝔐 and 𝔊. In line 6 יהוש[ע] is a supralinear insertion above ת̇[מו], implying that the text read [יהוש[ע וכל הגוי, not known from any of the textual witnesses. Alternatively, the added phrase may have belonged to a long addition, which may be reconstructed as [ככל אשר צוה משה א]ת̇ יהוש[ע], cf. 4:10 𝔐 (against 𝔊) in a similar context. In that case, however, it is not clear why [א]ת̇ should be written on the line, and יהוש[ע] above it (see NOTE for a third possibility).

4:1 (6–7) [ויהי כאשר תמו (כל הגוי) לעבור את הירדן] 𝔐𝔊] > $𝔊^{bjkl*na_2}$ (probably due to homoioteleuton)

4:3 (8) ל̇כם 𝔊*] +מזה 𝔐

Frg. 4 Josh 17:1-5

top margin

1 [הגורל למטה מנשה כי הוא בכ]ור יוסף֯[ל]מ֯כ֯י֯[ר בכור מנשה אבי הגלעד כי]

2 [הוא היה איש מלחמה] ו֯י֯הי לו ה֯[ג]ל֯עד֯[והבשן [2] ויהי לבני מנשה הנותרים]

3 [למשפחתם לבני]א֯ב֯יעזר֯ ול֯[בני] חל֯[ק ולבני אשריאל ולבני שכם ולבני חפר]

4 [ולבני שמיד]ע֯ אלה בני מ֯נ֯ש֯[ה בן יוסף הזכרים למשפחתם [3] ולצלפחד]

5 [בן חפר בן]ג֯ל֯ע֯ד֯ בן מ֯כ֯[יר בן מנשה לא היו לו בנים כי אם]

6 [בנות ואלה]ש֯מ֯ו֯ת בנתיו מ֯ח֯[לה ונעה חגלה מלכה ותרצה [4] ותקרבנה]

7 [לפני אלעז]ר֯ הכהן ולפני יהו֯[שע בן נון ולפני הנשיאים לאמר יהוה צוה את]

8 [משה לתת לנו נ]חלה [ב]תוך א֯[חינו ויתן להם אל פי יהוה נחלה בתוך אחי]

9 [אביהן [5] ויפ]ל֯[ו]ח֯ב֯[לי מנשה עשרה לבד מארץ הגלעד והבשן אשר מעבר]

The top margins of frg. 4 and frg. 5 have been preserved. Reconstruction of the text according to 𝔐 would require seven lines beyond the last preserved line, yielding sixteen lines for this column.

VARIANTS

17:1 (2) ו֯י֯הי לו ה֯[ג]ל֯עד֯] 𝔐] ἐν τῇ Γαλααδείτιδι καὶ ἐν τῇ Βασανείτιδι 𝔊

17:2 (4) בני מ֯נ֯ש֯[ה בן יוסף] 𝔐] > 𝔊*α′

17:3 (5) [בן]ג֯ל֯ע֯ד֯ בן מ֯כ֯[יר בן מנשה] 𝔐] > 𝔊*

17:3 (6) בנתיו 𝔐] τῶν θυγατέρων (υἱῶν $𝔊^{dp*t}$) Σαλπααδ 𝔊*

17:4 (7) [בן נון] 𝔐] > 𝔊*

Frg. 5 Josh 17:11-15

top margin

י]ה֯

1] [*vacat* וי֯שב ע[ין] דאר וב֯[נת]

2 [ויבלעם ובנותיה ו]את[ישבי ד]ר ו֯בנתיה וישב֯[י ת]ע֯נך

3 [ובנתיה וישבי מגד]ו֯ ובנותי[ה]של֯ש֯ת הנ֯פות [[12] ול]א֯ י֯[כלו]

4 [בני מנשה להוריש]את הערים האלה ויואל הכנעני לשב[ת]

5 [בארץ הזאת 13וי]הי כי חזקו בני ישראל ויתנו את הכנענ[י]

6 [למס והורש לא]הורישהו *vacat*

7 [14וידברו בני יו]סף אל י[ה]ושע לאמר מדוע נתתה ל[י] נחל[ה]

8 [גורל אחד וחבל אח]ד ואני עם רב אשר כה ברכני יהוה

9 [15ויאמר אליהם יה]ושע אם ע[ם רב]א[תה]עלה לך היערה

10 [ובראת לך שם בארץ]הפ[רזי והרפאים כי] אץ לך הר א[פרי]ם

L. 1 (17:11) There is an interval within verse 11; no interval 𝔐.
L. 6 (17:13) There is a long interval after verse 13; ס 𝔐^{A, L} .

VARIANTS

17:11 (1) וישב ע[ין] דאר וב[נת]ה] > 𝔊. This phrase represents עין דר of 𝔐 occurring later in the verse. The doublet of 𝔐 דאר / עין דר is not represented in 𝔊 (see below), and there probably is a connection between this doublet and the different sequence in 4QJosh^b.

17:11 (2) [ויבלעם ובנותיה] 𝔐] > 𝔊*

17:11 (2) ו[את] ישבי ד]ר ובנתיה 𝔐 (ואת ישבי דאר ובנותיה)] > 𝔊*

17:11 (2–3) [ובנתיה] וישב[י ת]ענך 𝔐 (and Judg 1:27)] > 𝔊^{B, mss}; added in 𝔊^{A, mss} after Megiddo

The sequence of the different elements is thus as follows:

𝔐	4QJosh^b	𝔊*
—	וישב ע[ין] דאר וב[נת]ה	—
ויבלעם ובנותיה	[ויבלעם ובנותיה]	—
ואת ישבי דאר ובנותיה	ו[את] ישבי ד]ר ובנתיה	=
וישבי עין דר ובנתיה	—	—
וישבי תענך	וישב[י ת]ענך	—

17:11 (3) שלשת 𝔐 (שְׁלֹשֶׁת)] καὶ τὸ τρίτον 𝔊 [= (ו)שְׁלִשַׁת?]

17:11 (3) הנפות] הַנָּפֶת 𝔐; τῆς Μαφετα (𝔊^{B,mss}) / τῆς Ναφετα (𝔊^{A,mss}) καὶ τὰς κώμας αὐτῆς 𝔊 (the Greek translator took הנפות as the name of a town). For the plural form of 4QJosh^b, cf. 𝔐 in 11:2 ובנפות דור, and see further G. Dahl, 'The Three Heights of Josh. 17.11', *JBL* 53 (1934) 381–3.

17:13 (6) הורישהו] הורישו 𝔐. Note the singular form of the suffix in both texts which is not impossible in biblical Hebrew, but it would suit better the parallel verse Judg 1:28, where the subject is ישראל.

17:14 (7) אל 𝔐^{mss}] את 𝔐

17:14 (8) אשר כה] עד אשר עד כה 𝔐. For the phrase of 𝔐 (doublet?) 𝔊𝔙 have merely καὶ /*et*; ℭ has a shortened version for אשר עד כה, viz., לסגי; like 4QJosh^b, 𝔐^{mss} omit עד 1°; 𝔐^{mss} and 𝔖 omit עד 2°.

17:14 (8) יהוה 𝔐] ὁ θεός 𝔊

17:15 (10) [שם בארץ]הפ[רזי והרפאים] 𝔐] > 𝔊*

Frg. 6 col. i

top margin

◦◦◦[1

ה̣◦[2

◦[3

◦ ◦[4

◦[5

The text of this fragment cannot be identified. There is no certainty that this fragment belongs to the same scroll as frgs. 1–5. The decay pattern of the letters differs from that of the other fragments. The ink has left white traces for the center of the lines, with only the borders remaining black.

Frg. 6 col. ii (5:4f.?)

top margin

אר̊ץ̊] 1

צ̊◦] 2

◦◦] 3

◦] 4

49. 4QJudg[a]

(PLATE XXXVI)

Preliminary publication: J. Trebolle Barrera, 'Textual Variants in *4QJudg[a]* and the Textual and Editorial History of the Book of Judges', *RevQ* 54 (1989) 229–45.

THE SOLITARY fragment preserved from 4QJudg[a], consisting of two contiguous pieces, contains portions of Judg 6:2-13. The leather of the manuscript is light brown with some darkening and it has suffered wrinkling from the top left side to the bottom right. The leather, 0.4 mm thick, measures 7.6 cm high and 4.8 cm wide. It is inscribed on the hair side as usual, and the back is also smooth and well-prepared. The surface is nearly worn away at the central portion of lines 1–3 and at the beginning of line 7. Traces of stitching can be observed at the lower right margin of the fragment, where a right margin of 1.1 cm and a bottom margin of 1.8 cm occur. A vertical ruling at the right margin is faintly discernible, although no traces of horizontal dry lines are visible. The distance between lines varies from 6 to 7 mm, and the height of the letters is 2 mm. The number of letters per line determined by reconstruction according to 𝔐 ranges between 59 and 65 letters per line. The space between words normally corresponds to the width of the letter *waw*.

The script is a late Hasmonaean or early Herodian book hand from *c*.50–25 BCE.

א. *ʾAlep* is the same size as the other letters, and made in three movements. The supralinear *ʾalep* in line 9 perhaps could have been made in two movements in the inverted-'v' form typical of the beginning of the Herodian period.

ב. *Bet* is generally penned in two movements. The base is a separate, left-to-right stroke. In line 4 the two forms of the *bet* typical of the late Hasmonaean or early Herodian formal hand (4QSam[a]) are found: in ארבה the base of the *bet* is made from right to left without lifting the pen; in לרב it is made in two strokes. In line 9 the base of the *bet* is a double stroke (from right to left and back) which is an uncommon trait.

ג. The left leg of *gimel* joins above the middle of the right leg.

ד\ר. The head of the *dalet* is well marked, distinct from that of the *reš*. The *reš* sometimes has a very distinct rounded head, as in line 6; in line 4, however, its head is more similar to that of the *dalet*.

ה\ח. The *he* is made in two movements. In ארבה line 4, יהוה line 5, אלהים line 8, the crossbar is a double stroke. The *ḥet* is probably penned in two movements in the two instances which occur in line 2, while in מחיה line 3 it is probably made in three movements.

ו\י. *Waw* and *yod* are very similar when one follows the other; otherwise their heads are different as in יהוה line 5. The *yod* of כי in line 3 has an inverted-'v' shape, while the older form of *yod* is preserved in line 5, and in עזרי- line 6 the *yod* is almost a triangle.

כ. *Kap* is long and narrow, in archaic fashion. The head of final *kap* is deep and well marked.

ל. *Lamed* is formed with a small loop in the arm, except perhaps for the *lamed* in the supralinear בישראל in line 3.

ם. Final *mem* is elongated and closed.

ן. Final *nun* is rather long and very vaulted, unlike that in 4QDeut[c], showing the facility of the copyist with the pen.

ס. The *samek* of שספרו in line 9 is square, very large, and fully closed, with the left leg looping into the crossbar in a shape very much like that of the early Herodian script.

ע. The examples of *ʿayin* in lines 1, 5, and 6 are very small, and they have a short and curved tail; the instance in גדעון in line 8 is an exception. The intersection of the two strokes is found almost at the bottom of the letter, which is a sign of archaism that makes it closer to the typical Hasmonaean script than to the early Herodian, in which the right arm is lengthened. Of the two forms of *ʿayin* found in 4QSam[a] (see Cross, p.138, Fig. 2 Line 3), the second is closer to that of 4QJudg[a].

פ. The head of *pe* is rather round, not yet the later triangular shape.

ק. The head of *qop* in line 2 is slightly open, in line 5 closed.

The manuscript preserves two orthographic differences from 𝔐:

Frg. 1 2 (6:4) וישחתו] וישחיתו 𝔐; orth.? (cf. *Hipʿil* להשחִתו 2 Kgs 18:25; ותשחִתו Ezek 16:47; ישחִת Prov 11:9; וישחִתו 2 Sam 11:1), or morph. var.? (cf. *Piʿel* לשחתה 𝔐 in v 5; לשחתה 𝔐, להשחיתה ш Gen 19:13; בשחת 𝔐, בהשחית ш Gen 19:29).

Frg. 1 9 (6:13) אבתינו] אבותינו 𝔐.

Two supralinear corrections, apparently by the original scribe, are preserved: בישראל in line 3, and *ʾalep* in line 9 correcting the word למר to לאמר.

This fragment represents a form of the text independent from any other known text-type, although it shares readings with the proto-Lucianic text. It is the only extant witness which does not include the literary insertion found in vv 7-10 of 𝔐𝔊, although 𝔐[mss] and the 𝔊[B] text also omit v 7a. Verses 8-10 have been generally recognized by modern critics as a literary insertion, attributed in the past to an Elohistic source (G. F. Moore, *ICC*, 1895) and now generally considered (e.g. Wellhausen, Gray, Bodine, Soggin) a piece of late Dtr. redaction. 4QJudg[a] can confidently be seen as an earlier literary form of the book than our traditional texts. For more detailed discussion of its textual character and its relationship to 𝔐, 𝔊[L], 𝔊[B], and the Old Latin, see the preliminary publication in *RevQ*.

Mus. Inv. 305. PAM 43.059.

Frg. 1 Judg 6:2-6, 11-13

Line	Text	Letters
1	[אשר]בׄהׄרים ואׄתׄ הׄמערות ואת[המצדות 3והיה אם זרע ישראל ועלה מדין ועמלק]	65
2	ובני קדם 4ויחנו על[י]הם וישחתו[את יבול הארץ עד בואך עזה ולא ישאירו]	63
	בישראל	
3	מחיה שה שור וח[מו]ר 5כי הם [ומקניהם יעלו ואהליהם וגמליהם יבאו כדי]	60
4	אׄרבה לרב ולהם אׄ[ין מספר וי]באו בא[רץ לשחתה 6וידל ישראל מאד מפני]	59
5	[מדין]ויׄזעקו בני יש[ראל אל] יהוה[11ויבא מלאך יהוה וישב תחת האלה אשר]	62
6	[בעפרה]אשר ליואש האביעזרי וג[דעון בנו חבט חטים בגת להניס מפני מדין]	64
7	[12ויר]אׄ אליו מלאך יהוה ויאמר[אליו יהוה עמך גבור החיל 13ויאמר אליו]	60
8	גדעון בי אדני ויש אלהים[עמנו ולמה מצאתנו כל זאת ואיה כל נפלאתיו]	63
	א	
9	שספרו לנו אבתינו למׄר[ ]	

bottom margin

Right and bottom margins are extant, with evidence of stitching observable in the bottom right corner.

L. 1 (6:2) The final *mem* of בהרים is complete. The *yod* to its right is certain, as is also the base of a letter like *bet*, with a trace of a ligatured letter (*he*). Enough ink remains to be confident of *reš*. Most of the vertical stroke of the *waw* of ואת remains, followed by the bottom of the right stroke of the *ʾalep*, and the bottom tips of the *taw*.

L. 1 (6:2) Of המערות, the lower portion of the right vertical stroke of the *he* is preserved. The following letters are certain although only partially preserved: traces of the base and left stroke of the *mem* are visible; the bottom of the *ʿayin* is ligatured with the *reš*. At the end of the line the traces of the *ʾalep* in ואת are faint but clear, and the lower portions of the two legs of the *taw* are visible.

L. 2 (6:3-4) On the edge of the leather traces of the head and bottom of the *waw* of ובני are extant. The surface of the leather where על[י]הם was inscribed is partly lost, but the upper part of *ʿayin* and the top of *lamed* are visible, while the top left portion of a *he* is virtually certain. At the end of the line the head of the final *waw* of וישחתו is preserved.

L. 3 (6:4-5) בישראל has been written supralinearly, apparently by the original scribe. Ink traces from the head and right leg of the *ḥet* of וח[מו]ר are visible before the damaged spot, and following it *reš* is certain, with the space between them large enough for *mem* and *waw* to be reconstructed. The head of the final *mem* of הם is preserved.

L. 3 (6:5) [וגמליהם]. Spatial reconstruction suggests that this MS included וגמליהם (understanding the following word as יָבֹאוּ, but note ובאו 𝔐^{q, mss}) in agreement with 𝔊^L La(Lucifer), but against 𝔐𝔊^{AGabckx} La(Lugdunensis) θ′ Arm Eth and 𝔊^B which do not include it. For יָבֹאוּ, note παρέφερον 𝔊^{LA+} + ἦγον 𝔊^L, *adferebant* La Luc + *ducebant* Luc (against παρεγίνοντο 𝔊^B).

L. 4 (6:5) The top left portion of the *ʾalep* of ארבה is preserved. Before the break the remains of the *ʾalep* of א[ין are preserved. The break in the leather is about 9–10 letter-spaces wide, and after it the left part of the *bet* of וי[באו is preserved (see VAR.). The damaged letters of בא[רץ at the edge of the fragment are the traces of the base, head, and vertical stroke of *bet* and the bottom of the oblique stroke of *ʾalep*.

L. 5 (6:6) Of ויזעקו, a minimal trace of the initial *waw* remains visible at the edge, but the top portions of *yod* and *zayin* and an identifiable part of *ʿayin* are certainly preserved. The break in the leather has destroyed about 6 letter-spaces.

L. 5–6 (6:6, 11) The text of 6:6 followed in the next line by that of 6:11 on the same piece of leather shows that vv 7-10 were not part of this MS; 4QJudg^a bears witness to a shorter, earlier text than that of 𝔐 (see VAR.), where the added text, generally agreed to be a literary insertion in Deuteronomistic (?) phraseology and concepts, is signalled by intervals (פ) before and after.

L. 6 (6:11) Of the *gimel* in וג[דעון only the right stroke is extant at the end of the line.

L. 7 (6:12) While the surface is partly worn away, the ink on the edge of the fragment could well belong to the *ʾalep* of ויר[א. Enough ink remains to identify the oblique and left strokes of the *ʾalep* of אליו, and despite wrinkling, traces of the top and bottom of the *lamed* are visible, as well as the triangular head of the *yod*. Although damaged by the wrinkling, the *mem* of מלאך is fully preserved.

L. 8 (6:13) The head of the *yod* in ויש is damaged, and the *šin* is faint but certain. At the end of the line, a trace of the characteristic head of the final *mem* of אלהים is preserved.

L. 9 (6:13) At the edge of the leather the ink trace may belong to the *reš* of ל^אמר, the *ʾalep* of which has been written supralinearly.

VARIANTS

6:3 (2) קדם] + ועלו עליו 𝔐; συνανέβαινον αὐτοῖς 𝔊^B; καὶ ἀνέβαινον ἐπ' αὐτόν 𝔊^A La(Lugdunensis, Lucifer) Syh. Origen's Latin version (*In librum Iudicum* Homilia VII.2) omits ועלו 𝔐: (*adscendebant Madian et Amalec et filii Orientis*) *super eos.*

6:4 (3) שה שור] ושה ושור 𝔐

6:5 (4) ולהם א[ין] ולהם ולגמליהם אין 𝔐. 4QJudg^a lacks ולגמליהם (see NOTES on lines 3 and 4), as does La *quorum* (*quoniam* Lucifer) *non erat numerus* (Lugdunensis, Lucifer).

6:6 (5) יהוה]] + 6:7-10 𝔐𝔊𝔖𝔙 (+ 6:7b-10 𝔐Ken. 4, 187 𝔊B𝔖𝔙) (see NOTE)

6:11 (6) האביעזרי 𝔊Agnpt('Αβιεζρι)] אבי העזרי 𝔐𝔊B+(πατρὸς τοῦ Ἐσδρεί). The prehexaplaric reading 'Αβιεζρι, attested by the Antiochian MSS, seems closer to the Qumran reading.

6:13 (8) אלהים] יהוה 𝔐𝔊

6:13 (9) שספרו] אשר ספרו 𝔐, cf. Judg 6:17; 7:12; 8:26. This use of -ש is characteristic of Qumran texts between Late Biblical and Mishnaic Hebrew.

50. 4QJudg[b]

(PLATE XXXVI)

Preliminary publication: J. Trebolle Barrera, 'Édition préliminaire de 4QJuges[b]. Contribution des manuscrits qumrâniens des Juges à l'étude textuelle et littéraire du livre', *RevQ* 15 (1991) 79–100.

ONLY three fragments of 4QJudg[b] remain, with portions of Judg 19:5-7 and 21:12-25. The leather of the manuscript is brown, especially dark in the upper part of the fragments and reddish where the leather has been torn. The leather is very fine, 0.3 mm thick, but quite worn and wrinkled, and the back is well-prepared and smooth. Frg. 1 measures 2.2 cm high and 3.7 cm wide, frg. 2, 5.2 cm high and 2.8 cm wide, and frg. 3, 10.7 cm high and 14.3 cm wide. The bottom margin of frg. 3 is preserved, with blank space measuring 5.3 cm from the bottom of the final letters, which correspond to the end of the book of Judges, to the lowest edge preserved. Horizontal dry lines, from which the letters are suspended, are visible on frg. 1, lines 2 and 4, but they are no longer visible on frgs. 2–3, although they surely existed since the writing is quite rectilinear. A comparison of characteristic letters such as *ʾalep*, *yod*, *reš*, and *taw* confirms that frg. 1 belongs to the same manuscript as frgs. 2 and 3. Frgs. 2 and 3, although not contiguous, preserve parts of three lines, 5–7, in common. The distance between lines of script is 6–7 mm, and the height of the letters is 2–3 mm. Spaces between words normally correspond to the width of *waw*. Frg. 1 averages 50–53 letter-spaces per line, but in frgs. 2–3 the lines reconstructed according to 𝔐 are very irregular in length, and the last seven lines diminish in length progressively.

The carefully written script is an early Herodian formal hand, dated to *c.*30–1 BCE.

- א. Almost upright, *ʾalep* is made in three movements. The left leg does not touch the axis at the peak (1 2; 2 2, 4; 3 8, 11).
- ב\כ. *Bet* (3 8) is distinct from *kap* (2 3). The head of the *kap* is small and its base oblique, very distinct from that of *bet* which is more square.
- ד\ר. The difference between the two is well marked (*reš* 1 2; 2 2; 3 6, 13; no clear *dalet* occurs).
- ו\י. The head of the *waw* is very small (1 2, 3, 4; 2 2; 3 8, 11, 12), while that of the *yod* is a large triangle (1 3[bis], 4; 2 3, 7; 3 7, 8, 9, 11, 12).
- ה\ח. The horizontal stroke of the *he* (2 2, 3, 6; 3 8, 10, 11) is a double stroke, first to the left and then a return. The *ḥet* is made in three strokes: the right vertical stroke followed by the horizontal and the vertical left stroke (1 2; 3 10).
- מ. *Mem* is angular and square (2 4, 6; 3 12). Final *mem* is very elongated, and the stroke of its head is well marked (1 3, 4; 2 2).
- נ. *Nun* is very square and angular (1 2).
- ע. *ʿAyin* has the long, well-defined early Herodian, not the short Hasmonaean, form (2 1, 3).
- ץ. The head of final *ṣade* is very small but very angular and therefore well marked (2 1).
- ק. The head of *qop* is wide and open (1 4).
- ש. *Šin* is made in three movements (1 3; 2 3).
- ת. The left leg of *taw* is angular, made separately or by turning back (2 6).

Only one orthographic variant is preserved, בני[מי]ן 3 8, cf. בנימן 𝔐; in the two other occurrences of that word, 4QJudg[b] and 𝔐 agree on the short form, לבני[מ]ן 2 3, ◦בְּנְיָמִן 2 4.

No intervals are extant, but an interval possibly occurred at frg. 2 1 (after 21:12); ס 𝔐.

One or possibly two supralinear corrections are preserved. At frg. 1 4 a *bet* is added by the original hand above לך to change it to לבך. At frg. 2 4 the trace of a supralinear letter may remain above the first letter of ◦בׄנׄיׄמׄן (cf. 𝔐 מבנימן אשה).

Mus. Inv. 1123. PAM 43.059, 43.157.

Frg. 1 Judg 19:5-7

1 [ ]◦[ ]◦[ ]

2 [ויקם ללכת ויאמר אבי הנ]עׄרה אל חתנו סׄ[עד לבך פת לחם ואחר] 53

3 [תלכו [6]וישבו ויאכלו שני]הם יחדׄ[ו] וישתו ויׄ[אמר אבי הנערה] 50

4 [אל האיש הואל נא ולין וי]טֹב לך(ב) [7]ויקם האׄ[יש]

L. 2 (19:5) Traces of the left stroke of *ʿayin* in הנ]עׄרה and the upper part of *samek* in סׄ[עד are extant.

L. 3 (19:6) At יחדׄ[ו], the fragment now has a rectangular hole, but a piece of the surface, measuring *c*.5 mm, has flaked off and rotated, confusing the picture. On that piece the lower part of *waw* and the upper stroke of the supralinear *bet* in the next line are still visible, although covered by the leather of the main fragment. In ויׄ[אמר the lower portion of the *yod* remains at the left edge of the fragment.

L. 4 (19:6) A portion of the *lamed* in לׄ(ב)ך is extant.

Frgs. 2–3 Judg 21:12-25

1 (13) [ ]אׄרץ כׄנען[ ]

2 (14) [ ]קראו להם [ ]

3 (15,16) [ ]מׄן כי עשה יהׄ[ ]

4 (18) [ ]◦בׄנׄיׄמׄן (]◦[) [17]ויׄאמרו יׄרׄ[ ]

5 (19) f.3 [ ]◦[ ]הׄ חׄ[ ]יׄהוׄה בשׄ[ ]

6 (20) [ ]זרח הׄ[ ]ש [ ]הׄעׄלה מׄ[ ]ת אׄ[ ]

7 [ ]כׄ[ר]מׄיׄם[[21]]אׄ[ ]וׄהנה אׄם י[ ]

8 [ ]יׄ[ ]מׄי[[22]]וׄהיה[ ]יבאוׄ אבותׄיׄהׄ[ ]

9 [[23]]לׄק[ ]אׄש[ ]מׄלׄחׄמׄה כׄי[ ]

10 [ ]שׄאׄ[ ]שׄיׄ[ ]ם מהמחללׄ[ ]

11 [ ]נוׄ את [ ]ים וׄישׄבוׄ בׄהׄם [24]ויתהלכׄ[ ]

12 [ ]טׄו ולמשפחׄ[ ]צׄאוׄ מׄשׄ[ ] אישׄ[ ]

13 [[25]]הׄהׄם אׄי[ ]לׄך בׄישראׄ[ ]ש [ ]נׄיׄ[ ]יׄ[ ]

bottom margin

Reconstruction of Judg 21:12-25

1 [ויביאו אותם אל המחנה שלה אשר ב]ארץ כנען[*vacat* [13]וישלחו כל העדה וידברו]

2 [אל בני בנימן אשר בסלע רמון וי]קראו להם [שלום [14]וישב בנימן בעת ההיא ויתנו להם הנשים אשר חיו מנשי יבש גלעד] 96

3 [ולא מצאו להם כן [15]והעם נחם לבני]מן כי עשה יה[וה פרץ בשבטי ישראל [16]ויאמרו זקני העדה מה נעשה] 84

]◦[

4 [לנותרים לנשים כי נשמדה]◦בנימן [17]ויאמרו יר[שת פליטה לבנימן ולא ימחה שבט מישראל [18]ואנחנו לא נוכל לתת להם
נשים מבנותינו כי נשבעו בני ישראל לאמר ארור] 141

f.3 5 [נתן אשה לבנימן [19]ויאמרו הנ]ה ח[ג]יהוה בש[לו מימים ימימה אשר מצפונה] 61

6 [לבית אל מ]זרח ה[שמ]ש [למסלה]העלה מ[בי]ת א[ל שכמה ומנגב ללבונה [20]ויצו את בני בנימן לאמר] 77

7 [לכו וארבתם ב]כ[ר]מים[[21]ור]א[יתם]והנה אם י[צאו בנות שילו לחול במחלות ויצאתם מן הכרמים וחטפתם לכם איש אשתו מבנות] 102

8 [שילו והלכתם אר]ץ [בני]מי[ן [22]]והיה [כי] יבאו אבותיה[ם או אחיהם לרוב אלינו ואמרנו אליהם] 76

9 [חנונו אותם כי לא]לק[חנו איש] אש[תו ב]מלחמה כי[לא אתם נתתם להם כעת תאשמו] 66

10 [[23]ויעשו כן בני בנימן וי]שא[ו נ]שי[ם למספר]ם מהמחלל[ות אשר גזלו וילכו וישובו] 67

11 [אל נחלתם ויב]נו את [הער]ים וישבו בהם [24]ויתהלכ[ו משם בני ישראל בעת] 59

12 [ההיא איש לשב]טו ולמשפח[תו וי]צאו מש[ם] איש[לנחלתו] 44

13 [[25]בימים]ההם אי[ן מ]לך בישרא[ל אי]ש [הישר בע]ני[ו]י[עשה] 44

bottom margin

A bottom margin is preserved. The final words conclude the Book of Judges, and the distance from the bottoms of the final letters to the lowest edge is 5.3 cm. On the plate the distance between frgs. 2 and 3 appears to be greater than it was on the original. Since the leather is worn and wrinkled, when the two fragments are joined, the writing in lines 6 and 7 seems to be not quite rectilinear, as it is in the other lines. Therefore, it is impossible to establish with absolute accuracy the spatial relation between the two fragments. Furthermore, the reconstructed line-lengths vary widely between 61 and 102 letter-spaces. On frg. 3, lines 8 through 13 decrease gradually in length from 76 down to 44 letter-spaces. The irregularity in the number of characters per line may be explained by the fact that frgs. 2–3 belong to the last column of the book, where the copyist did not need to respect left and bottom margins; other reasons should also be considered. 4QJudg^b may not have had כי נשבעו בני ישראל לאמר ארור נתן אשה לבנימן (21:18b 𝔐) in lines 4–5, in so far as the clause was possibly an 'editorial repetition' of 21:1 (G. F. Moore, *ICC*, 450). The reading of the Greek text in v 18a, οτι 𝔊^B and και οτι 𝔊^{A,L} (𝔐 -ו), reflects the duplication of causal clauses . . . כי . . . כי. Line 4 would then have 94 letters, matching the average number of letters per line in lines 1–7.

The preserved readings of 4QJudg^b are very close to 𝔐. The reconstruction of its lines shows, however, that 4QJudg^b possibly knew a variant shorter text or presented a text arrangement different from that of 𝔐. The fragments of Judges from Cave 1 (1Q**6**) have similar problems in their relation to 𝔐 (cf. *DJD* I. 62–64, Pl. XI).

L. 1 (21:12) The *reš* of ב[א֯רץ is certain and most of the head and tail of final *ṣade* remains, but only a point of ink at the right edge of the leather is preserved from *ʾalep*. The *ʿayin* of כ֯נ֯ען is certain and the two ink traces before it could well be the lower extremities of *nun* and *kap*, while at the end of the line enough ink remains to be confident of final *nun*.

L. 2 (21:13) The tail of the *qop* of וי[קראו is preserved, and most of the final *mem* of להם remains.

L. 3 (21:15) The final *nun* of לבני[מ֯ן is damaged but certain, while on the edge of the leather the ink spot belongs to the head of *mem* and the thin stroke to its base. A wrinkle defaces the tops of the letters of כי and the *ʿayin* of עשה, but at the end of the line the *yod* of יה֯[וה is sure and the small dot on the torn edge corresponds to the head of *he*.

L. 4 (21:16-17) The last four letters of ו֯י֯אמרו are certain, although only the upper portion of the final *waw* is preserved. The traces to the left of ו֯י֯אמרו quite likely belong to the tops of *yod* and *reš* of י֯ר֯[שת. To the right of the *ʾalep* of ו֯י֯אמרו faint traces of *yod* and *waw* are visible. To the right of ו֯י֯אמרו, even though the surface of the leather is quite damaged, two traces of the top and bottom of the final *nun* of ◦ב֯נ֯י֯מ֯ן[are visible. Spatial reconstruction suggests that a faint trace to the right is possibly from the right side of *mem*, while an ink point above and another below may be from *yod* and *nun*. Another ink spot to the bottom right can correspond to the right tip of the base of *bet*, while the ink on the edge of the leather possibly corresponds to the left tip of the head of a *mem* that bends down. Finally, a supralinear ink trace above the word probably is from one of the letters of אשה (cf. מבנימן אשה 𝔐).

L. 5 (21:19) Part of the head and base of the *bet* in ב֯ש֯[לו is discernible, and the ink trace that follows can belong to the upper right part of *šin*. The letters of the tetragrammaton can be identified from left to right: the horizontal and right vertical strokes of *he*, a portion of the top of *waw*, the horizontal stroke and upper right angle of *he*, and the ink spot on the edge of the hole probably belongs to the upper left portion of *yod*. At the right edge of the line, higher and lower traces of ink correspond to the left portion of the *he* of ה֯[נ]ה, while to the left the ink spot below is probably the remainder of the right leg of the *ḥet* of ח֯[ג. On frg. 3, only a point of ink is preserved, which possibly belongs to one of the last letters of the word לבנימן.

L. 6 (21:19) On frg. 3 at the right edge of the line, the letters of מ[זרח are certain. To the left, the vertical trace may belong to the right stem of the *he* of ה֯[שמ]ש, but the space for word-division seems very narrow, and therefore a reading without the locative *he* or a haplography may be possible. The *šin* of ה֯[שמ]ש is partly preserved. On frg. 2, the *lamed* and *he* of ה֯ע֯לה[are certain; the ink stroke to the right is quite likely the remains of the upper right portion of *ʿayin*, and the horizontal stroke may correspond to the top portion of the intital *he*. After a space for word-division the vertical stem and base of the *mem* of מ֯[בי]ת are very likely, and after a lacuna of two middle-sized letters the *taw* is certain. Traces of the *ʾalep* of א֯[ל are identifiable, but it is impossible to determine if these letters formed one word or two (מבית אל or מביתאל).

L. 7 (21:20-21) At the right edge of frg. 3, tops of letters in ב[כ֯[ר]מ֯י֯ם are identifiable, while only traces of further letters are visible. On frg. 2 the *nun* of ו֯ה֯נה֯[alone is certain; the two traces to the right of *nun* belong to the head of *he*, and the next ink point may correspond to the top of *waw*; to the left of *nun* the right downstroke of the second *he* is visible. Ink traces are all that remain of א֯ם֯: the ink stroke on the left edge of the hole can be understood as the remains of *ʾalep*, and it is followed by a portion of the head and a point of the base of the final *mem*. At the end of the extant line, the *yod* of י[צאו is certain.

L. 8 (21:21-22) The trace at the beginning of the line belongs to the middle portion of a letter that, according to spatial reconstruction, could be the final *ṣade* of אר[ץ֯. The *yod* of בני[מ֯י֯ן, under the hole, is certain, and to its right the ink dot below probably corresponds to the base of *mem*. A trace of the *waw* is visible at the beginning of ו֯היה. The ink stroke before the *bet* and *ʾalep* of י֯באו֯ probably belongs to *yod*, and the vertical stroke after them corresponds to *waw*. After a space for word-division, the first three letters of אבות֯י֯ה֯[ם are certain; a horizontal ink trace is the only remaining portion of the left leg of *taw*, and the two small traces that follow correspond to the bottom of *yod* and the right leg of *he*.

L. 9 (21:22) The *yod* at the end of the line is certain, and to its right an ink trace visible on the leather could well be from the *kap* of כ֯י. Before it, the remains of the characteristic head and base of the second *mem* of ב[מ֯ל֯ח֯מ֯ה֯ are visible, followed by portions of the top right angle of a *he*, and preceded by the right leg of the *ḥet* and the characteristic head of the first *mem*. At the beginning of the line, ל֯[ק]חנו[is

preserved in the traces of the tail and head of *qop* and the base of the hook of *lamed*. Two ink traces in the middle of the line are the only remainders of the top and bottom right side of a possible *ʾalep* of אש]תו. To its left an oblique trace is the only remains of the right stroke of a *šin*.

L. 10 (21:23) At the left side of the fragment, the bottom of a *lamed* from מהמחלל̊[ות is certain, and an ink trace on the edge of the leather probably corresponds to the bottom of the second *lamed*. Enough ink remains of four other letters to be confident of the sequence -מהמח-: the *ḥet* is certain; to its right the head and base of the *mem* are extant; the horizontal and right vertical strokes of the *he* remain; and a trace of the base of a *mem* is still identifiable. The left vertical stroke and left top of the final *mem* of למספר[ם are also clearly visible. Spatial reconstruction allows the identification of some ink traces at the right side of the fragment as some of the letters of וי[שׂא]ו נ[שׁי̊ם.

L. 11 (21:23-24) Ink traces of the *waw* of ויב]נ̊ו remain on the right edge of the leather, and under that *waw* the bottom of a *nun* remains ligatured. The following את is clear. To the left of the hole traces of the *yod* and the almost complete final *mem* of הער[ים are preserved. The *yod* of וי̊שׁב̊ו is certain, and an ink dot to its right very probably belongs to the initial *waw*; spatial reconstruction permits identifying the minimal ink traces as the remainder of this word. The base of the final *mem* of ב̊ה̊ם is clear, with the first two letters being mere traces. The first five letters of ויתהלכ̊]ו are certain, although only the bottom part of *lamed* is preserved; the vertical stroke of the *kap* is extant on the edge of the leather.

L. 12 (21:24) At the right edge of the fragment the left stem of *ṭet* and the top of *waw* in the word לשב]ט̊ו are preserved. The first four letters of the next word, ולמשפ̊ח̊[תו, are mutilated but clear, with the *šin* having only the top left portion preserved; the next ink dot probably belongs to the head of *pe* and the following one to the right angle of *he*. Spatial considerations allow some of the following ink traces to be assigned to the letters of וי[צ̊א̊ו מ̊ש̊[ם. The *ʾalep* and *yod* of איש̊ are certain, but only the top right portion of the *šin* is extant.

L. 13 (21:25) The ink dot at the right edge of the fragment probably belongs to the upper angle of the initial *he* of]ה̊ה̊ם; the base of the following *he* is lost, but the typical trait of the head of the final *mem* is visible. The *ʾalep* of אי̊[ן is almost complete, and the following point of ink belongs to the upper part of *yod*. After three spaces of medium size the bottom of the *lamed* of מ]ל̊ך̊ is preserved, and the left tip of the head and the bottom of the tail of a final *kap* are visible. Two points of ink signal the place of the first two letters in ב̊י̊שרא̊[ל, and the characteristic left arm of *śin* is visible before *reš*, while on the edge of the hole an ink dot signals the upper right tip of *ʾalep*. At a distance of five spaces three small dots of ink probably signal the place of the *šin* of אי̊ש̊. After a tear in the leather two ink points can be construed as belonging to the *nun* and *yod* of בע[נ̊י̊]ו. Finally, at the left edge of the leather an ink spot probably corresponds to the *yod* of the word]י̊[עשה.

VARIANTS

21:17 (4) וי̊אמרו י̊ר̊[שת 𝔐] καί πῶς ἔσται 𝔊^gnw (Antiochian) 𝔊^koy; καὶ εἶπαν πῶς ἔσται 𝔊^ptv (Antiochian). In 4QJudg^b there is no room for the proposed correction איך instead of or after ויאמרו 𝔐.

21:19 (6) מ]זרח ה̊[שמ]ש] מזרחה השמש 𝔐; cf מזרח שמש Deut 4:47 (מזרחה שמש 𝔐^ms; מזרח השמש 𝔐^mss ɯ 𝔗^OJ; מזרחה השמש ɯ^mss; cf 𝔖) and מזרחה שמש Deut 4:41 (מזרח השמש 𝔐^ms ɯ^mss 𝔗^OJ; מזרחה השמש 𝔐^ms ɯ; cf 𝔖).

21:22 (8) אבות̊י̊ה̊[ם] אבותם 𝔐. The same form of the pronoun is found in the noun that follows, או אחיהם 𝔐.

21:23 (10) וי[שׂ̊א̊]ו 𝔐] +להם 𝔐^Ken 150, 180, 250; ἑαυτοῖς 𝔊^gh 𝔖. There is no room for להם between וי[שא]ו and נ[שי]ם

21:23 (10) מהמחלל̊[ות] מן המחללות 𝔐. The Massoretic MSS all have מן but have orthographic variations in the substantive: המחלות 𝔐^Ken 150, המחוללות 𝔐^Ken 30, 89, 101, 102, 174, 187, 264, המחולות 𝔐^Ken 96, המחוללת 𝔐^Ken 70, 154.

54. 4QKgs

(PLATE XXXVII)

Preliminary publication: Julio Trebolle Barrera, 'A Preliminary Edition of 4QKings (4Q**54**)', *Madrid*, 1. 229–46.

THE leather of the manuscript is thick, *c*.0.4 mm, and light brown in the upper part of columns 1–2 (frgs. 1–4) but dark brown in the lower part (frgs. 5–7). The largest fragments are frg. 5 (maximum height 9.9 cm, width 4.7 cm) and frg. 6 (height 5.5 cm, width 7.5 cm). The leather is wrinkled and thus present measurements do not correspond to original measurements. Lines of script curve upwards on some fragments due to the severe horizontal wrinkling (frg. 6 is also wrinkled vertically).

The surface is torn, particularly on frg. 5. The leather is also worn at an oblique angle on frgs. 2, 3 and 5; this is an important datum for the reconstruction of the text. Frgs. 1 and 5 are further damaged by small holes.

Frg. 5 preserves traces of stitching with suture holes along a right margin measuring *c*.6 mm. The bottom margin reaches a maximum of 1 cm. Frg. 6 preserves a left margin and frg. 2 a margin between two columns measuring 9 mm.

Traces of the vertical ruling are quite visible on the right margin of frg. 5, whereas in the left margin of frg. 6 they are less apparent. The horizontal ruling on frg. 6 is very faint. Frg. 1, line 2 also preserves traces of horizontal ruling, although in the first line they are discernible only in the spaces between the letters. The copyist has inscribed the letters slightly under the horizontal ruling. The distance between lines is 7 mm on frg. 1, 6–7 mm on frg. 5, and 6 mm on frgs. 2, 3, and 6, although this last is wrinkled in all directions.

The first seven fragments contain portions of 1 Kings 7–8 from two contiguous columns (see Table 1). An additional fragment (frg. 8) probably does not belong to this manuscript, but it had been grouped with these fragments and is published here in the absence of a more appropriate place.

TABLE 1: *Contents of 4QKgs*

Col.,	Frg.	Passage	Col.,	Frg.	Passage
I	1	1 Kgs 7:20-21	II	2	7:50 or 51?
	2	7:25-27		6	7:51–8:9
	3–5	7:29-42		7	8:16-18

The reconstructed number of lines per column is 30–32. The number of letters per line, reconstructed according to 𝔐, is normally *c*.48–56, although two or three more letters should be added because of the fuller spelling of 4QKgs (see the reconstruction of lines and columns below).

The script is sometimes bizarre and in general exhibits transitional features. It displays both archaizing traits and cursive features. Various forms of a letter often occur, as well as features peculiar to the copyist's hand. This script can be assigned to the late Hasmonaean book hand in the process of transition to the early Herodian. It can thus be dated to the middle of the first century BCE.

The writing is very angular, as can be seen especially in *bet*, *dalet*, *yod*, and *mem*.

א. *ʾAlep* is made in three movements, e.g. frg. 5 7; 6 7, 10; in 6 8 this is visible only on the leather. In some cases *ʾalep* could have been made in two movements since the left leg reaches the top of the axis as in the Herodian inverted-'v' form, אחת 5 8; את 6 5. Sometimes the *ʾalep* is narrow and square, at times rather elongated.

ב. *Bet* is small but very wide, and made in two or possibly three movements. The base is clearly independent in הבית 6 8 and הבדים 6 10 and made from left to right in האבנים 6 11. In other instances it is made in only one movement and in an angular form, ברית 6 3, בחג 6 4.

ג. *Gimel* is normally very upright and long. Its form, however, is strange in עגלות 5 2, and narrow in ומסגרתיה 5 6. Usually the left leg joins in the middle of the right leg, בחג 6 4; נגיד 7 1.

ד. The head of *dalet* is angular, profoundly marked, and very big if compared with the leg, 5 6, 9; 6 8, 10. *Dalet* is quite square, and very different from *reš*.

ה. *He* is made in three movements, יהוה 6 3, 5. The horizontal stroke is very curved, a characteristic that attracted round forms as in 6 8, with a tendency for the right end of the horizontal stroke to bend downwards, announcing a cursive or a ligatured form, הלוים 6 6.

ו\י. *Waw* and *yod* generally differ from each other, but when they are together the difference almost evanesces, 3 1; 7 2, but 4 2. The *yod* has no head, is small in size, and rather elongated, but sometimes it is a very small triangle, יספרו 6 7; עמי 7 2.

ח. *Ḥet* is made in the form of a capital *N*, 5 4.

ט. It is difficult to establish if *ṭet* is made in one or two movements, 6 2. It is slightly archaizing, but not very.

כ. *Kap* is bizarre, because its head is imperceptible, 2 2; 3 2; 5 5, 10; 6 9. It clearly differs from *bet*, which is wider. The head of *kap* is very oblique, and its base tends to become horizontal, 5 10. The head of the final *kap* is not yet profoundly marked, as it tends to be in the late Herodian formal script.

ל. The stem of *lamed* ends in a big loop. The leg is rather cursive, and almost imperceptible, שלמה 6 6, while in 7 2 the leg is very elongated.

מ. *Mem* is bizarre and very angular, and no one *mem* is the same as another. Its base is sometimes rounded, but at times very long and plain. In 5 6, 11 it might be made in three movements. The normal type is found in המטות 6 2, והמלך 6 6, and מקמו 6 8. A less typical, thicker example occurs in the second *mem* in משמאלו 5 11.

The final *mem* is closed in והלוים 6 6, but open in כהנים 6 6. Here the lower horizontal stroke goes up in a strange way. Normally it descends as in והלוים 6 6. It is open also in מקום 6 9, normal in כנפים 6 9.

נ. *Nun* is rather angular, 5 10, and final *nun* is almost upright, lacking a head, 1 1; 2 2.

ס. *Samek* is always closed, although not completely in 6 7. Triangular in 2 2, square in 5 6, 12, it seems to exhibit transitional features.

ע. There are two types of *ʿayin*: one small, placed above the line, and a little square, עשה 5 13, the other showing a tendency to lengthen, ממער 5 7; מעיר 6 3. Both types are found in 2 3. *ʿAyin*, made as a small 'v' with a short tail, seems to be in a transitional state.

פ. The head of *pe* is well marked and its base is horizontal, 2 2; 6 7.

צ. The head of *ṣade* is deep, and the bottom trace is angular, 5 8; 6 7.

ק. The prolongation of the head of *qop* is always open. This is a constant feature, as can be seen in 5 4, 8; 6 7, 8, 9, 10.

ר. *Reš* is rather small. It differs clearly from *dalet*, which has a very big head, although the head of the *reš* in 6 3 is also rather large.

ש. Very cursive, *šin* is made in two movements. The central stroke is short and very high. It is never found on the lower angle, 2 2; 5 14; 6 6, 7, 8, 10, which is a peculiarity of the copyist's hand.

ת. The foot of the left leg of *taw* is made in three different ways. It is almost imperceptible in 5 7, normal and rounded in 6 2, and angular in 5 10.

No intervals are found in the preserved fragments, although the scribe left a small gap of 7 mm in frg. 5 3, apparently due to a defect in the leather. The reconstruction of columns allows us to suppose that 4QKgs had intervals at the same points as 𝔐: after 7:22 (פ), 7:26 (פ 𝔐, apparently ס in 4QKgs), 7:37 (ס 𝔐^{L}, פ 𝔐^{A}), 7:39 (ס), 7:50 (פ), 7:51 (פ), 8:11 (פ) (cf. below).

The orthography is fuller than that of 𝔐 (which is itself not consistent), except for one case, although the orthography of 4QKgs is still not very full.

7:21 (1 2) העמוד̇י̇ם̇[2 Chr 3:17] העמדים 𝔐, cf. the use in the surrounding context: עמודים 7:2, 3, 6, 15, 16, 17, 18, 19, 20, 22bis, 41, 42; but עמדים 7:6, 21, 41bis

7:30 (3 2) כתפות] כתפת 𝔐

7:30 (4 2) לכיור] לכיר 𝔐𝔊 τῶν λουτήρων (כירות), cf. 𝔐 (ה)כיור in 1 Kgs 7:38ter and 2 Chr 6:13

7:34 (5 5) המכונה] המכנה 𝔐, cf. 𝔐 מכונה 7:27, 28, 30, 32, 35, 38; מכנה 7:34bis, 35

7:36 (5 7) ותמרות] ותמרת 𝔐

7:38 (5 10) המכונות] המכנות 𝔐

8:6 (6 8) מקמו] מקומו 𝔐

Reconstruction of Columns and Lines

There is enough evidence at our disposal to fix the positions of the seven extant pieces of 4QKgs in two columns of the scroll and to establish the number of lines in each column. The evidence is three-fold. Firstly, the bottom margin of frg. 5, the left margin of frg. 6, and the central margin of frg. 2 are preserved. Secondly, the shapes of damage of frgs. 5 and 6 correspond to each other (the lines 5 1 to 6 5, and 5 7 to 6 11; i.e. I 16 = II 15, and I 22 = II 21). Thirdly, the 𝔐 text of 1 Kings 7–8 serves as a parallel for reconstruction, because in the main it is faithfully reproduced in the extant pieces of 4QKgs. The goal of this reconstruction is to try to establish the exact position of the word לשכו̇ת̇ (2 ii) in the second column and consequently to identify the verse in the 𝔐 (7:50 or 51?), to which this word could belong or be related.

Mus. Inv. 1108. PAM 43.079 (42.279).

Frg. 1 1 Kings 7:20-21

]הבטן א[		1
]העמודים[	(21)	2
]הע[מ]וד[		3

L. 2 (7:20) Traces of the heads of the letters forming the sequence -ודי- and an ink trace of the final *mem* are preserved.

L. 3 (7:21) The ink traces at the right edge of the leather probably belong to a *he*. Because of wrinkling on the left edge of the leather the letters *waw* and *dalet* cannot be seen in the photograph but are almost completely preserved in the original. They become visible by unfolding the leather. The wrinkling prevents one from seeing the ink, as is also the case in line 1. The rest of *dalet* is similar in form to that of line 2.

Frg. 2 i–ii 1 Kings 7:25-27

Col. ii	Col. i		
	]שלשה פנים[		1
	]שה שפת כוס פרח שושן[	(26)	2
לשכו[			
	]ת עשר נחשת ארבע[	(27)	3

L. 1 (7:25) The *lamed* of שלשה is no longer visible on the leather and on PAM 43.079, but it can still be seen in the older photograph PAM 42.279; similarly the top right portion of the second *šin* is visible only in that photograph. The *nun* of פנים, although damaged, is certain; it is followed by an ink trace that probably belongs to the bottom of the *yod*; the base of the final *mem* remains.

L. 2 (7:26) The *šin* of]שה is probable, although deformed by wrinkling. The letters composing the word שושן have suffered because of surface damage to the leather.

L. 3 (7:27) The ink trace on the right edge, more visible in PAM 43.079, probably belongs to the left upper part of a *taw*. In נחשת the characteristic traces of the *šin* are preserved, and the head of the *taw* is certain. *Reš* in ארבע is almost complete.

Col. ii The leather has been torn obliquely. It is still possible to observe on the leather that the stem of the *lamed* continued upwards. The head of the *kap* is well preserved (compare with 2 2; 3 2; 5 5, 10). The ink on the edge of the leather could be *bet, he* or *waw,* probably *waw.*

VARIANT

Col. ii לשכו[ ] See discussion under Reconstruction below.

Frgs. 3–4 1 Kings 7:29-31

]יות מעש[ה מורד [30]וא[רב[		1	f.4
[כתפות להם מת]חת לכיור		2	
]עלה בא[מה ופיה ע[ג]ל	(31)	3	

The blank space at the end of line 2 is part of the left margin.

L. 1 (7:29) מ֯ע֯ש֯]ה. The ink traces may belong to the lower parts of an *ʿayin* and of a *šin*.

L. 1 (7:30) וא[רב]. The traces of the *reš* and *bet* are faint but certain.

L. 3 (7:31)]ע֯לה ב֯א֯[מה. The first ink trace signals the upper left tip of an *ʿayin*. The *he* is certain. A faint trace of the head of a *bet* is probable. An ink trace on the edge, which is more clear on the leather, may correspond to the upper right portion of an *ʾalep*.

L. 3 (7:31) ע֯[ג]ל֯. The letter space count allows us to attribute the ink spots to traces of an *ʿayin* and the stem of a *lamed* in the expected עגל.

Frg. 5 1 Kings 7:31-42

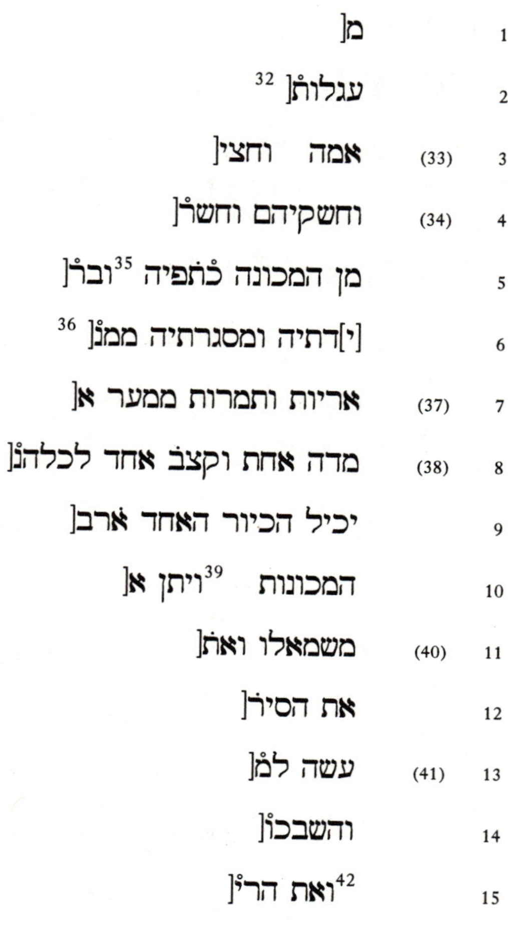

1 מ[

2 עגלו֯ת֯[32

3 (33) אמה וחצי[

4 (34) וחשקיהם וחשר֯[

5 מן המכונה כ֯תפיה 35 ובר֯[

6 י]דתיה ומסגרתיה ממנ֯[36

7 (37) אריות ותמרות ממער א[

8 (38) מדה אחת וקצב֯ אחד לכלהנ֯[

9 יכיל הכיור האחד ארב[

10 המכונות 39 ויתן א[

11 (40) משמאלו ואת֯[

12 את הסיר֯[

13 (41) עשה למ֯[

14 והשבכו֯[

15 42 ואת הר֯[

bottom margin

The right margin with a stitched edge is extant, as well as part of the bottom margin.

L. 2 (7:31) עגלו֯ת֯[. Only the lower portion of the *lamed* and *waw* are preserved. A part of the right leg of the *taw* is visible.

L. 3 (7:32) A small space of 7 mm separates אמה from וחצי[. The leather has a hole, skipped over by the scribe, which on the photograph gives the impression of ink traces.

L. 4 (7:33) וחשר֯[. An ink trace on the edge of the break is the only remainder of a possible *reš*.

L. 5 (7:34) כ̊ת̊פיה. Only two ink traces probably corresponding to the head of a *kap* are preserved, followed by the left upper part of a *taw*.

L. 5 (7:35) ובר̊[. As in the preceding line the bottom of a possible *reš* remains.

L. 6 (7:35) The *yod* is lost because of damage to the leather at this point and on the margin. The *gimel* is almost completely preserved. The bottom of a probable *nun* is visible.

L. 8 (7:37) The base of the *bet* is almost certain. Four points signal the extremities of an *ʾalep*. On the leather an ink trace of a *nun* is visible.

L. 9 (7:38) Only the left stroke of an *ʾalep* is preserved. The *bet* has lost its base.

L. 11 (7:39) The top right angle of a probable *taw* is visible.

L. 12 (7:40) A faint trace of the vertical stroke of a *reš* is visible.

L. 13 (7:40) The *mem* is certain although only its right side is preserved.

L. 14 (7:41) On the leather an ink trace of the bottom of the *kap* forms a ligature with the *waw*.

L. 15 (7:42) The trace of ink to the left of *reš* could be either a *yod* or a *mem* (cf. הרמנים 𝔐).

VARIANTS

7:36 (7) ממער] כמער 𝔐. Cf. the equally obscure parallel מעבר in 𝔐 at 7:30; and note the similar מ/כ change in כאפס 1QIsa[a]/מאפס 𝔐 at Isa 40:17.

7:37 (8) טס וקצב] קצב 𝔐. 𝔊 omits קצב אחד of 𝔐; the addition of *waw* could be an attempt better to integrate this gloss in the context (cf. 6:25).

7:40 (12) הסיר̊[ות 43 MSS Kenn. 𝔊𝔖𝔙 2 Chr 4:11] הכירות 𝔐, cf. v 45 הסירות.

Frg. 6 1 Kings 7:51–8:9

1]ת̊ בית̊[

2 (8:1)]א̊שי המטות נשי̊א̊[

3 (2)]ברית יהוה מעיר ד[

4 (3)]ם בחג הוא חדש הש[

5 4]ע̊לו את ארון יהוה ואת אה[

6]כ̊הנים והלוים 5והמלך שלמה וכ̊[

7]בחים צאן ובקר אשר לא יספרו ולא

8 (6)] יהוה אל מקמו לדביר הבית אל קדש

9 (7)]י̊ם פרשי כנפים אל מקום הארון ויסכו

10 (8)]ראשי הבדים מן הקדש

11 (9)]ר̊ק̊ שני הלחות האבנים

The left margin is extant.

L. 1 (7:51) The base of the *bet* is preserved. The bottom of the *yod* forms a ligature with the *bet*, and the lower part of its head is visible. The two vertical strokes and the base of the left leg of the *taw* are partly preserved. An ink trace visible on the right of the leather probably belongs to the base of another *taw*.

L. 2 (8:1) Only the left stroke of the *ʾalep* is preserved. The *śin* is partly lost but certain. Faint traces of *yod* and *ʾalep* are visible on the leather.

L. 5 (8:4) An ink spot on the edge of the leather may belong to an *ʿayin*.

L. 6 (8:4) The left tip of the head of a *kap* is still visible. *Kap* is preferable to *waw* (כ]והנים).

L. 11 (8:9) The extant ink traces probably correspond to the top of *reš* and *qop*.

VARIANTS

8:2 (4) חדש] החדש 𝔐 2 Chr 5:3

8:6 (8) לדביר] אל דביר 𝔐 2 Chr 5:7

8:7 (9) פרשי] פרשים 𝔐 2 Chr 5:8

8:7 (9) אל 𝔐] על 𝔊 (ἐπί) 2 Chr 5:8

8:7 (9) ויסכו 𝔐] ויכסו 𝔊 2 Chr 5:8

8:9 (11) הלחות 2 Chr 5:10] לחות 𝔐. The duplication of the article in this MS (הלחות האבנים) probably reflects the double reading לחות האבנים (𝔐-Kgs)/לחות הברית* (𝔊), which developed from a shorter reading הלחות (4QKgs, 𝔐-Chr), cf. the similar duplicate in 2 Kgs 7:13 ישראל...המון ישראל (המון 𝔐^{q})ההמון.

Frg. 7 1 Kings 8:16-18

]היות נגיד על עמ֯[

(17)]להיות על עמי על[

]שראל 18ויאמר[

All letters are certain, although many of them are damaged. In line 3 an ink trace above the *śin* is visible.

VARIANTS

8:16 (1) ל]היות נגיד על עמ[י 2 Chr 6:5] > 𝔐𝔊. The text partially preserved by this MS belongs to a reading lost by homoioteleuton in 𝔐, but preserved in the parallel text 2 Chr 6:5b-6a:

להיות שמי שם ולא בחרתי באיש להיות נגיד על עמי ישראל ואבחר בירושלם
להיות שמי שם ואבחר בדויד להיות על עמי ישראל

The second part of the reading lost by 𝔐-Kgs is attested also by 𝔊-Kgs καὶ ἐξελεξάμην ἐν Ἰερουσαλὴμ εἶναι τὸ ὄνομά μου ἐκεῖ (cf. the reconstruction of lines below).

8:16 (2) על] > 𝔐𝔊 2 Chr 6:6

Frg. 8 Unidentified Fragment

כ]והנ֯י֯ם֯[1

א]שר כו֯ל[2

]י֯חוה ◦[3

(left? or) bottom margin

Frg. 8 preserves either a left margin or more probably a bottom margin, which would reach 18 mm. A further line may have existed beneath line 3, traces of which would not have been preserved if the line ended before an interval. The distance between lines varies from 6 to 7 mm.

Frg. 8 is physically very similar to frgs. 1–7 of 4QKgs. The script here, however, seems more Herodian than the still transitional hand of frgs. 1–7. The letters on this fragment are of greater caliber and more elongated, and particularly *kap* and *šin* differ from those on the other fragments. The big head of the *kap* on frg. 8 contrasts with the imperceptible head of the other exemplars. The *šin* is made in three movements, not in two, as on the other fragments. The size of the *reš* is greater and not as angular. Although the *he* may be the same, the probable *yod* of line 1 differs from the *yod* with the angular head of the other fragments (cf. 7 2).

It is therefore not certain that this fragment belongs to 4QKgs, although it is not impossible. The fragment appears with frgs. 1–7 on PAM 43.079 but not on the older PAM 42.279. Moreover, the preserved text has no counterpart in 𝔐 of Kings; given the strong 'massoretic' character of the other fragments, this fact can be a further argument that this fragment did not belong to 4QKgs.

There is now an additional fragment located with frgs. 1–8 in the museum, although it has not been photographed and is therefore not on Plate XXXVII. Measuring 2.5 mm high and 3 mm wide, it preserves only the letter *reš* which is more similar in shape to the *reš* on frg. 8 than to those of the other fragments.

L. 1 The vertical stroke forming a ligature with the *nun* could belong to a *yod*. An ink trace on the edge could belong to a final *mem*, possibly completing the word כוהנים, 'priests'.

L. 2 The final letter may be a *waw*, although a *yod* is also possible. The reading א]שר כו֯ל is probable.

L. 3 There is a trace of an unidentifiable letter on the left edge of the leather. The *ḥet* is damaged but certain. The preceding ink spot could signal the head of a *yod*.

Reconstruction of the Columns

The evidence and clues discussed below help us see how the extant fragments fit into two contiguous columns, and also permit us some further speculation. I am grateful to Prof. Hartmut Stegemann of Göttingen who provided the following data and analysis.

The evidence of the originals of the extant fragments clearly shows that frg. 6 was on the layer above frg. 5 in a pile of similarly shaped fragments.

The text of frg. 5 comes from 1 Kgs 7:31-42.

The text of frg. 6 comes from 1 Kgs 7:51–8:9.

Therefore, (a) frg. 6 comes from a place *left* of frg. 5 and (b) this scroll was damaged at a time when the beginning of the text was outside and the end of the text inside the scroll.

The reconstruction of the biblical text left of frg. 5 5 and right of frg. 6 results in columns about 11.5 cm wide.

The distance between correspondent points of damage in frg. 5 and frg. 6 is then about 21 cm.

Since the patterns of damage in the upper left part of frg. 5 and the upper left part of frg. 6 are very similar and the texts on the two fragments are very near to one another, there would have been no other fragment intervening between them.

Therefore, the relatively large distance of about 21 cm between corresponding points of damage clearly demonstrates that those fragments were very far from the end of the scroll when the scroll sustained its damage.

Up to this point, every statement is quite exact and in no way 'speculative', but the following arguments are more hypothetical.

The two columns of this scroll represented by frgs. 1–7 cover roughly the text of four pages of *BHS*. Therefore, one may conclude that, on the average, one column of 4QKgs corresponds to approximately two pages of *BHS*.

From the text represented by frgs. 1–7 (1 Kgs 7:19–8:19) to the end of the book of 2 Kings, there are in *BHS* (p. 674 minus p. 574 =) 100 pages; this corresponds to 50 columns in this scroll. In 4QKgs, one column plus the margin between it and the next column measured *c.*12.5 cm, thus eight complete columns would measure one meter of the scroll, and the 50 columns would measure 6.25 meters.

This evidence is illuminated by the *Temple Scroll* (11QT^{a}), where the width of the columns (including margins) similarly averages *c.*12.5 cm, even though individual column widths vary. 11QT^{a} had 66 columns, plus a 'long' handle sheet at its end; and 11QT^{a} was also damaged with the end of its text inside (like 4QKgs).

The fiftieth column before the end of 11QT^{a} is its col. XVI. Here the distances between corresponding points of damage are about 14 cm, as opposed to the 21 cm for 4QKgs. The leather of 11QT^{a} is very thin: evidently, each turn of this scroll took 1 mm more than the preceding turn, or, in other words, the distances between corresponding points of damage increase 1 mm after each turn, from one layer of the scroll to the next one.

The leather of the fragments of 4QKgs is a little bit thicker than that of 11QT^{a}. Therefore, it seems plausible that the 'increase' from turn to turn in the 4QKgs scroll was about 1.5 mm. In that case the scroll would end with the conclusion of the Book of 2 Kings—50 columns (or 6.25 meters) to the left of the column represented by frg. 5.

Reconstruction Col. II 1 Kings 7:42–8:19

Letters	Text	Frg. line
55	לכסות את שתי גלת הכתרות אשר על פני העמודים 43ואת המכונות עשר ואת הכירת	
52	עשרה על המכונות 44ואת הים האחד ואת הבקר שנים עשר תחת הים 45ואת הסירות	
57	ואת היעים ואת המזרקות ואת כל הכלים האהל אשר עשה חירם למלך שלמה בית יהוה	
54	נחשת ממרט 46בככר הירדן יצקם המלך במעבה האדמה בין סכות ובין צרתן 47וינח	
54	שלמה את כל הכלים מרב מאד מאד לא נחקר משקל הנחשת 48ויעש שלמה את כל הכלים	
55	אשר בית יהוה את מזבח הזהב ואת השלחן אשר עליו לחם הפנים זהב 49ואת המנרות	
55	חמש מימין וחמש משמאול לפני הדביר זהב סגור והפרח והנרת והמלקחים זהב	
54	50והספות והמזמרות והמזרקות והכפות והמחתות זהב סגור והפתות לדלתות	
	הבית הפנימי לקדש הקדשים לדלתי הבית להיכל זהב *vacat*	
55	51ותשלם כל המלאכה אשר עשה המלך שלמה בית יהוה ויבא שלמה את קדשי דוד אביו	
	את הכסף ואת הזהב ואת הכלים נתן באצרו[ת̊ בית̊] יהוה *vacat*	6 1
54	8:1אז יקהל שלמה את זקני ישראל את כל ר[אשי המטות נשיא̊]י האבות לבני ישראל	6 2
56	אל המלך שלמה ירושלם להעלות את ארון [ברית יהוה מעיר ד]וד היא ציון 2ויקהלו	6 3
52	אל המלך שלמה כל איש ישראל בירח האתני[ם בחג הוא חדש הש]ביעי 3ויבאו כל	6 4
51	זקני ישראל וישאו הכהנים את הארון 4וי[עלו את ארון יהוה ואת אה]ל מועד	6 5
54	ואת כל כלי הקדש אשר באהל ויעלו אתם ה[כ̊הנים והלוים 5והמלך שלמה וכ̊]ל עדת	6 6
54	ישראל הנועדים עליו אתו לפני הארון מז[בחים צאן ובקר אשר לא יספרו ולא	6 7
52	ימנו מרב 6ויבאו הכהנים את ארון ברית [יהוה אל מקמו לדביר הבית אל קדש	6 8
56	הקדשים אל תחת כנפי הכרובים 7כי הכרוב[ים פרשי כנפים אל מקום הארון ויסכו	6 9
57	הכרבים על הארון ועל בדיו מלמעלה 8ויארכו הבדים ויראו [ראשי הבדים מן הקדש	6 10
63	על פני הדביר ולא יראו החוצה ויהיו שם עד היום הזה 9אין בארון [ר̊ק̊ שני הלחות האבנים	6 11
51	אשר הנח שם משה בחרב אשר כרת יהוה עם בני ישראל בצאתם מארץ מצרים 10ויהי	
54	בצאת הכהנים מן הקדש והענן מלא את בית יהוה 11ולא יכלו הכהנים לעמד לשרת	
	מפני הענן כי מלא כבוד יהוה את בית יהוה *vacat*	
50	12אז אמר שלמה יהוה אמר לשכן בערפל 13בנה בניתי בית זבל לך מכון לשבתך	
51	עולמים 14ויסב המלך את פניו ויברך את כל קהל ישראל וכל קהל ישראל עמד	
52	15ויאמר ברוך יהוה אלהי ישראל אשר דבר בפיו את דוד אבי ובידו מלא לאמר	
51	16מן היום אשר הוצאתי את עמי את ישראל ממצרים לא בחרתי בעיר מכל שבטי	
54	ישראל לבנות בית להיות שמי שם ולא בחרתי באיש ל[היות נגיד על עמ̊]י ישראל	7 1
52	ואבחר בירושלם להיות שמי שם ואבחר בדוד [להיות על עמי על] ישראל 17ויהי	7 2
52	עם לבב דוד אבי לבנות בית לשם יהוה אלהי י[שראל 18ויאמר] יהוה אל דוד אבי	7 3
50	יען אשר היה עם לבבך לבנות בית לשמי הטיבת כי היה עם לבבך 19רק אתה לא	

Reconstruction Col. I 1 Kings 7:19-42

Letters	Text	Frg. line
52	באולם ארבע אמות [20]וכתרת על שני העמודים גם ממעל מלעמת]הבטן א[שר לעבר	1 1
54	שבכה והרמונים מאתים טרים סביב על הכתרת השנית [21]ויקם את]העמודים[לאלם	1 2
52	ההיכל ויקם את העמוד הימני ויקרא את שמו יכין ויקם את] הע[מ]וד[השמאלי	1 3
50	ויקרא את שמו באז [22]ועל ראש העמודים מעשה שושן ותתם מלאכת העמודים *vacat*	
55	[23]ויעש את הים מוצק עשר באמה משפתו עד שפתו עגל סביב וחמש באמה קומתו וקוה	
53	שלשים באמה יסב אתו סביב [24]ופקעים מתחת לשפתו סביב סבבים אתו עשר באמה	
53	מקפים את הים סביב שני טורים הפקעים יצקים ביצקתו [25]עמד על שני עשר בקר	
56	שלשה פנים צפונה ושלשה פנים ימה ושלשה פנים נגבה ו]שלשה פנים[מזרחה והים	2 1
55	עליהם מלמעלה וכל אחריהם ביתה [26]ועביו טפח ושפתו כמע]שה שפת כוס פרח שושן	2 2
	אלפים בת יכיל *vacat* [27]ויעש את המכנו]ת עשר נחשת ארבע	2 3
56	באמה ארך המכונה האחת וארבע באמה רחבה ושלש באמה קומתה [28]וזה מעשה המכונה	
54	מסגרת להם ומסגרת בין השלבים [29]ועל המסגרות אשר בין השלבים אריות בקר	
56	וכרובים ועל השלבים כן ממעל ומתחת לאריות ולבקר ל]יות מעשה מורד [30]וא]רב[עה	3–4 1
57	אופני נחשת למכונה האחת וסרני נחשת וארבעה פעמתיו] כתפות לה[ם מת]חת לכיור	3–4 2
52	הכתפות יצקות מעבר איש ליות [31]ופיהו מבית לכתרת ומ]עלה בא[מה ופיה] ע[ג]ל	3–4 3
48	מ]עשה כן אמה וחצי האמה וגם על פיה מקלעות ומסגרתיהם מרבעות לא	5 1
62	עגלות[[32]וארבעת האופנים למתחת למסגרות וידות האופנים במכונה וקומת האופן האחד	5 2
49	אמה וחצי[האמה [33]ומעשה האופנים כמעשה אופן המרכבה ידותם וגביהם	5 3
51	וחשקיהם וחשר]יהם הכל מוצק [34]וארבע כתפות אל ארבע פנות המכונה האחת	5 4
54	מן המכונה כתפיה [35]ובר]אש המכונה חצי האמה קומה עגל סביב ועל ראש המכונה	5 5
49	[י]דתיה ומסגרתיה ממנ]ה [36]ויפתח על הלחת ידתיה ועל ומסגרתיה כרובים	5 6
53	אריות ותמרות ממער א]יש וליות סביב [37]כזאת עשה את עשר המכונות מוצק אחד	5 7
	מדה אחת וקצב אחד לכלהנ]ה *vacat* [38]ויעש עשרה כירות נחשת ארבעים בת	5 8
53	יכיל הכיור האחד ארב]ע באמה הכיור האחד כיור אחד על המכונה האחת לעשר	5 9
50	המכונות [39]ויתן א]ת המכונות חמש על כתף הבית מימין וחמש על כתף הבית	5 10
49	משמאלו ואת[הים נתן מכתף הבית הימנית קדמה ממול נגב *vacat* [40]ויעש חירום	5 11
52	את הסיר]ות ואת היעים ואת המזרקות ויכל חירם לעשות את כל המלאכה אשר	5 12
57	עשה למ]לך שלמה בית יהוה [41]עמודים שנים וגלת הכתרות אשר על ראש העמודים שתים	5 13
45	והשבכו]ת שתים לכסות את שתי גלת הכתרות אשר על ראש העמודים	5 14
50	[42]ואת הרי]מנים ארבע מאות לשתי השבכות שני טורים רמנים לשבכה האחת	5 15

But the question now is how to determine where the original scroll began.

Most of the more than 800 scrolls from the Qumran caves are badly damaged, and usually only a few fragments of each survived. Statistically, about half of those 'remaining fragments of a particular scroll' come from the middle layers of the scroll as it had been deposited, i.e., the outer as well as the inner layers of those scrolls were destroyed—mainly by humidity—and only some fragments which were roughly equidistant from the inner hole of the scroll and from its outmost layer could survive.

If indeed, as the statistical evidence indicates, the fragments surviving from 4QKgs also come from the middle layers of the original scroll, this scroll must have been a very large one, containing the books of Joshua, Judges, 1–2 Samuel, and 1–2 Kings.

From the beginning of the book of Joshua (p. 354 in *BHS*) to the 4QKgs fragments (p. 574 top), there are about 220 pages. This would correspond to about 110 columns in our scroll, agreeing very well with the position of the surviving fragments in what had been the middle of the scroll:

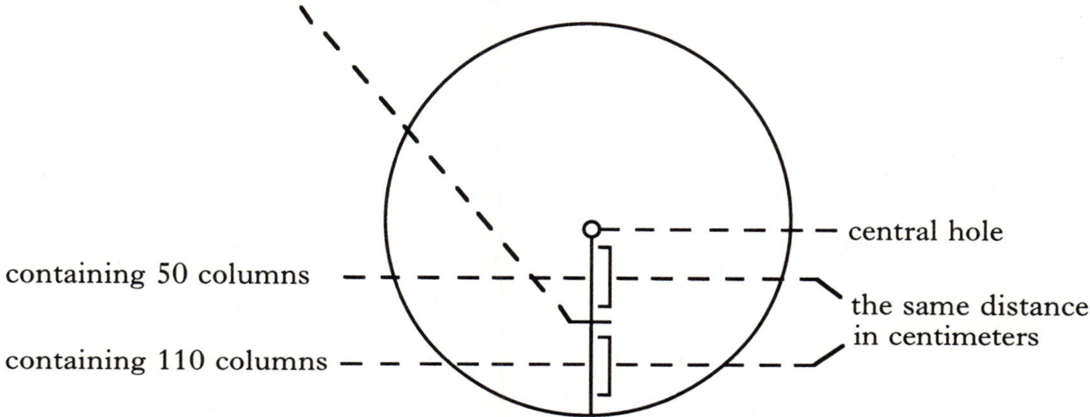

In this case, the scroll would have contained a total of 160 columns, and its length would have been 160 x 12.5 cm = 20 meters. This is highly speculative; but it may not be impossible (Torah scrolls were still longer!).

Reconstruction of the Lines

On most scrolls, the number of lines per column is the same within a given sheet. In the complete Isaiah scroll (1QIsa[a]), however, there are three sheets which contain columns with differing numbers of regular lines (see M. Burrows, *The DSS of St. Mark's Monastery* [New Haven: ASOR, 1950] pp. xvii-xviii):

Sheet	Col. (= plate)	Number of lines	Sheet	Col. (= plate)	Number of lines	Sheet	Col. (= plate)	Number of lines
IV	XII	31	VIII	XXVI	32	XII	XXXVII	29
	XIII	31		XXVII	29		XXXVIII	30
	XIV	32					XXXIX	31
	XV	32					XL	32

Also in 4QKgs, col. II may have had one line, or two lines (!), more than col. I within the same space from the top to the bottom of the column (see the reconstruction of cols. I–II above). The lines of frg. 6 were evidently closer together than those of frg. 5 (see frg. 2 i–ii, where the line with לשכות in the left column is slightly higher than the third line in the right column with ארבע; thus it is closer to the top of its column). Therefore, line II 15 of our final reconstruction will have been still closer to the top of its column than the corresponding line I 16. According to Prof. Stegemann's estimation, col. II had 32 lines; but the distance from line II 32 to the bottom of the scroll would have been the same as that from I 30 to the bottom. For similar evidence, see 4Q**405** (*Shir Shabbat*) frg. 3A (Carol Newsom, *Songs of the Sabbath Sacrifice: A Critical Edition* [Atlanta: 1985], Pl. VI).

The main consequence of this reconstruction is that we are able to establish that the letters לשכו̇[in frg. 2 ii are to be fixed at the beginning of line 9 (or 10) of the column that follows frgs. 2–5. These letters form the word לשכות, which is not found in the 𝔐 of Kings but is present in a parallel passage of 1 Chr 28:12 (הלשכות). Both the passage in Kings (vv 48-51) and that in 1 Chronicles 28:12-18 contain the same terms but they are more developed and occur in a different order in Chronicles: cf. כל הכלים (1 Chr 28:13), מזבח הזהב (v 18), השלחן (v 16), המנרות (v 15), המזרקות (v 17), הקדשים (v 12), אצרות (v 12).

Conclusion

This manuscript stands in the proto-rabbinic textual tradition. The positive evidence is provided by the readings ויסכו and אל at frg. 6 9 (8:7), in agreement with 𝔐 against 𝔊 and Chr. The negative evidence is stronger. 4QKgs agrees with 𝔐 Kgs (and Chr) against 𝔊 in all the frequent and substantial variants which give to the *Vorlage* of the Old Greek its very strong character and which reflect an intensive editorial activity: the omissions in 7:20b, 30b-32a, 38b; 8:1a, 2, 3a, 4, 5-8b, the additions in 7:45b and 8:1a, the transpositions in 7:26 (placed before 𝔐 7:25); 7:51 followed by 7:1a, 2-12, 1b; 8:12-13 (placed after 𝔐 8:53), and other textual variants such as 7:27 (ארבע 4QKgs𝔐, πέντε 𝔊), etc.

4QKgs agrees, however, with certain Massoretic manuscripts 𝔊𝔖𝔙 and 2 Chr against the erroneous 𝔐 in הכירות at 7:40. The addition of *waw* in וקצב at 7:37 in agreement with 𝔖 and 𝔙 could have arisen independently in each witness. 4QKgs presents two peculiar variants that represent inferior readings: חדש in 8:2 and פרשי (st. cstr.) in 8:7. Another peculiar reading of 4QKgs is that of ל- for אל in 8:6. It cannot therefore be said that 4QKgs is completely deprived of its own character.

The most important reading of 4QKgs is the preservation of a substantial original reading of Kings, lost by homoioteleuton in 1 Kgs 8:16, but preserved in the parallel text of 2 Chr 6:5b-6a and partially preserved in the Old Greek text of 1 Kings 8:16.

INDEX OF BIBLICAL PASSAGES

INDEX OF THE CONTENTS OF THE MANUSCRIPTS

4QDeut[n]

8:5-10
5:1-33
6:1

4QDeut[o]

2:8
4:30-34
5:1-5, 8-9
28:15-18, 33-36, 47-52, 58-62
29:22-25

4QDeut[p]

6:4-11

4QDeut[q]

32:9-10?, 37-43

4QJosh[a]

8:34-35
5:X, 2-7
6:5-10
7:12-17
8:3-14, 18?
10:2-5, 8-11

4QJosh[b]

2:11-12
3:15-17
4:1-3
17:1-5, 11-15

4QJudg[a]

6:2-6, 11-13

4QJudg[b]

19:5-7
21:12-25

4QKgs

1 Kgs 7:20-21, 25-27, 29-42, 50?, 51
8:1-9, 16-18

PLATES

28. 4QDeut[a]

Column II

Column I

1

2 ii

2 i

4

3

Column III

5

6

7

8

29. 4QDeut[b]

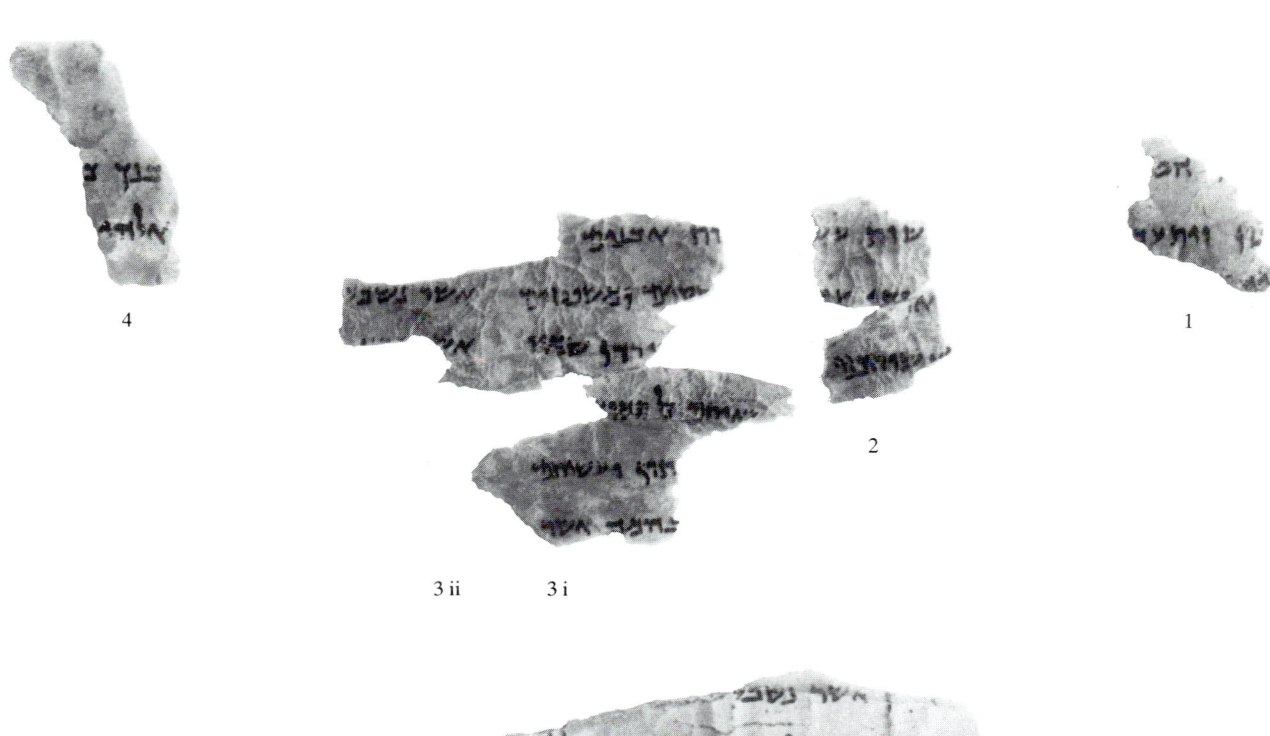

5

7

6

8

30. 4QDeut[c]

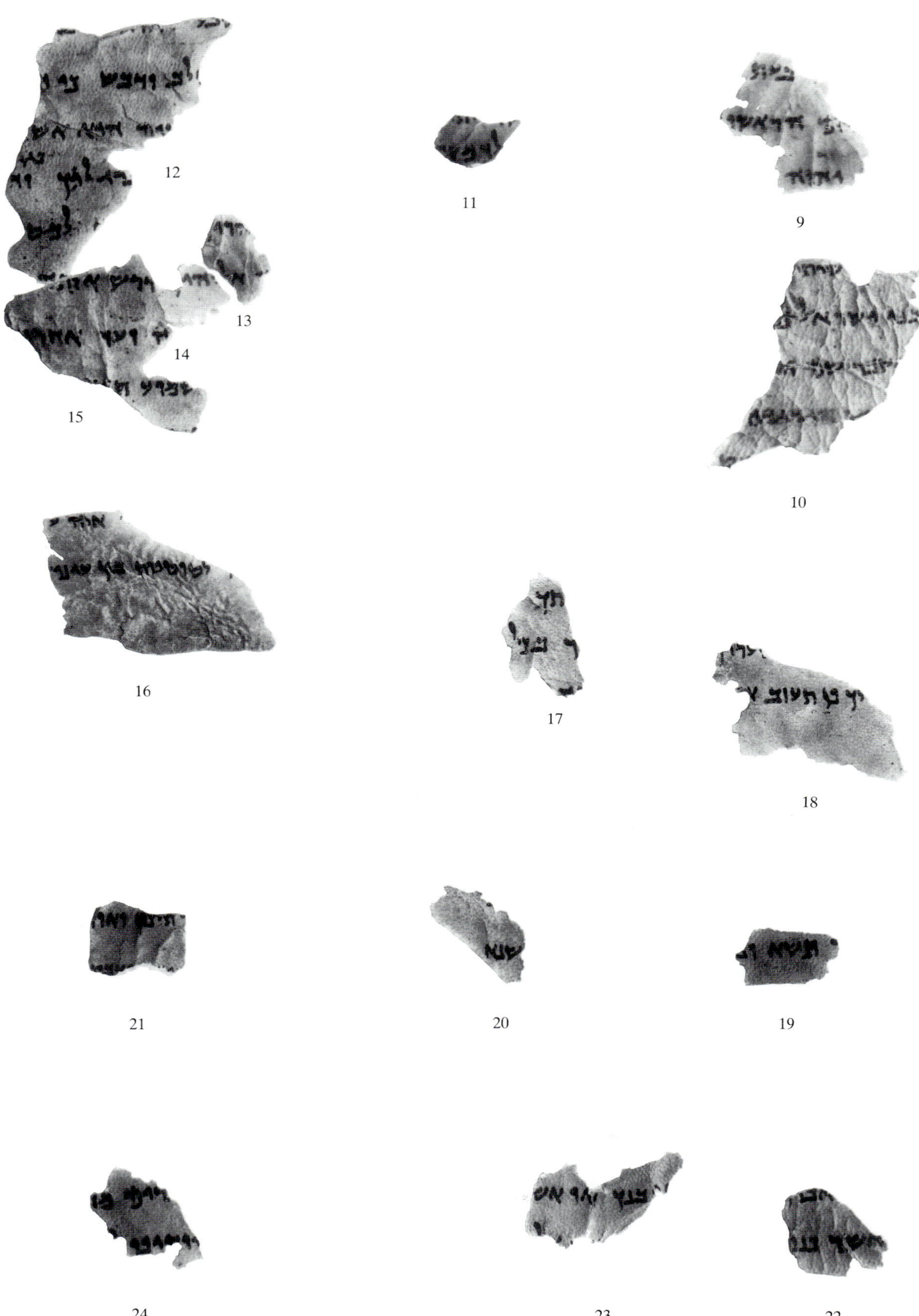

30. 4QDeut[c]

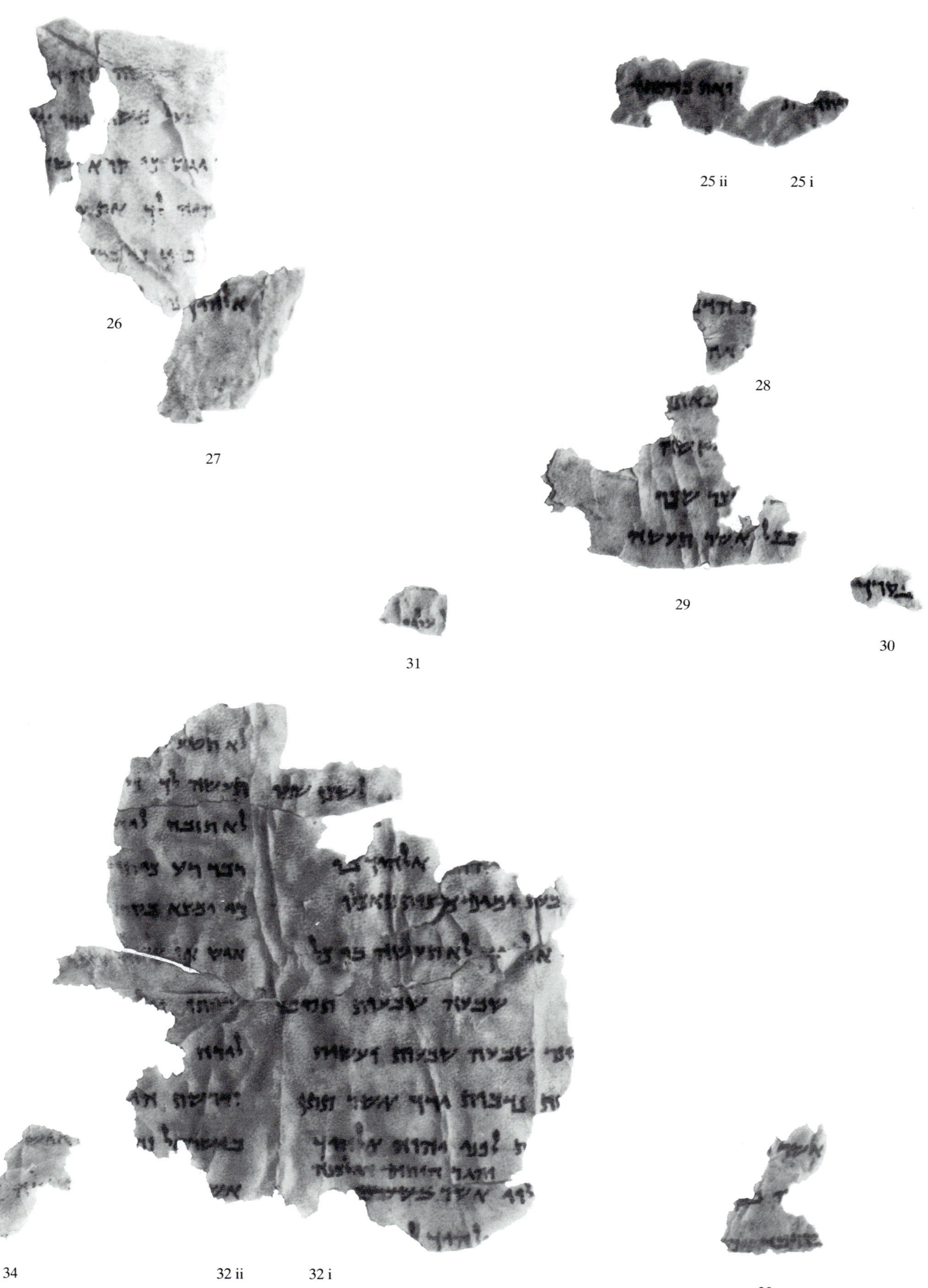

30. 4QDeut[c]

35

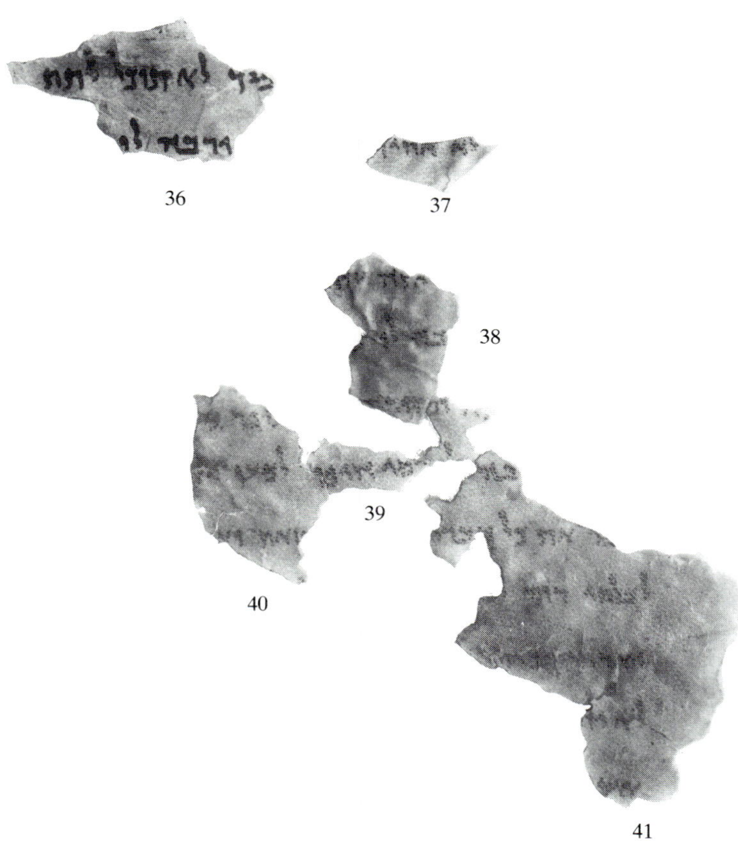

36 37 38 39 40 41

42

30. 4QDeut^{c}

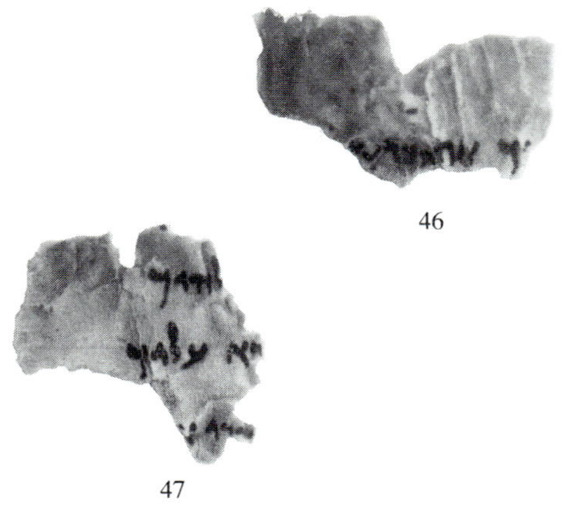

46

47

48

49

43

44

45 ii

45 i

30. 4QDeut^{c}

52 51 50

53

55

54 ii 54 i

30. 4QDeut^{c}

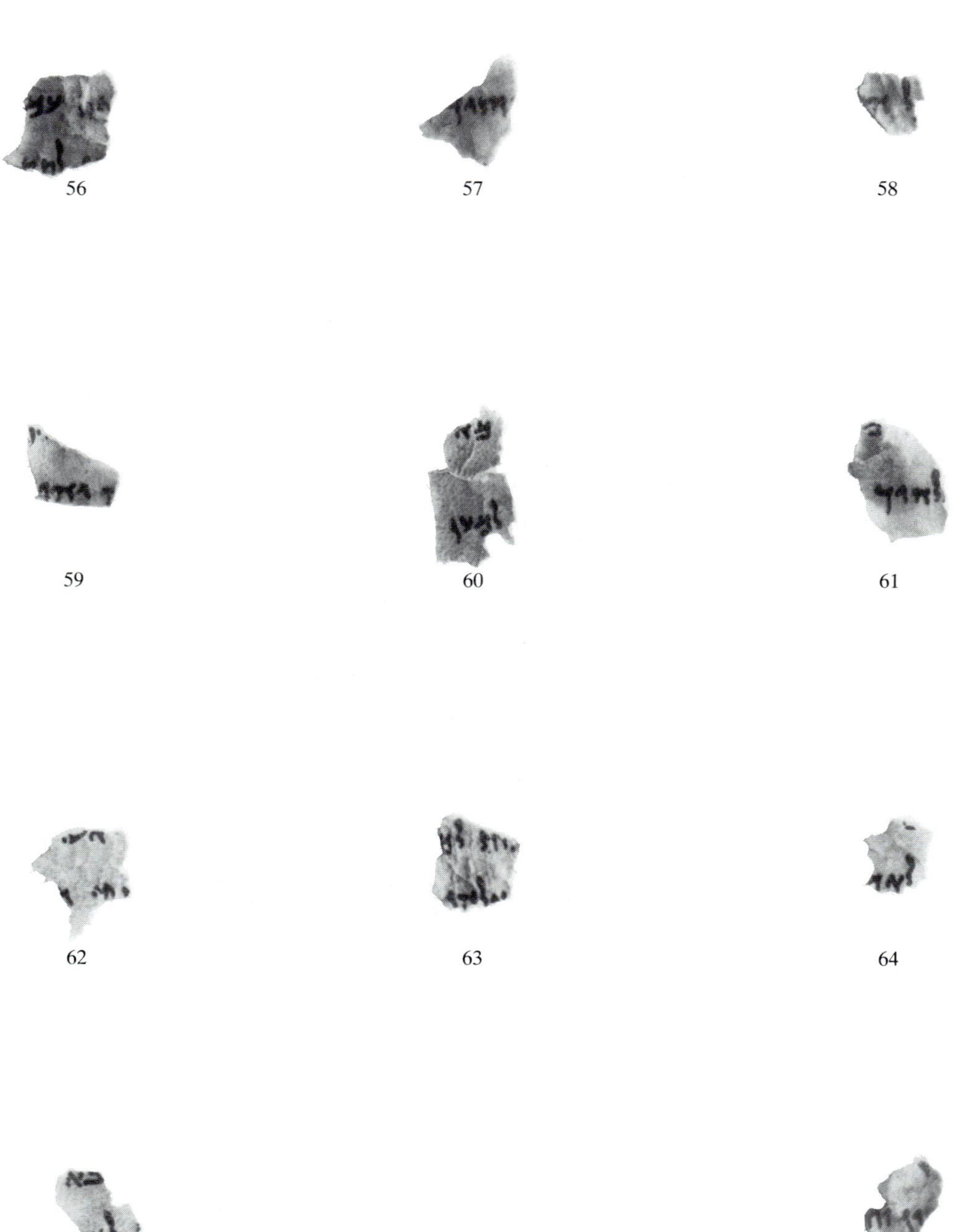

56 57 58

59 60 61

62 63 64

65 66

30. 4QDeut[c]

PLATE X

Column I

Column II

31. 4QDeut[d]

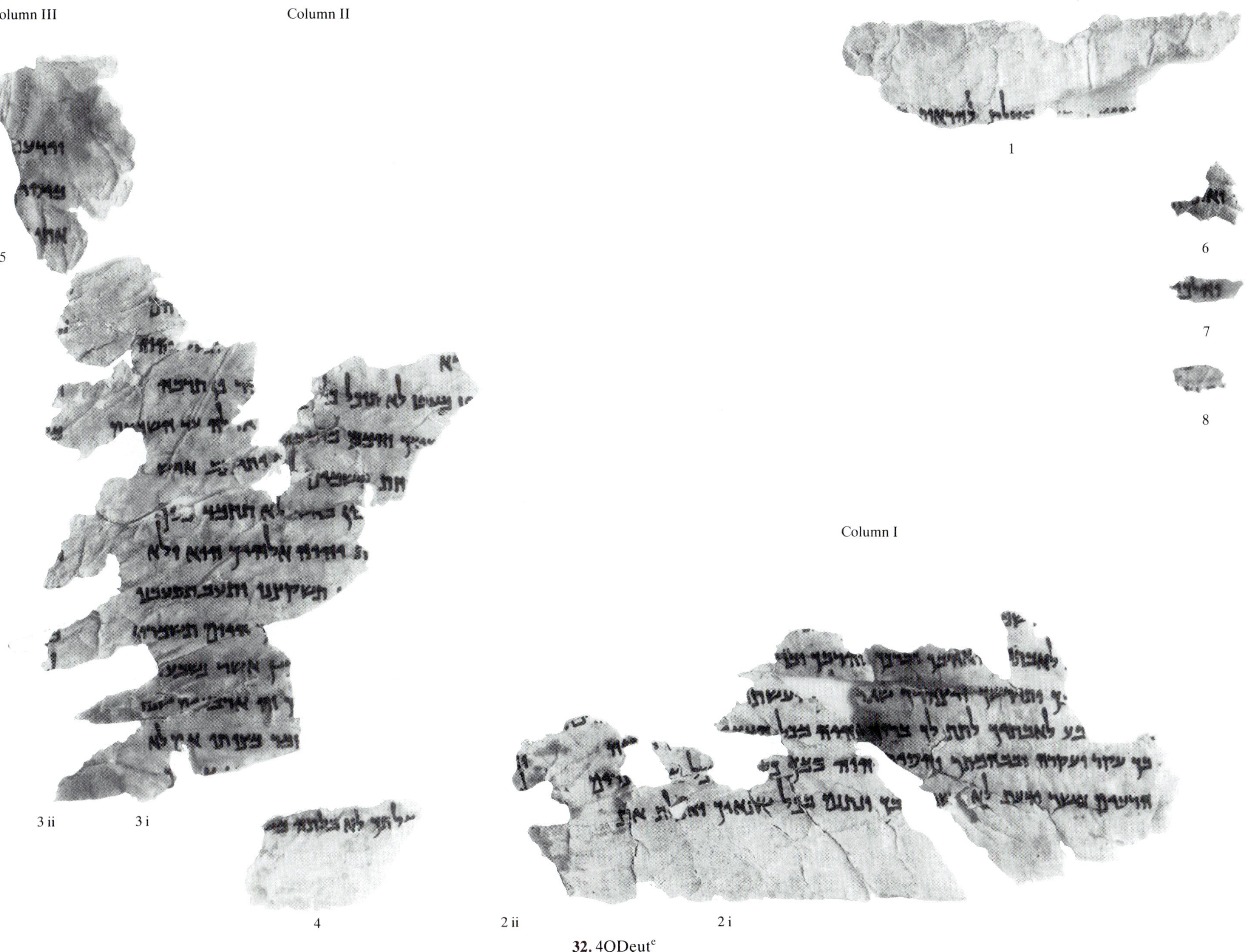

32. 4QDeut^{e}

33. 4QDeut[f]

33. 4QDeut[f]

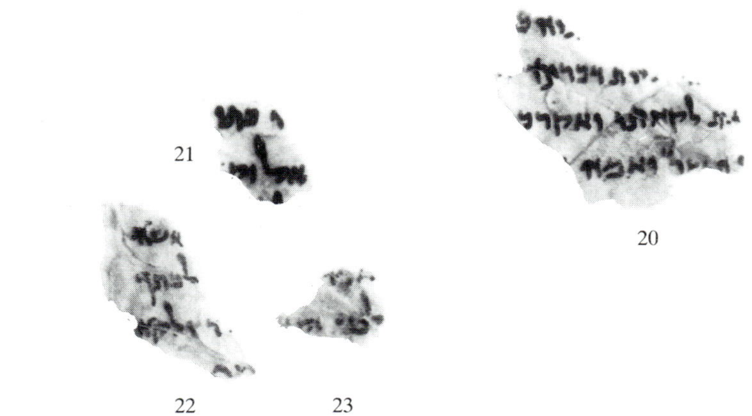

20 21 22 23

24 25 26 27 28 29 30 31

33. 4QDeut[f]

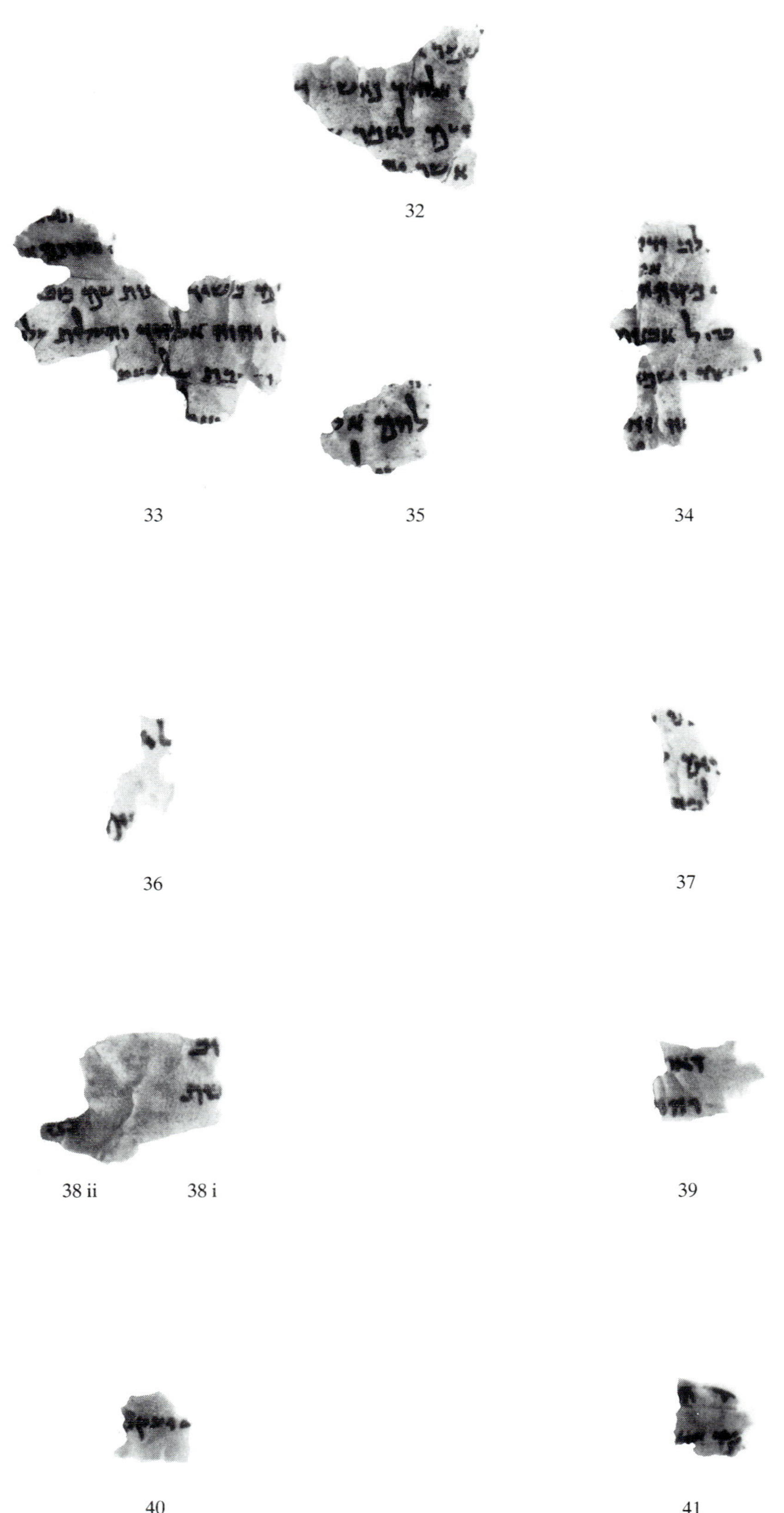

32

33 35 34

36 37

38 ii 38 i 39

40 41

33. 4QDeut[f]

3 2 1

10 5 4

11 9 8 7 6

34. 4QDeut[g]

2

1

3

4

5

6

35. 4QDeut^{h}

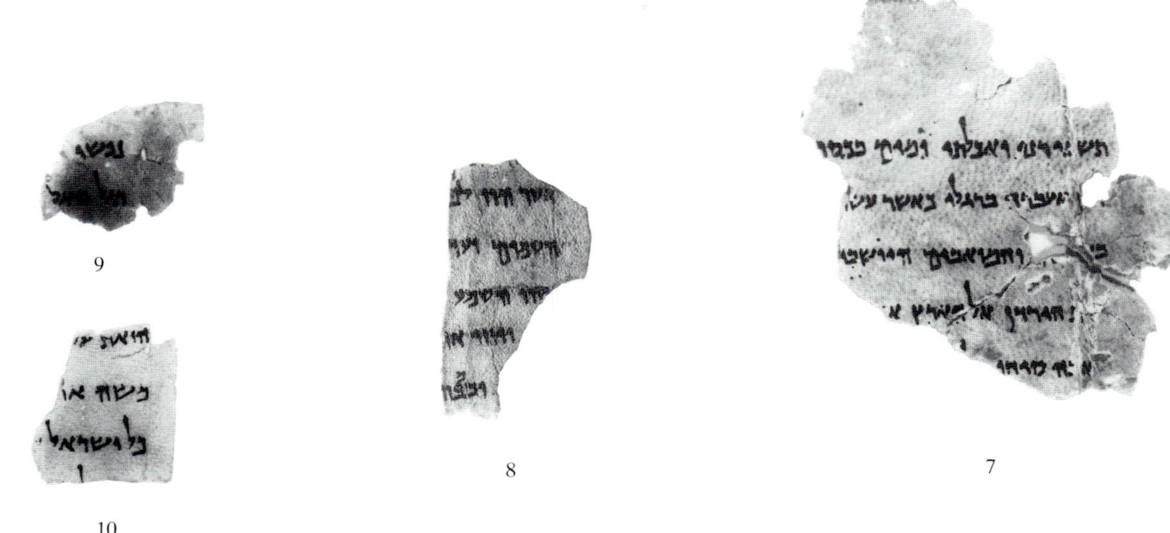

9 10 8 7

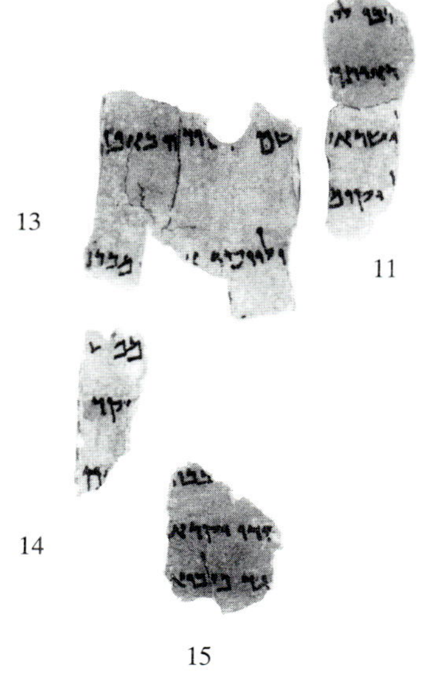

13 11 14 15

12

35. 4QDeut^{h}

2 ii 2 i 1

4

3 ii 3 i

5 ii 5 i

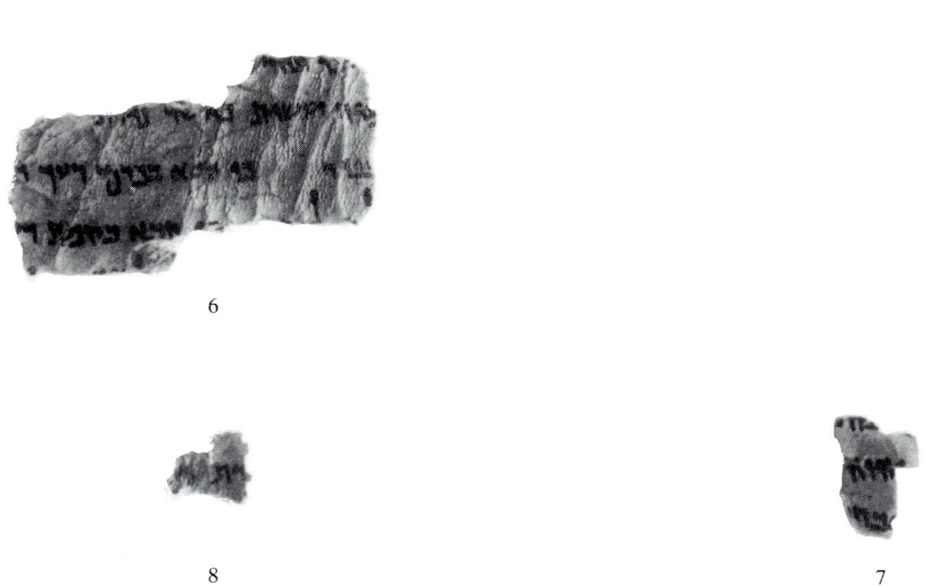

6

8 7

36. 4QDeut[i]

Column I

1

2

3

4

5

6

7

8

Column II

9

10

37. 4QDeut[j]

Column IV

Column III

37. 4QDeut^{j}

Column V

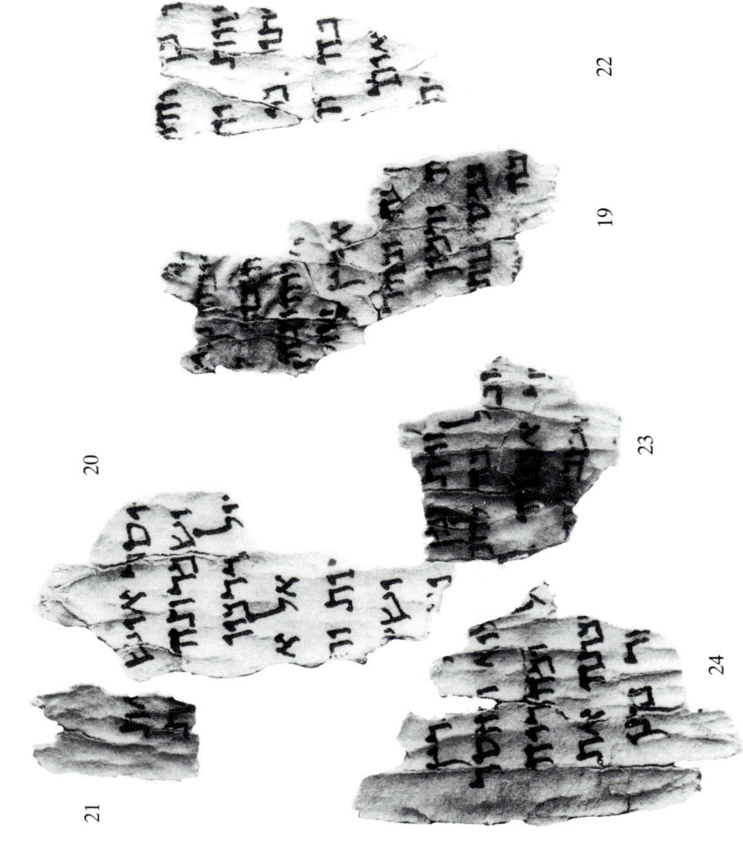

19 20 21 22 23 24

Column VIII

25 26

37. 4QDeut[j]

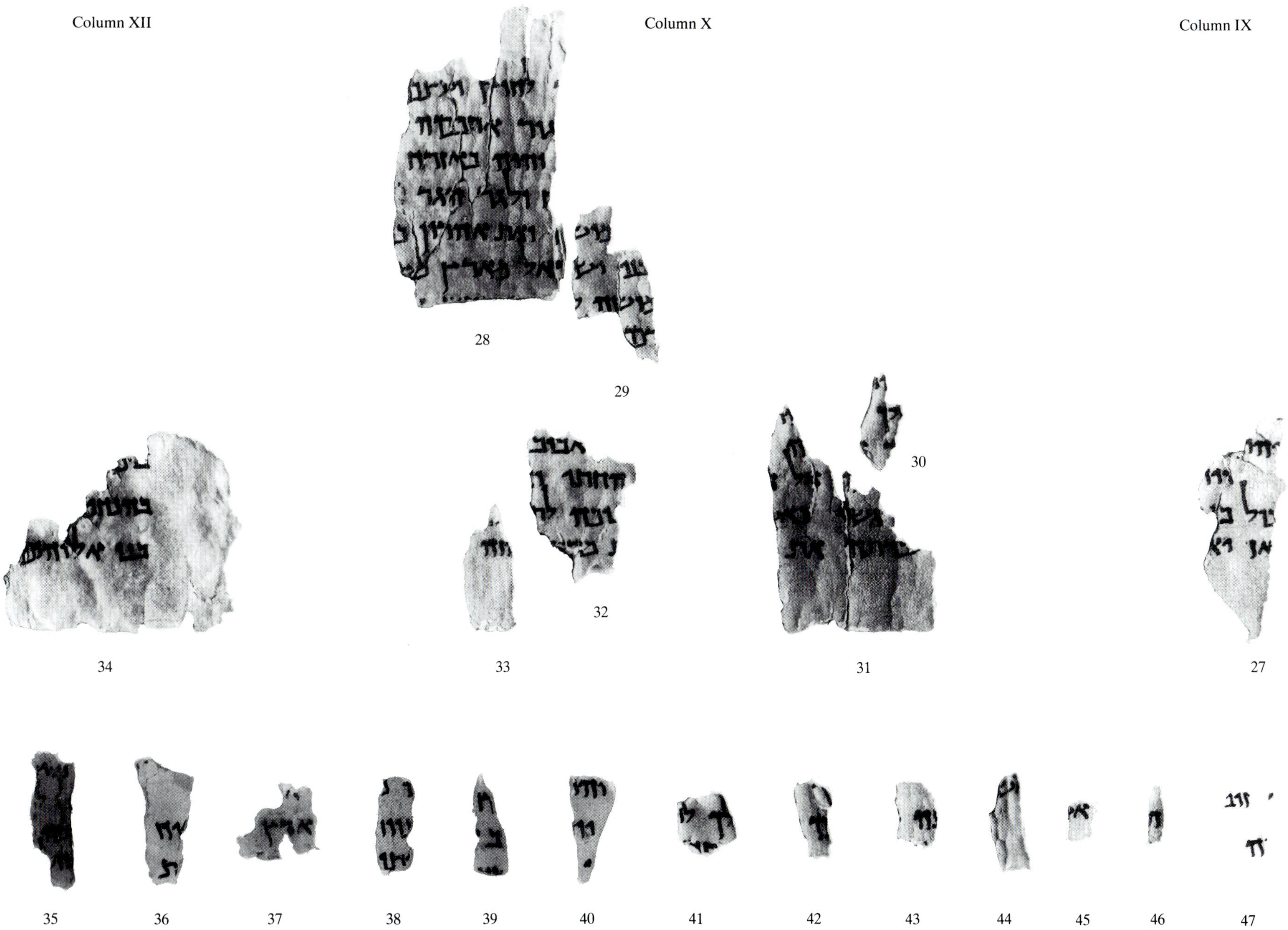

Column XII

Column X

Column IX

28

29

34

33

32

31

30

27

35 36 37 38 39 40 41 42 43 44 45 46 47

37. 4QDeut[j]

1

3

4

5

2

frgs. 1–5 (PAM 43.056)

0 1 2 3 4 cm

38. 4QDeut[k1]

38a. 4QDeut^{k2} 38b. 4QDeut^{k3}

frgs. 6–9, 11 (PAM 43.052)

frgs. 1–5, 10 (IAA 204.599)

39. 4QDeut[l]

2

3

1

4

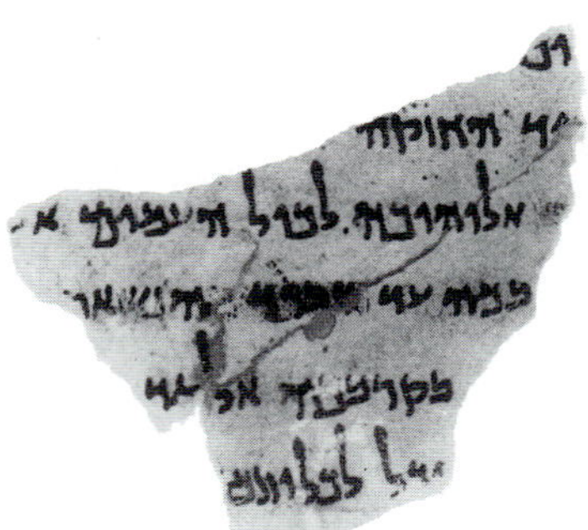

5

40. 4QDeut^{m}

PLATE XXVIII

Column I

Column II

Column III

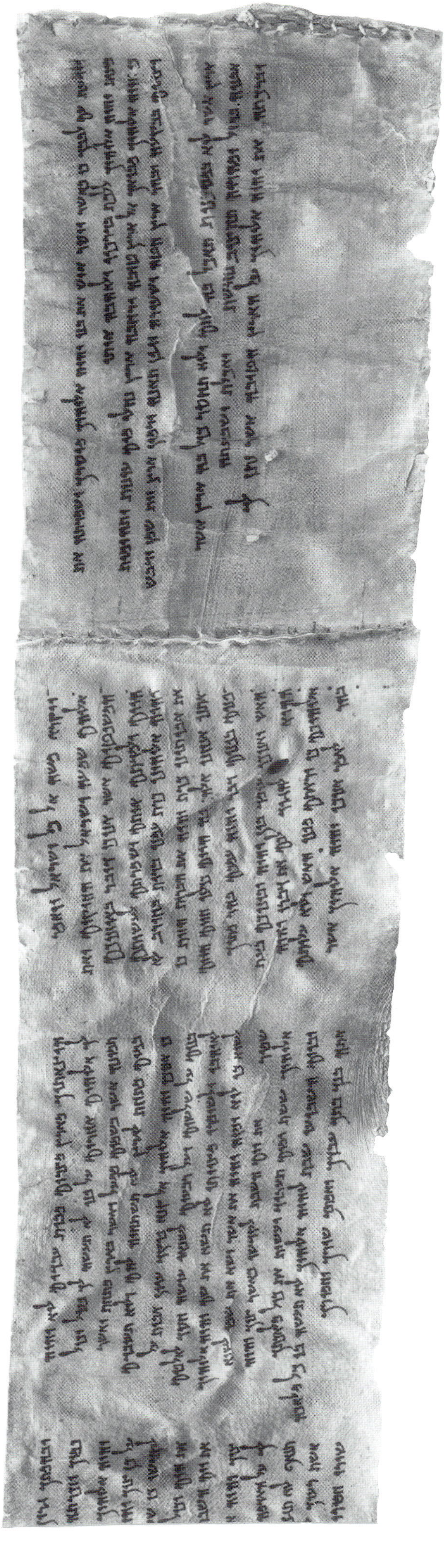

cols. I–III (PAM 42.642)

0 1 2 3 4 cm

41. 4QDeut^{n}

Column VI

Column V

Column IV

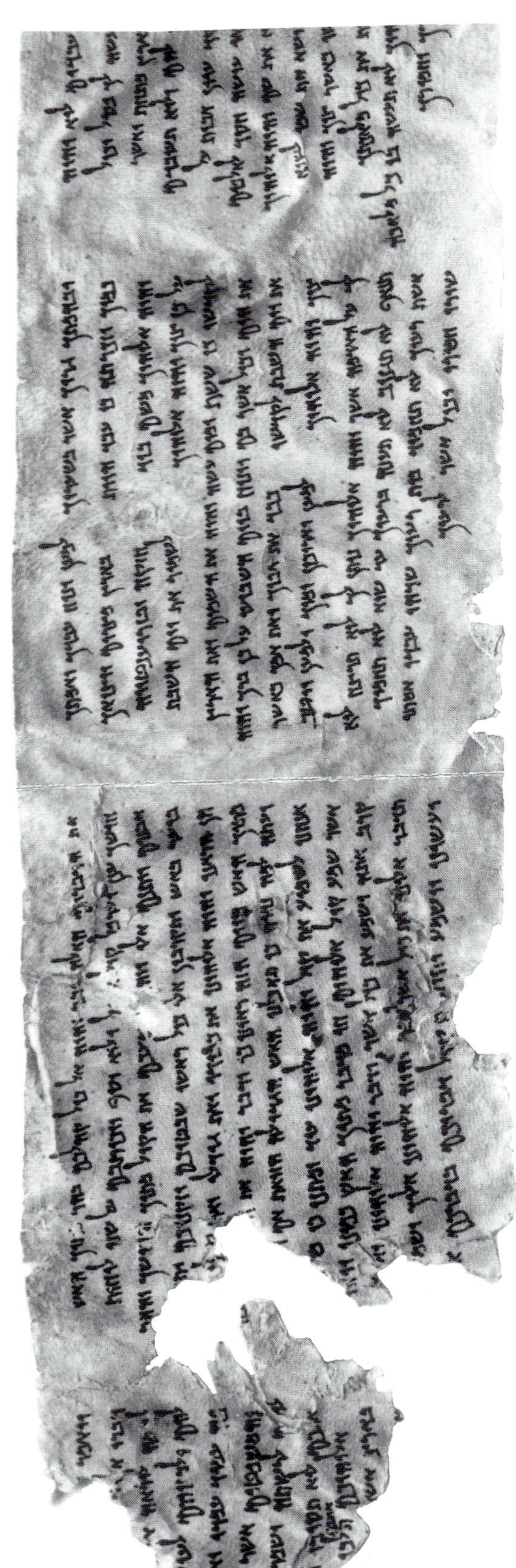

41. 4QDeut^{n}

cols. IV–VI (PAM 42.642)

42. 4QDeut°

43. 4QDeut^{p} **44.** 4QDeut^{q}

Column II
Column I
6
4
5
3
1
7
8
2
frgs. 4–8 (PAM 43.060)
0 1 2 3 4 cm
frgs. 1, 3 (PAM 41.201), frg. 2 (IAA 329.237)
0 1 2 3 4 cm

47. 4QJosh[a]

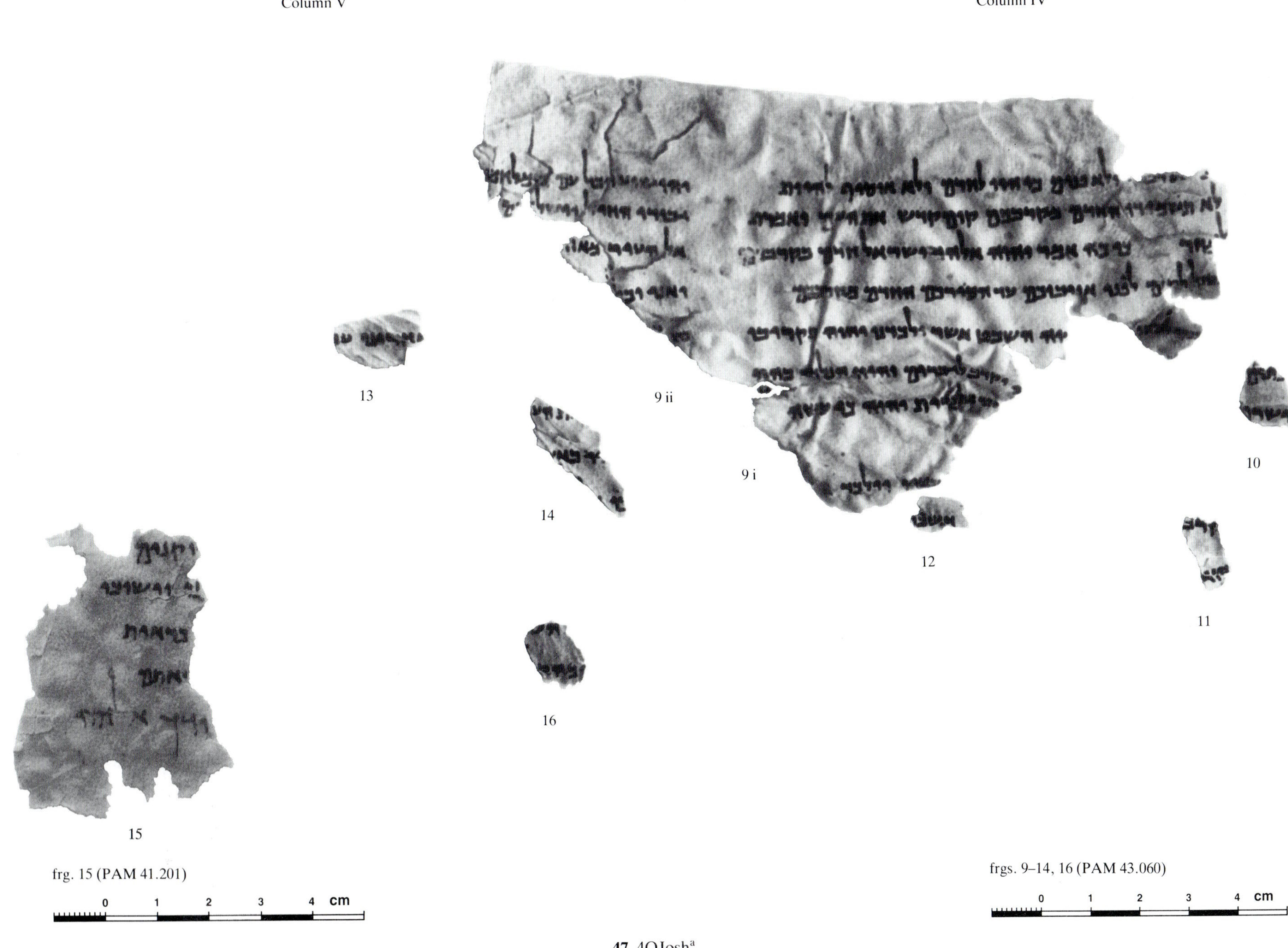

frg. 15 (PAM 41.201)

frgs. 9–14, 16 (PAM 43.060)

47. 4QJosh[a]

Column VII?

18 17

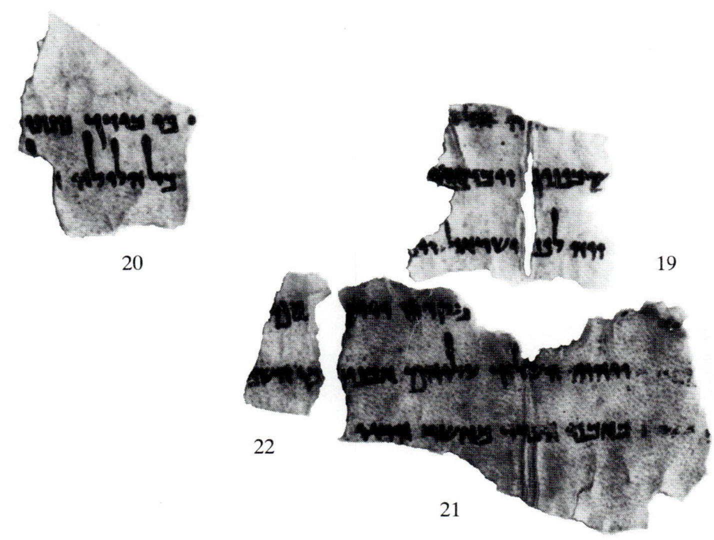

20 19 22 21

frgs. 17–22 (PAM 43.057)

0 1 2 3 4 cm

4

1

5

2

3

6 ii 6 i

frgs. 1–5 PAM 42.274 (43.061, 41.302)
frg. 6 43.061 Mus. Inv. 392

0 1 2 3 4 cm

48. 4QJosh[b]

4QJudg[b] frgs. 1, 3 (PAM 43.059)

4QJudg[b] frg. 2 (PAM 42.157)

49. 4QJudg[a] **50.** 4QJudg[b]

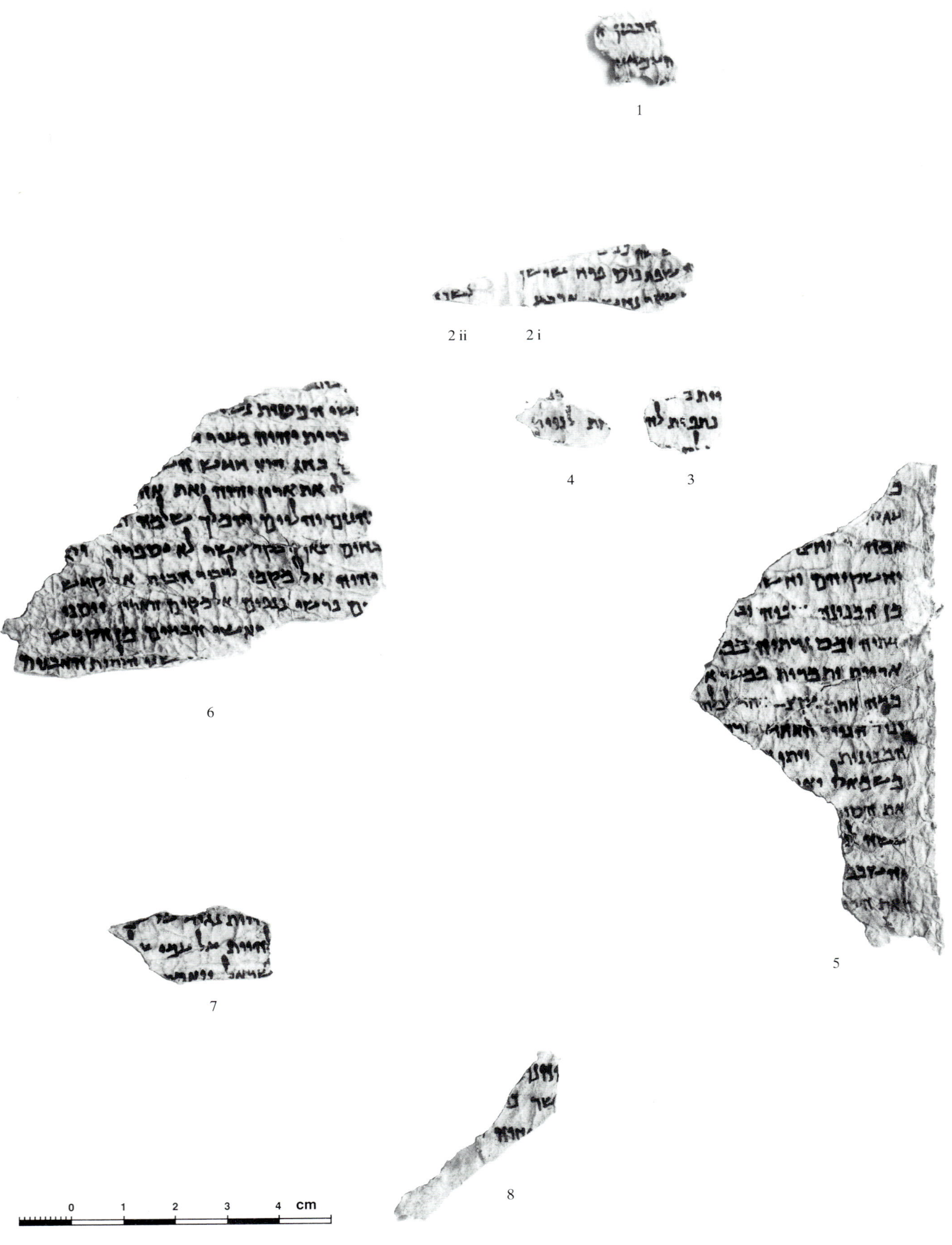

1

2 ii 2 i

4 3

6

5

7

8

54. 4QKgs